Lost Cricket Stickers

Lost Cricket Stickers

In Search of 1983's World of Cricket Sticker Album Heroes

Matthew Appleby

Foreword by
Jim Carter OBE

First published by Pitch Publishing, 2024

Pitch Publishing
9 Donnington Park,
85 Birdham Road,
Chichester,
West Sussex,
PO20 7AJ
www.pitchpublishing.co.uk
info@pitchpublishing.co.uk

© 2024, Matt Appleby

Every effort has been made to trace the copyright. Any oversight will be rectified in future editions at the earliest opportunity by the publisher.

All rights reserved. No part of this book may be reproduced, sold or utilised in any form or transmitted in any form or by any means, electronic or mechanical, including photocopying, recording or by any information storage and retrieval system, without prior permission in writing from the Publisher.

A CIP catalogue record is available for this book from the British Library.

ISBN 978 1 80150 691 5

Typesetting and origination by Pitch Publishing
Printed and bound in Great Britain by TJ Books, Padstow

Contents

Foreword by Jim Carter. 7
1. Is There Something I Should Know? 9
2. Sign of the Times 15
3. Cruel Summer, Timeline 1983. 17
4. Roger Binny 19
5. Enid Bakewell 29
6. John Holder 34
7. The Counties. 39
8. Derbyshire: Ole Mortensen 42
9. Essex: David Acfield and Derek Pringle. 56
10. Glamorgan: Mike Selvey. 73
11. Gloucestershire: Jack Russell and David Graveney 89
12. Hampshire: Kevin Emery 109
13. Kent: Chris Cowdrey. 125
14. Lancashire: Graeme Fowler 137
15. Leicestershire: Nick Cook 149
16. Middlesex: John Emburey 160
17. Northamptonshire: Geoff Cook 175
18. Nottinghamshire: Peter Such 187
19. Somerset: Nigel Popplewell 200
20. Surrey: Graham Monkhouse. 221
21. Sussex: John Barclay 238
22. Warwickshire: Norman Gifford 250
23. Worcestershire: Tim Curtis 264
24. Yorkshire: Simon Dennis and Geoff Boycott . . 279
25. Faces for the Future 304
26. Conclusion: Everything Counts 307
Postscript Mike Brearley 315
Acknowledgements. 319
Bibliography 320

Foreword

By Jim Carter OBE, actor, Yorkshire CCC fan and Hampstead CC president

MATTHEW APPLEBY's look back at the 1983 cricket season is a great read for all cricket lovers.

I have to say that through gritted teeth as it's tough for a Yorkshireman who had been brought up on a diet of almost undiluted success in the late 50s and 60s to be reminded of the season when God's Own County was bottom of the County Championship with only a single victory to their name.

This was also the year that India won the World Cup – played over 60 overs in white clothing and with a red ball. It was a moment when the world shifted slightly on its axis.

Cricket fans will relish the interviews with many of the main players of the age and be able to reflect on how much the game has changed in the course of a single generation.

Chapter 1

Is There Something I Should Know?

'CAN WE have a word please? We're police officers.'

I looked up from my scrap of paper.

'We've observed you for the past half hour acting suspiciously. You've been looking and wandering around making notes in a manner we regard to be suspicious. You'll understand how this looks. Can you explain your behaviour? You were observed at the other gate and then at the ticket office and then walking to the tube station and back.'

Standing in the shade opposite the Hobbs Gates at The Oval, while June 2023's World Test Championship final between India and Australia went on inside, I had to talk fast.

'Well, I'm waiting to speak to a cricketer, well, a cricket guy. I've been emailing him for the past few days. I'll just check if he's emailed back.'

'Do you have any form of ID on you?' asked the shorter cop.

'Do you have a criminal record?' asked the bearded one. 'It will help us look up your details.'

'Err, no.' I passed them my staff card. 'I can't afford a ticket. They're 85 quid! If he's emailed back, then I'll buy one. But I'm not gonna if he hasn't.'

'Why are you taking notes?'

'I'm actually writing a book about the 1983 cricket season. I'm making a few notes, for colour, you know – it was sunny, the crowds were pouring in, that sort of stuff.'

'Why is 1983 important?'

'Ah, well, India won the World Cup. And that changed the global balance of power from Lord's to India. I'm waiting to talk to a guy called Roger Binny who was in the team then and is BCCI president now. He's a real gent. He's a great guy. He's been really helpful with the book but I just want to meet him and here's a good chance if he can get away. He's in there now.' I pointed to the back of The Oval pavilion.

'What do you do?'

'Well, I'm a gardening journalist.'

'If you asked us about rugby or football, we'd know what you were talking about. We don't know much about cricket.'

'Well, it's about the Panini cricket sticker album in 1983. You know them? They usually did football. They only did one for cricket. I'm tracking down players from then and Binny's one of them. I know it sounds so convoluted that I couldn't be making it up.'

'You'll understand we have to check these things.'

'Why don't you get a ticket off a tout?'

'Isn't that illegal?'

'Not for you, and we're not after them.'

'Are they still around?'

'They're here all day.'

'I've only got £15 on me. Can you send one over?'

'Yeah, we'll have a word. You can include us in this book of yours. Say you got questioned by two handsome cops. That'll be a good bit.'

'I'll do that. Can you tell your colleagues that I'm writing a book so they don't think I'm acting suspiciously? It's out next year. You gonna buy one?'

'Maybe, if we're in it. What's it called? *Cricket Stickers*? Good title. You sound like you should have a pass to be in there.'

'I did once, but it was a long time ago.'

'We're satisfied with who you say you are. Have a good day.'

They walked back to the gates. I stood still next to the Boris Bikes, not daring to look up. Certainly not to make notes. What did they think I was? A terrorist? In 1983, the IRA was active. The Harrods bombing was in 1983, and the Maze Prison escape. The Brighton bomb was in 1984. On 29 June 2023, an Extinction Rebellion Just Stop Oil Ashes protestor was carried off Lord's by England's Jonny Bairstow.

I looked up. England player Reece Topley walked by. I made a note. No one else noticed him.

A guy caught my eye.

'You alright? You want something?' he demanded.

'Yeah, just waiting for the day's play to end.'

I stood stiller and longer and looked down lower.

Eventually, I remembered once seeing the surreal comedian Chris Morris on his bike watching the match from outside The Oval gate opposite the derelict Cricketer's pub, in front of the gasometer. This was close to where I was lurking.

There were some delivery bike guys looking through the gate. You could see a bit of the pitch as well as the replay screen. There was strength in numbers. I breathed deep. I checked my emails. No reply.

India lost their greatest, Virat Kohli, caught high at slip by Australia's top man, Steve Smith. There was a collective groan. Fans in their Virat shirts and tricolour wedding turbans walked between us looking through the gate's bars and at the game. There were uniforms everywhere: police, traffic wardens, security, stewards, St John Ambulance, chefs, bar staff, the service team, the pitch team.

'Hello, Matthew,' said a friendly voice on a bike passing by. 'Met the Queen today?' I asked. I knew the new (since the coronation a month before) Queen Camilla had opened an exhibition that morning at the museum the cyclist ran in nearby Lambeth Palace Road. 'Yes, she was very nice. Alan was there too.' He meant TV gardener Titchmarsh.

'I just nearly got arrested.'

'What for?'

'Waiting outside the ground making notes.'

'Can you be arrested for that?'

I told my condensed Binny story.

Ravindra Jadeja was caught at slip by Steve Smith for 48. The crowds, drunker Aussies, posher Brits and excited Indians with ice creams went back and forth. I saw a guy in a shirt with Kapil Dev written on the shoulders. Kapil was captain of his 'devils' in 1983. Most India shirts said 'Virat' or 'Kohli'.

There were two coaches outside the ground. One drove to where the players must be coming out. I followed it. India fans crowded the coach. 'Kohli, Kohli,' they chanted. A voice behind me asked: 'Did you get your interview?' It was a different plainclothes policeman, casually dressed, with a backpack, leaning on a different gate. 'No. Maybe tomorrow.' The crowd engulfed me.

I extricated myself and walked to a different gate. Indian commentators were being surged. Surrounded and loudly lauded by hundreds of fans were the smartly dressed Sourav Ganguly, slim Harbhajan Singh, a smiling Sunil Gavaskar (a 1983 World Cup winner, though he scored just two in the final) and a stern Ravi Shastri (who played five of the eight 1983 World Cup matches, but not the final). There were more stars I couldn't see. Phones were held aloft. The famous men in suits or blazers were led through the throng to cars with blacked-out windows. There was former Australia captain Ricky Ponting too, less adulated by this crowd.

Almost 40 years before, Binny (21 and 4-29) had been man of the match in a 118-run knockout World Cup win against Australia. He took 18 wickets in the finals, more than anyone else, even the superstars Kapil Dev, Malcolm Marshall, Michael Holding, Richard Hadlee, Imran Khan and Ian Botham. Of those, one was knighted, one became a Lord and one a prime minister, while Holding is an influential campaigner against racism. For Binny, it was the presidency of the Board of Control for Cricket (BCCI) in India, the richest cricket governing body in the world, which oversees the national sport of 1.4 billion people.

I asked a guy if he'd seen Binny. 'No, not him.' The man walked off. Thinking he might be another undercover cop, I walked too.

Chapter 2

Sign of the Times

THE FIRST cricket sticker album was issued in 1983. Ian Botham's on the front, blootering one, sans helmet. *World of Cricket 83* is the title, though it's about county cricket, not international cricket. Test and County Cricket Board (TCCB) approved, inside the front cover are the Schweppes County Championship and John Player League fixtures, tabulated. Under them are Benson & Hedges Cup and NatWest Bank Trophy schedules and England v New Zealand Test dates. There are no World Cup players (though there are eight shiny badges and a cup sticker to collect) or New Zealand tourist sections, though there are some lovely images of bucolic county grounds, Canterbury, Worcester, Taunton, Cheltenham.

Recently retired Middlesex and England captain Mike Brearley wrote the foreword. He mentions getting his mum or even his great-aunt to bowl at him, the only references to women in the album. 'To my mind no game compares,' he wrote. He is featured below the County Championship and Ashes stickers. Then there are the 17 counties each with a foil shiny badge, a team photo and a list of honours.

There's a pen portrait for 12 players per team, listing where and when they were born, batting and bowling style, international honours and best performances.

There are 268 stickers, including 28 foils in the Panini publication. The album cost 20p. Stickers were 10p for a packet of six. The history of cricket cards went back to Victorian times, collected by generations and still cherished today.

Having Mike Brearley introduce this book would provide a nice link, mirroring his foreword to the album back then. My dad wrote to him after attending a lecture 30 years before and I had Brearley's letter of reply and address. Typed and posted, I thought that would appeal to the intellectual Brears.

> Dear Mr Brearley,
>
> I'm writing a book about the 1983 cricket season based on the Panini cricket sticker album of that year, which you wrote the introduction to: 'What is there about cricket? For me it's been a life-long love … ' The album helped fuel my love of cricket. My new book includes interviews with county players about then and now.
>
> I wondered if I could talk briefly about differences between then and now in the game (e.g. India won the World Cup in 1983 starting the shift of the game from Lord's). Perhaps you could write a few words to introduce my new book?
>
> Regards, Matthew Appleby

On Easter Monday, a blow: Brearley wishes me all the best but he's really sorry, he's too busy to take on a new project.

This book was going to be harder than I thought.

Chapter 3

Cruel Summer, Timeline 1983

New Year's Honours: F.G. Mann CBE, Brian Johnston OBE
February 28: Final match of England Australia and New Zealand tour.

30 April: County Championship season starts.

30 May: Surrey 14 all out v Essex at Chelmsford.

6 June: World Cup starts. England beat New Zealand by 106 runs at The Oval.

9 June: Margaret Thatcher's Conservatives win the General Election.

9/10 June: India shock West Indies in the World Cup with a 34-run win at Old Trafford.

18 June: Kapil Dev hits 175 not out for India against Zimbabwe at Tunbridge Wells.

22 June: India beat England in the World Cup semi-final at Old Trafford.

22–24 June: Yorkshire v Derbyshire at Sheffield. Ole Mortensen takes 11-89.

24 June: A 41-minute hundred by Nigel Popplewell for Somerset v Gloucestershire at Bath.

25 June: India win the World Cup final at Lord's against West Indies.

14–18 July: England win first Test against New Zealand, at The Oval. Graeme Fowler scores a century.

23 July: Benson & Hedges Cup final, Middlesex beat Essex

1 August: Headingley: New Zealand beat England for the first time in a Test in England.

11–15 August: Nick Cook (5-35 and 3-90) helps England beat New Zealand at Lord's by 127 runs to take a 2-1 lead in the series.

13–16 August: Geoff Boycott scores 140 not out and 97 against Gloucestershire and is reprimanded for slow scoring.

17 August: Somerset beat Middlesex in the NatWest semi-final having lost fewer wickets. Nigel Popplewell takes 3-34 and scores 46.

20–23 August: Geoff Boycott scores 163 and 141 not out against Nottinghamshire.

25–29 August: Nick Cook takes 9/150 in the match to seal a 3-1 series win for England v New Zealand at Trent Bridge.

28 August: John Player League, Yorkshire beat Derbyshire at Bradford. Simon Dennis hits Ole Mortensen for six to win the match.

3 September: NatWest Trophy: Somerset beat Kent.

10–13 September: Essex win the County Championship after drawing with Yorkshire as Middlesex's game is abandoned.

11 September: John Player League, Yorkshire v Essex, no result. Yorkshire won the league.

13 September: A 35-minute hundred by Steve O'Shaughnessy for Lancashire v Leicestershire.

Chapter 4

Roger Binny

IN THE 1975 inaugural World Cup, India only beat minnows East Africa. They lost by 202 runs to England, plodding to 132/3 in 60 overs chasing 335, with opener Sunil Gavaskar going through 'mental agony' and scoring 36 off 174 balls. India lost all their games in the 1979 World Cup. In 1983 it was very different for Kapil Dev's team, which began as 66/1 outsiders.

One of the squad was all-rounder Roger Binny, who I remembered from his stint in 1982 as pro for Carlisle, my home city. He's come a long way since then and became much respected in both the playing and administration of cricket.

He was an India Test player when he joined Carlisle. His swing bowling suited English conditions and his club won the North Lancashire League that year. Binny ran in so smoothly and then unfurled a strong action, not unlike Kapil Dev.

In *Indian Cricket* 1983, between adverts for The Great Eastern Hotel in Calcutta, Clevite quality bearings and Raleigh Bicycles from the Cycle Corporation of India,

Binny is named one of the cricketers of the year, alongside Mohinder Amarnath and Balwinder Sandhu. *Indian Cricket* notes Binny's talent was first noticed alongside Kapil Dev's at a cricket camp at Binny's home city Bangalore in 1974. In England in 1983, now 27 and three years after his India debut, 'a confident-looking Binny appears certain to return with rich harvest. That would really elevate his status in Indian cricket.'

On the way to the World Cup final against West Indies, in the group stage, Binny scored 27 and took 3-48 in a win against the Windies at Old Trafford. He had the world's best batsman, Viv Richards, caught behind for 17. In the semi-final win over England, on a dusty pitch at the same venue, England's Paul Allott complained the surface suited the India spinners (India selected no frontline spinner, though Kirti Azad's off breaks did take 1-28 in 12 overs). Binny removed openers (and top scorers) Chris Tavare and Graeme Fowler, taking 2-43 in a six-wicket win. Carlisle team-mate Chris Packham remembers how the 'gentlemanly, immensely popular bloke' gave the club 20 tickets for the semi.

In the final, three days later on 25 June 1983, a turning point came when, off a full-length Binny (10-1-23-1) delivery, Kapil Dev caught Clive Lloyd at mid-off to leave West Indies stricken on 66/5. Kapil had just caught Richards over his shoulder off a miscued pull from the bowling of Madan Lal. The crowd spilled onto the pitch, and they did so again and again until the greatest India victory of all time was complete.

I contacted Binny via the BCCI, using the Carlisle connection as an 'in'.

'Hi Matthew, Sorry for delay in replying back. I will be available after the 11th for a reply or an interview. It's great to be in contact with someone from Carlisle. Cheers, Roger Binny.'

I realised June is when the World Test Championship final was to be held at The Oval.

The next email: 'Hi Matthew, I have already reached London and staying at [...] Maybe day two of the Test? Is that okay? Did you get the mail on the questions you sent?'

I hadn't. I was mortified: 'Sorry I did not receive the mail on the questions I sent. Can you resend please? I live in London and day two would certainly be okay though I'm sure you have a lot of official engagements.'

At 6.43am the day before the World Test final, he emails back with answers, originally sent on 16 May and lost in the ether: 'Thank you, Roger! Best of luck for the big match!'

Roger had emailed: 'My stint to Carlisle was done in the last minute as I was dropped from the 1982 tour of England. It was a wonderful experience to play league cricket in very pretty surroundings. I truly enjoyed that stint and to cap it all I was back next year for the biggest event of my career and had great success.

'When the 1983 cricket season started I was trying to make a comeback to the Indian team as I was dropped from the 1983 tour of the West Indies which happened just before the World Cup. I had a good domestic season and got back into the team. My aim at the World Cup was to establish my place in the team and I tried very hard with great success.

'India were never rated in the past two World Cups and we didn't look good as a team for this format due to various reasons. The team too didn't have too many thoughts when we travelled to England. The first was the mind changer when the West Indies lost to us and there was a sudden transformation in the team which was very noticeable. We started playing a different brand of cricket.

'West Indies were such a dominant force in cricket in the 1970s and early 80s. Very few teams challenged them for the top post. England was the ideal place for the West Indies. Maybe the pitches in India didn't suit their game. Australia had some success in Tests against them in the mid-70s.

'Our win in 1983 changed the mindset of the other teams and they believed they could do it too. India became a very confident team after that win.

'Our win changed the face of Indian cricket. It gave our board a big boost and a lot of things changed. We were able to take control of the game with the ICC as we had the infrastructure and the players so that gave our board the confidence to go ahead.

'There has been a very big change in the game and players are more exposed. Players now are very well paid and don't need to work for a living like we did. The facilities have changed and there are a lot of opportunities for the cricketers to get back into the game.'

Of the World Cup teams, while West Indians Gordon Greenidge, Desmond Haynes, Richards, Lloyd, Malcolm Marshall, Andy Roberts, Joel Garner and Michael Holding (and group stage players Wayne Daniel and Winston Davis) were the leading county players in the 1970s and 1980s, of the Indians only Kapil Dev (40 first-class matches between 1981 and 1985 for Northamptonshire and Worcestershire) and Sunil Gavaskar (Somerset 1980) played first-class county cricket in England, and both not for long. Cup final man-of-the-match Mohinder Amarnath was with minor counties Durham and Wiltshire.

Binny told me: 'I never tried hard enough to play county cricket as that was our off-season time and we had time to spend with the family.'

In 1983, India were such big outsiders that even Kapil Dev said his team were only 'capable of a surprise or two'. Lord's rang out to the cymbals and bongos of West Indies' fans and dholaks and temple bells of Indian supporters. The miracle at Lord's was Indian cricket's finest hour.

Prime Minister Indira Gandhi telegrammed the players: 'My slogan is India can do it. Thank you for living up to it.' That message was displayed at state-owned petrol stations India-wide. At a reception when they returned home Mrs Gandhi said she was surprised the English press had underplayed the achievement.

The Cricketer magazine headlined with 'Indian inherit the earth' – Indians around the globe celebrated their famous victory with fervent joy. A triumph 'not just for India but for the game'. In August 1983 Kapil was on the front cover, alongside Mohinder Amarnath. Pakistan captain Imran Khan said Binny and Amarnath had 'amazing temperaments' and 'won it for India in the final, on soft English wickets'.

Early in 1983, India, without Binny, lost 2-0 in the Tests and 2-1 in the ODIs in the West Indies. Kapil Dev had taken over from Gavaskar as captain. In winter 1983, West Indies toured India and had their revenge. India lost the one-dayers 5-0 and 3-0 in the Test series. Binny played in all the Tests and took seven wickets. Better days were to come.

In 1985 he totalled 17 wickets in the World Series one-dayers in Australia and in 1986 he took 5-40 and 2-18 as India beat England by 279 runs at Headingley. He then took four wickets in the 1-1 Texaco Trophy draw, including those of Graeme Fowler, featured later, and David Gower, England's best batsman of the 1980s.

In *The Cricketer* an anonymous county cricketer observed that the World Cup reinvigorated public interest and served as a reminder how much counties rely on overseas players. India 'captured hearts' said *Wisden* editor John Woodcock.

An Indian TV special 40 years on from 1983 saw all 11 players 'bringing back the goosebumps.' Syed Kirmani is characterised as 'the angler – catch of the day', while all-rounder 'Jimmy' Amarnath is the 'silent assassin'. Binny is the 'gentle giant', still quietly going about his job.

Kapil said the love and affection from the people was enough and no money can buy that. They were paid a 1,500 rupee match fee, plus 200 rupees a day. Kapil had a 'pleasure not pressure' mantra.

Amarnath said in the previous World Cups India were 'just participating' but in 1983 the team was ready, coming together after having played tough series in Pakistan and West Indies.

The self-confidence was there, with the right team for the right conditions. It was India's moment.

The winning players have had a WhatsApp group for 15 years. The bond is still there. There is some disquiet about how little the BBC covered India matches. The turning point was when Kapil scored 175 off 138 balls against Zimbabwe at Tunbridge Wells after going in at 17/5: 'God has created certain days for you,' Kapil said. Kapil catching Richards was pivotal, said Sandhu. 'He always made it look so easy.'

Before that, swashbuckling opener Kris Srikkanth and Binny smiled to each other in the covers when the leader asserted they would win. 'It looks like the match will be over by tea. The boss has gone mad.' But the sense of determination, aggression and self-confidence which Kapil brought gave them belief.

On the TV programme, Srikkanth gets Amarnath to sing. Kapil has Srikkanth singing. Binny does not speak.

Another TV show, *Indian Cricketers and Cast of 83*, hears how the actors portrayed the players in the film *83*, which was directed by Kabir Khan and was the first movie to celebrate Indian cricket. 'Tickling the nipple' with the ball was the secret to acting as Kapil said Ranveer Singh. Amarnath was all about the shoulders. Gavaskar was in the walk, like a tiger.

He described it as a 'triumph of the human spirit. Grown up men will start crying all over again.'

Sandeep Patil is played by his son Chirag, who imitates his father's shambling walk. Kirti Azad is a 'cool dude', Dilip Vengsarkar 'the colonel'. Madan Lal is played by former India under-19s cricketer Hardy Sandhu, who points out three of the World Cup winners who coached him. There is a minute's silence for Yashpal Sharma, who died of a heart attack in 2021.

Sardesai tried to bring in Binny, 'as quiet as ever'. He just says he's looking forward to the film. He praises actor Nishant Dahiya, 'who has done a fantastic job' but isn't there so can't explain how he played the all-rounder.

They recall how in 1983, before the first game in Manchester, against West Indies, India were playing bad cricket. They had three warm-up games and lost all of them but then at Old Trafford something clicked. Everyone was throwing themselves around in the field and it got them going in the tournament.

At Tunbridge Wells, before anyone could finish their coffees, India lost five wickets for 17 runs. Finally, Kirmani (24 not out) and Kapil put on 126 for the ninth wicket, with Kapil's sixes flying out of the ground. They forget that Binny and Kapil added 60 for the fifth wicket, and without Binny's contribution India's tournament would have been over. Everyone was a captain and the team played together.

After India won the final, Tory grandee Lord Carr of Hadley, on behalf of sponsor's Prudential, presented Kapil, 24, with the trophy. It was a visual representation of the handover of power from London to Bombay. India won £20,000 but the bigger prize was to lead the world. India and Pakistan hosted the World Cup in 1987. Kapil weeps at the end of *83*: 'It's about character.' On the actors: 'They bring back our lives.'

✲ ✲ ✲

In eight World Cup matches, Roger Binny scored 73 runs at 12.16 and took 18 wickets at 18.66 with an economy rate of 3.81. He went on to play 27 Tests and 72 one-day internationals.

World Cup final 1983, Lord's, India v West Indies

Sunil Gavaskar c Dujon b Roberts 2
Kris Srikkanth lbw Marshall 38
Mohinder Amarnath b Holding 26
Yashpal Shaa c sub (Logie) b Gomes 11
Sandeep Patil c Gomes b Garner 27
Kapil Dev c Holding b Gomes 15
Kirti Azad c Garner b Roberts 0
Roger Binny c Garner b Roberts 2
Madan Lal b Marshall 17
Syed Kirmani b Holding 14
Balwinder Sandhu not out 11
Extras 20
183 all out 54.4 overs
Bowling: Roberts 10-3-32-3; Garner 12-4-24-1; Marshall 11-1-24-2; Holding 9.4-2-26-2; Gomes 11-1-49-2; Richards 1-0-8-0.

West Indies

Gordon Greenidge b Sandhu 1
Desmond Haynes c Binny b Madan Lal 13
Viv Richards c Kapil Dev b Madan Lal 33
Clive Lloyd c Kapil Dev b Binny 8
Larry Gomes c Gavaskar b Madan Lal 5
Faoud Bacchus c Kirmani v Sandhu 8
Jeff Dujon b Amarnath 25

Malcolm Marshall c Gavaskar b Amarnath 18
Andy Roberts lbw Kapil Dev 4
Joel Garner not out 5
Michael Holding lbw Amarnath 14
140 all out 52 overs
Bowling: Kapil Dev 11-4-21-1; Sandhu 11-4-21-1; Madan Lal 12-2-31-3; Binny 10-1-23-1; Amarnath 7-0-12-3; Azad 3-0-7-0.

Chapter 5

Enid Bakewell

THE 1983 Panini album, as well as including no World Cup player stickers, includes no women. *Wisden* 1984 was 1,290 pages long, featuring two pages on women's cricket, compared to 96 pages in 2022.

Nottinghamshire-born Enid Bakewell, an inspirational cricketing pioneer, first played for the county aged 14. Born in 1940, the top order batter/slow left-armer played 12 Tests from 1968–79 averaging 59.78 with the bat, as well as taking 50 wickets. In Tests she made four hundreds and seven fifties. Her wickets came at an average of 16.62. She also played 23 ODIs from 1968–82.

In 1973, she was a member of the first World Cup-winning team, scoring 118 in the decider. The first men's World Cup was not until 1975 and England men did not win it until 2019. Bakewell scored 264 runs and captain Rachael Heyhoe Flint 256. All the teams were invited to 10 Downing Street for a reception with Prime Minister Ted Heath.

Her last international match came in the 1982 World Cup in Australia and New Zealand when England lost in the final by three wickets to Australia. Aged 41, she bowled 12 overs and took 0-26. In 2012 she became the third women's ICC Hall of Fame inductee, after Heyhoe Flint and Australian Belinda Clark.

From the mining village of Newstead, Bakewell is a former Labour councillor. That's how I tracked her down.

On 17 June 2023, just as Ben Stokes has Steve Smith lbw in the first Ashes Test, a letter lands on the mat.

Dear Matthew, many thanks for your letter. I shall look forward to reading your book.

'My vivid memories are the 4 ½ months Tour of Oz & NZ Dec 1968–April 1969. During that tour Rachael [Heyhoe Flint's] team did not lose one match and we met people in their homes when not playing Test matches.

'Before we departed we were hosted by ex-England player Con [Constance] Holden who was a board member at Edgbaston. Con hosted all 17 players at her house and even invited men from Warwickshire for the girls who were not married. She even took off her shoes and bowled to us in the Edgbaston nets.'

The tourists did not lose a game until they played on matting in the USA against a men's team. Bakewell scored 1,031 runs and took 118 wickets on tour.

'I remember the match at Edgbaston when we beat the Oz in a 60 overs game [the de facto final in the 1973 World Cup]. Captained by Rachael and sponsored by Sir Jack Hayward. The trophy was presented by Princess Anne, who gave me an MBE a few years ago [2019]. I scored a century and took two wickets (I think) [118 and 2-28 off 12 overs] but was accompanied by my father Len

Turton [Turton is Enid's maiden name] with his rug to keep him warm. He was a councillor, not an athlete, but gave GREAT encouragement. [There were 1,500 people at the final.] All the players were amateurs.'

She says she does not remember losing to Australia in the 1982 final. THE game was in 1976 – the first at Lord's. 'When I first went to Lord's there was a large notice board saying "Gentlemen ONLY allowed up these stairs" on the stairs leading to the BELL! We were not sure we would be allowed in the changing rooms or the LONG ROOM but Rachael opted to field as she would then be the first woman to step onto Lord's. I scored 50 that day then got myself out [run out] so that Rachael could bat!' England with 162/2 won the ODI by eight wickets, Bakewell taking 2-30 and Heyhoe Flint scoring 17 not out.

'WOMEN'S CRICKET has taken great strides forward thanks to Rachael who had MUCH OPPOSITION from women who had worked for Women's Cricket for years without being paid. She was dropped from [the] captaincy without being told why. She had played the ukulele near Lord's to tell folk that women played cricket – we played matches v men to let folk know. She also entertained us after games with the ukulele. CRICKET has made SO MUCH progress and APPEALS to YOUNG BOYS & GIRLS. Enid x.'

Bakewell was educated at a girls' grammar school where they only played rounders. The PE teacher saw her talent and put her in touch with a cricket club in Nottingham where she attended weekly nets.

Dartford College of Physical Education had been a cradle of the women's cricket game since the 1920s. Bakewell was there from 1962, when England wicketkeeper Ruth Westbrook was a lecturer (1959–64, played for England 1957–63). Ex-England captain Mary Duggan (1925–73, England 1948–63, college lecturer 1953–59 and deputy principal 1963–73) was there too.

'I got known by those two,' recalled Enid. 'Had I not gone down there I wouldn't have been chosen. You've got to get yourself seen and I suppose they realised how competitive I was.'

Rachael Heyhoe, Sheila Plant, Mary Pilling, Jill Cruwys, Heather Dewdney, Pam Ferdinand and Chris Watmough were Dartford graduates who played with Enid for England.

Heyhoe Flint was called the W.G. Grace of women's cricket by writer Scyld Berry, but Bakewell dismisses a parallel with leading all-rounder Garfield Sobers: 'I wouldn't compare myself with a man.'

When did she realise she could play?

'I scored a century in my first Test!' But before that? 'I never worried about being good. All I wanted for us to do was to win. I once ate lunch with the team of Australians we were playing. I got myself out when I went out to bat because I'd lowered my guard and wasn't as competitive as normal; I'd imagine that you are born competitive.'

Cricket had to be fitted between having three children: 'Four with my husband because he'd been brought up like a child by his mother who did everything for him. She waited on him hand and foot!

'I don't know whether I would have coped with full-time cricket.' On the long 1973 Australia, New Zealand, USA tour, she managed: 'But I'd left a two-and-half-year old with my mother and father during the week and my husband at the weekend and he said it was too long.'

After the 1982 World Cup, aged 42, her England career was over.

She continued to play for East Midlands, and later Surrey, for another decade, and then coached and played club cricket into her 80s.

Bakewell says she made life-long friends all over the world through cricket; the only was regret being banned after playing in South Africa, where she was alarmed to see servants living in what were effectively garden sheds at the bottom of gardens in the houses they visited. She became a Labour councillor, but back then she says political discussion was off-limits: The 'men only' board in the Lord's pavilion has gone, 'but you feel it's still upper class'.

She'd do it all over again: 'I would have to play differently though because I never hit the ball in the air.'

Her hopes for women's cricket? 'That we just progress and we involve more and more people and people accept it more.

'It's amazing how they've got so many more people to help them. It's so much more professional now – and they let them play at Trent Bridge! We did play at Trent Bridge eventually.'

It's 18 June 2023. The women's Ashes Test is next week and Bakewell will ring the bell to begin the match. She says she'll give me a wave.

Chapter 6

John Holder

I'M AT the Cheltenham Cricket Festival for the Professional Cricketers' Association (PCA) annual former players' day. Autograph hunters, all middle-aged rather than the kids who collected them in 1983, descend on their old heroes. There's 20-plus that I recognise from the sticker album, including Kevin Emery, John Steele, Bob Taylor, David Graveney, David Lawrence, Norman Cowans, Andy Brassington, Alan Jones, Tim Tremlett, John Barclay, Nick Cook, Paul Jarvis, Kevin Saxelby and Norman Gifford. Trying to spot men you haven't seen for 40 or more years is a team effort. The stalkers exchange notes. Many have books and memorabilia to sign, brought along in carrier bags on the basis of a list of attendees given by the PCA.

Gloucestershire have played under the honey stone of the Victorian chapel and library since W.G. Grace's early days in 1872, making it the longest-running outground cricket festival. I first visited when Mike Procter took a hat-trick of Yorkshire lbws back in 1979.

The cider flows and the match is secondary. Distracting spectators is Jonny Bairstow's 99 not out in the fourth

Ashes Test at Old Trafford, shown via satellite on the marquee TVs rather than listened to on transistor radios which would have been clasped to ears in 1983.

John Holder comes in, still with what looks like his umpire's hat on, and is keen to talk: 'In my first year [1982] I was lucky that Alan Whitehead [a first-class umpire from 1970–2005] was my mentor. We spent a week at Fenner's when Cambridge University played Middlesex and then Warwickshire and he talked to me about umpiring, he was outstanding. I was on the reserve list then I got the letter telling me I was on the first-class panel for 1983 and I wrote to Alan to thank him for the help he gave me.'

For Holder, a £5,000 salary plus expenses wage was more attractive than working in an asbestos factory.

'In my first year [on the first-class list] we had the incident at Chelmsford when Surrey got bowled out for 14. We had rain on the Saturday and we lost some play, then we had a Sunday game, then on the Monday Essex batted and got almost 300. Keith Fletcher [110] and Kenny McEwan [45] got runs and they declared and left Surrey with 65 minutes to bat. A chap called Norbert Phillip, the overseas player, was bowling from my end at Hayes Close, and Neil Foster, making his debut, was bowling from the River End. When Essex batted, the ball hardly did anything, even Sylvester Clarke didn't cause too many terrors. It was an easy-paced pitch, but when Surrey batted all of a sudden the ball started to swing like a boomerang. Almost every ball could have been a wicket. They were playing and missing. They were nicking it. The atmosphere was unbelievable because you had a big Essex crowd and almost every ball could have got someone out. My colleague was a fella from Australia, Bill Alley, and I thought to myself what have I done to deserve this sort of pressure? I've just started learning the job. And they got bowled out for 14!

'I gave three lbw and Alley gave one and in 65 minutes they were all out and then following on the next day they batted out the overs, hardly lost a wicket and the ball did nothing. The interesting thing was after that session everyone wanted to look at the ball but it wasn't any different from another used ball, it just hooped around. [Surrey captain] Roger Knight came into bat and Norbert Phillip was bowling and he said "John, is the ball swinging?" and I said "Yes." First ball he pads up and I gave him out.'

Another memorable game for John was when Middlesex played Somerset at Lord's on August 20–23. Ian Botham wasn't happy they started after rain. Phil Edmonds (5-19) and John Emburey (4-28) rolled the away team on a drying pitch. Somerset's spinners Vic Marks (3-17) and Paul Booth (4-26) dispatched Middlesex for 93 (requiring 126) and Botham turned 'good as gold'. Holder was ranked 13th out of 26 umpires that year and his new career was up and away.

Holder had played for Hampshire from 1968–72 as a fast bowler having moved to England from Barbados in 1963 to work on the Underground and play cricket.

'My career got cut short by a back injury in 1970. I played for a couple of seasons at Hampshire but in my first-class career I didn't feel fulfilled. I was playing in the leagues in Lancashire and didn't really achieve much and I started to miss first-class cricket. I thought it's too late to come back as a player, so umpiring it was and it's the best decision I ever made.'

There were very few black umpires in the county game when he began (in the domestic game he stood in 421 first-class matches and 449 List A matches, while from 1988–2001 he stood in 11 Tests, plus five as a TV umpire, 19 ODIs and from 2005-2009 in six women's ODIs). Vanburn Holder, also Barbados-born, was the next black umpire after Holder and there have been none since.

'One thing with me, I'm a black man and I know I'm a black man, but that's not something I worry about,' John said. 'I walk about as a human being. That has never concerned me. I've never felt inadequate, I've never had the negativity thinking life is tough because I'm black, because it's never concerned me.

'But I've been disappointed that there's not been many other black umpires following me. I think it's been a deliberate policy. Even now the last black umpire taken on by the TCCB/ECB was Vanburn Holder in 1992. I think that was a deliberate policy because the powers that be they wanted people who looked like them. When I was taken on my boss was John Carr's father [TCCB secretary D.B. Carr]. But some of my bosses were not competent and some were bigots. I was already established so I suppose it would have caused a big thing if they kicked me out because I was always near the top of the markings. But I loved umpiring and I wanted to be one of the best.

'That decision to become an umpire for me in terms of career satisfaction and achievement was the best decision I've ever made. If I was 30 again I'd have no hesitation but now I'd get paid a lot better, especially if I was on the elite panel.'

Holder, who was 78 when we met, is now retired. He has macular degeneration and can no longer drive. The problem first manifested itself in 1995 when he was umpiring at The Parks, and has seen a very gradual degeneration.

In March 2023, the ECB created a new 34-strong professional umpires' team following an independent review.

Holder had accused the ECB of 'years of racism' when appointing umpires. Five umpires have since been added to the list: Naeem Ashraf, Jack Shantry, Anthony Harris, Sue Redfern and Surendiran Shanmugam.

Chapter 7

The Counties

Derbyshire: Barry Wood, Ian Anderson, Alan Hill, Peter Kirsten, John Hampshire, Kim Barnett, Geoff Miller, Bob Taylor, Bernard Maher, Paul Newman, Steve Oldham, Colin Tunnicliffe.

Essex: Keith Fletcher, Graham Gooch, Brian Hardie, Ken McEwan, Keith Pont, Derek Pringle, David East, Norbert Phillip, John Lever, Stuart Turner, Ray East, David Acfield.

Glamorgan: Mike Selvey, Alan Jones, John Hopkins, Javed Miandad, Rodney Ontong, Charles Rowe, Alan Lewis Jones, Arthur Francis, Terry Davies, Malcolm Nash, Greg Thomas, Barry Lloyd.

Gloucestershire: David Graveney, Chris Broad, Andrew Stovold, Zaheer Abbas, Paul Romaines, Phil Bainbridge, Alastair Hignell, Andy Brassington, John Shepherd, Franklyn Stephenson, Richard Doughty, John Childs.

Hampshire: Nick Pocock, Gordon Greenidge, Chris Smith, Mark Nicholas, Trevor Jesty, Nigel Cowley, David Turner, Tim Tremlett, Bobby Parks, Malcolm Marshall, Kevin Emery, John Southern.

Kent: Chris Tavare, Neil Taylor, Laurie Potter, Bob Woolmer, Mark Benson, Christopher Cowdrey, Derek Aslett, Alan Knott, Graham Dilley, Kevin Jarvis, Richard Ellison, Derek Underwood.

Lancashire: Clive Lloyd, Fowler, Cockbain, David Lloyd, Chris Maynard, John Abrahams, David Hughes, Steve O'Shaughnessy, Jack Simmons, Paul Allott, Colin Croft, Ian Folley.

Leicestershire: Roger Tolchard, Chris Balderstone, John Steele, Nigel Briers, Brian Davison, David Gower, Tim Boon, Mike Garnham, Andy Roberts, Les Taylor, Gordon Parsons, Nick Cook.

Middlesex: Mike Gatting, Wilf Slack, Keith Tomlins, Graham Barlow, Roland Butcher, Clive Radley, Paul Downton, Phil Edmonds, John Emburey, Wayne Daniel, Norman Cowans, Simon Hughes.

County Grounds: Lord's, Canterbury, Bath, The Oval, Taunton, Trent Bridge, Cheltenham, Chesterfield, Worcester.

Northamptonshire: Geoff Cook, Wayne Larkins, Richard Williams, Allan Lamb, Peter Willey, Robin Boyd-Moss, David Steele, Kapil Dev, George Sharp, Neil Mallender, Jim Griffiths, Tim Lamb.

Nottinghamshire: Clive Rice, Tim Robinson, Basharat Hassan, Derek Randall, Mark Fell, John Birch, Bruce French, Mike Hendrick, Kevin Cooper, Kevin Saxelby, Eddie Hemmings, Peter Such.

Somerset: Brian Rose, Jeremy Lloyds, Peter Roebuck, Viv Richards, Peter Denning, Ian Botham, Vic Marks, Phil

Slocombe, Trevor Gard, Joel Garner, Hallam Moseley, Colin Dredge.

Surrey: Roger Knight, Alan Butcher, Grahame Clinton, David Smith, Monte Lynch, Andy Needham, Jack Richards, Sylvester Clarke, Robin Jackman, Kevin Macintosh, Dave Thomas, Pat Pocock.

Sussex: John Barclay, Gehan Mendis, Allan Green, Paul Parker, Imran Khan, Colin Wells, Ian Greig, Ian Gould, Paul Phillipson, Garth Le Roux, Tony Pigott, Chris Waller.

Warwickshire: Bob Willis, Dennis Amiss, David Smith, Alvin Kallicharran, Andy Lloyd, Asif Din, Geoff Humpage, Anton Ferreira, Gladstone Small, Willie Hogg, Chris Old, Chris Lethbridge.

Worcestershire: Phil Neale, Martin Weston, Alan Ormrod, Mark Scott, Younis Ahmed, Tim Curtis, Damian D'Oliveira, Dipak Patel, David Humphries, Paul Pridgeon, John Inchmore, Alan Warner.

Yorkshire: Ray Illingworth, Geoffrey Boycott, Richard Lumb, Bill Athey, Jim Love, Stuart Hartley, Martyn Moxon, Kevin Sharp, David Bairstow, Graham Stevenson, Arnie Sidebottom, Phil Carrick.

Faces for the Future: Colin Cook, Nigel Felton, Neil Foster, Richard Illingworth, Paul Jarvis, Hugh Morris, Chris Penn, Tony Wright, 'Jack' Russell.

The Prudential Cup

England, West Indies, Australia, Zimbabwe, India, New Zealand, Pakistan, Sri Lanka.

Chapter 8

Derbyshire: Ole Mortensen

DERBYSHIRE'S DANE was a trailblazer as cricket tentatively moved beyond England's imperial colonies in the 1970s and 1980s, the era when the MCC lost control of the game to the ICC. And it was in the momentous year of 1983 when Mortensen broke new ground when he signed for Derbyshire: 'I can't run away from the fact that I'm not born in England,' he says, 40 years on.

Michael Foot's Labour Manifesto 1983 promised to open negotiations to prepare for Britain's withdrawal from the EEC. Surprisingly, given Brexit in 2016, Margaret Thatcher's Conservatives said leaving the European Union would mean job losses, isolation and export and investment declines: 'Withdrawal would be a catastrophe for this country.'

While the UK was finding some sort of stability under Thatcher's government, Derbyshire CCC was in chaos. Captain Barry Wood resigned in the first week in May and then left. The 22-year-old Kim Barnett took over. He steered the team back to equilibrium, helped by new players such as Mortensen, who took 84 wickets in all competitions for the county in 1983 with his accurate and angry fast bowling. West Indian paceman Michael Holding was injured in a World Cup final pitch invasion and hardly played (though he took 21 Championship wickets at 12.47 when he did). Mortensen bowled at the other end to medium pacers Roger Finney, Colin Tunnicliffe and Steve Oldham. Yet in his debut season of 1983 his 66 Championship wickets were 26 more than for any of his team-mates.

The majority of counties still used home-grown players. Nine of Derbyshire's 13 who played more than ten first-class games were born in Derbyshire, Staffordshire or Cheshire. Oldham and Hampshire were Yorkshire imports. All Yorkshire players had to be Yorkshire-born until their rules were relaxed in 1992. Nine of Essex's Championship-winning 15 were local-born. Typically, there were a couple of overseas imports (West Indian Holding and New Zealander John Wright at Derbyshire). No county could play more than one England unqualified player unless they had been registered before the 1979 season. There were no loans and few transfers between counties (and then usually for opportunity rather than money).

In 1982, a new rule allowing the counties to field just one overseas player in Championship matches was introduced. In 1991, that was tightened to one per squad, bringing a new threat to a long-established Ole. But Mortensen won a legal action, citing the Treaty of Rome, which guaranteed equal employment rights to all European Union citizens.

Although Mortensen was considered a home player rather than an overseas one for Derbyshire, he still couldn't play for England, nor could the top eight players in the 1983 bowling averages. This was because they were foreigners or banned for touring South Africa in 1981/82.

Rules allowing overseas players had originally been relaxed in 1968. Garry Sobers and Nottinghamshire were among those benefitting, with Nottinghamshire paying the world's leading all-rounder £7,000 plus a flat and car for the summer.

Mortensen had arrived in Derby as a 25-year-old income-tax inspector, taking a pay cut. He'd impressed Derbyshire cricketer/footballer Ian Buxton, who knew Denmark's New Zealand-born coach Peter Hargreaves, at a trial.

Denmark became an ICC associate member in 1966 and first played in the ICC Trophy (World Cup qualifier) in 1979 (losing in the semis to eventual winner Sri Lanka at Birmingham with 21-year-old Mortensen scoring five as an opener and taking 1-58 to complete a tournament joint-second-best ten wickets at 12.90.

He'd had a trial for Derbyshire in 1981, having previously been considered by Kent, but EEC players qualified as overseas and Derbyshire already had Wright and Peter Kirsten.

Denmark were not involved in 1982 when Zimbabwe (Sri Lanka now had Test status) qualified for the 1983 World Cup and although Mortensen had averaged 7.2 for his country over the last three years, with a best bowling of 8-7, he looked to be lost to a bigger stage, until Derbyshire re-ignited interest.

Derbyshire's historian David Griffin and fan Steve Dolman put me in touch with Ole.

'Cricket is a minority sport in Denmark and I'd never anticipated that I was going to make a career in county cricket. I came to England for six months to enjoy myself and that's about it. So there wasn't an awful lot of pressure. I took the opportunities as they came along.

'I was honoured to be given the opportunity to have a trial with Derby. I was also meant to have a trial with Kent but Derby signed me on the spot and as I had a wonderful time with Derby so I don't regret not going to Kent.'

He took 7-12 against Lincolnshire for the seconds a couple of weeks after signing a contract, was in the first team by the end of May and took 4-59 against Hampshire in early June.

'The Viking' knew he had made it when he pillaged Yorkshire at Sheffield in mid-summer. It was Derbyshire's first Championship win against their northern neighbours since 1957. On a dodgy pitch later reported as substandard, a hostile Mortensen made the ball lift unpleasantly, said *Wisden*. When he had last man Simon Dennis caught just 22 runs shy of the 256 target, he had 11-89 from 40.5 overs in the match. Only Geoff Boycott, who carried his bat for 112, evaded him. 'That was the turning point when I thought that I could make an impact in English county cricket,' he recalls.

Mortensen remembers how veteran England keeper Bob Taylor, 42 the next month, advised him where to bowl and what the batsmen's weaknesses were. That year Yorkshire were fragile, captained by 51-year-old Ray Illingworth but with the strings being pulled by Boycott, banned by England, and determined to bat forever for his county.

'He was a very tough competitor and a legend and to get him out was a bit of a coup but I also remember a Sunday League game [at Bradford]. I got Geoffrey out in the first over and that was a big, big mistake. I nearly got crucified when I got to the boundary edge by the Yorkie supporters because they didn't like seeing me taking their Geoffrey in the very first over.

'It was all in the good spirit. They like to see Boycott get some runs, but it was a beautiful delivery and he nicked it.' Yorkshire won by two wickets after Bill Athey, injured in a car accident the previous evening, added 21 for the ninth wicket with Simon Dennis, who hit the winning run off Mortensen.

As basically the first Kolpak, Mortensen (known as Stan after the 1950s Blackpool and England footballer) was only an honorary Briton with the TCCB because Denmark was in the EEC. If Labour had won the 1983 election, Mortensen would probably have left as he would have been behind overseas players Holding and Wright, who were both away for the World Cup for most of 1983.

'In those days, all counties had two overseas world-class players. It was just a great education for me to go up in the bar on the second or the third day to talk to these great players. We had Richard Hadlee, Imran Khan, Vivian Richards, Clive Lloyd, Allan Border. They were all playing in that same era and I still look back and think how lucky I was to play in that era with some really outstanding players. I had the opportunity to open the bowling with my very good trusted friend Michael Holding and you know that's fantastic. Michael Holding, the Rolls-Royce, and me, the Reliant Robin, the plastic pig!'

He did it all with little backroom backup: 'We had one physiotherapist and he basically put Deep Heat on all parts of your body. There were no dieticians. There was no psychologist. You played day in day out and only Sunday was different because it was a two o'clock start. One day you were in Scarborough, the next you're in Canterbury, the next you're at Lord's and the next The Oval. You were just going up and down the country.

'Basically, you had the pre-season, from April Fool's Day. And then you bowled to get match fit. The senior pros Bob Taylor, Geoff Miller, Colin Tunnicliffe and Michael Holding and John Hampshire gave advice on how to read the pitch, the opposition, their strengths and weaknesses. But I had the gift that I could swing the ball and put it on the same spot again and again and if I hit the seam at the same time, the ball would jack in or out.

'Mikey Holding always told me, bowl straight and they miss and you hit then the pressure is on the batter and not you, and every batter has only got two arms and two legs so every delivery counts. You had to be consistent and believe in yourself and then you have more good days than bad.'

He was known for his desire to succeed: 'The Viking spirit is part of my DNA. I never give up. I was definitely competitive, but I've never been personal towards a batsman. My secret was, if I was really agitated and really pissed with myself, I would curse in Danish and the umpire and the opposition wouldn't know what I was talking about. I always played within the spirit of the game and I wanted to give value for money. I wasn't trying to go in and play half-hearted, because I was proud to play for Derbyshire. Sometimes it was really hard work. But it was a privilege to play first-class cricket, out in the fresh air, travelling around playing against some of the best players in the world, staying in nice hotels, reading the newspaper in the morning, together with your scrambled egg and smoked salmon. It was a good lifestyle.'

He's still involved, volunteering with young cricketers in Denmark. When he retired he became Denmark national coach from 1995–2000 and coached in France and Germany (2002-05) and Norway (2006–10): 'It's been great to pass on some of my knowledge and experience and watch smaller cricketing nations progress. If I can give something back to Danish cricket and the cricketers in Denmark, I'm happy to do so.'

T20 status began for full ICC members in 2005 and the ICC extended this to all its 105 members in 2019.

Denmark in the 1980s 'were basically competing with Ireland and Scotland and Holland. But today the national team sadly, they're playing in what the ICC call Division Four. And like lots of places in Europe a lot of the native guys don't take up cricket anymore. Because we live in a global village, players from Pakistan, Sri Lanka, Afghanistan and India make up the majority of the Denmark team and some of them are very talented.

'But I'm slightly concerned about Test cricket. As long as the ICC is in a position to secure big sponsor deals I think it will survive, but I can see T20 slowly but surely taking more and more of the limelight, because it's entertaining and very flashy. It's great to watch and only takes three hours, but for me it's not what cricket is all about. I can see Test cricket played in England or Australia and maybe one or two other places for a number of years but T20 is the competition which is going places. It's great to watch and I commentate on it for Eurosport, but it's not really my cup of tea.'

He would have loved to have played T20: 'It could be quite entertaining. I would have to expand my armoury with a slower ball and maybe be a bit more agile in the field. But it's a different game now, isn't it? The players have got four or five psychologists, they've got the personal trainers, they've got the two or three physiotherapists, they've got dieticians. There's almost more backroom staff than there are players. Guys are a lot fitter than when I was playing. But I think the playing standard or the challenge and the characters in the game are really missing, which is sad and it is more money-orientated. When I played there were characters who played for the love of the game, and you don't see that very often though these days.'

A cricketing trailblazer and committed and talented professional, Mortensen was a Denmark regular who was surely good enough for an England that tried 29 seam bowlers between 1983 and 1994: Tony Pigott, Jon Agnew, Richard Ellison, Arnie Sidebottom, Les Taylor, Greg Thomas, Neal Radford, Gladstone Small, Phil DeFreitas, David Capel, Paul Jarvis, David Lawrence, Phil Newport, Angus Fraser, Devon Malcolm, Alan Igglesden, Chris Lewis, Neil Williams, Steve Watkin, Dermot Reeve, Tim Munton, Neil Mallender, Paul Taylor, Andy Caddick,

Mark Illott, Martin McCague, Martin Bicknell and Craig White.

Does Mortensen wish he'd had the opportunity to have played Test and international cricket against the best? 'My good mate Mike Gatting said that I should try to qualify to play for England and the same happened when I was in New Zealand for one season [1983/84]. They made an inquiry if I wanted to take up nationality.'

Nonetheless, he reflects happily on his career: 'With my background I bought into it and enjoyed every single day playing for Derbyshire and putting my name in the history book, playing county cricket. I played for the love of the game and I'd have played for free.

'Salary-wise, it was peanuts compared with what guys are getting paid today. And when I look at some of the players playing county cricket, you know they wouldn't even get in the first team when I was playing. These days, players are moving around, with T20. Moving around [teams] has been basically the trend in the last ten to 15 years now but I have no regrets. I played at a time where some of the all-time great cricketers from all over the globe were playing in county cricket.'

In 1983, Mortensen took 66 Championship wickets at 24.31 in 18 matches, with 76 runs at 9.50. In the Sunday League in 1983 he took 13 wickets for 340 runs and in the NatWest Trophy 4-47 in two matches. Overall, in List A matches in 1983 he took 18 wickets at 22.61. In his career, he took 434 wickets at 23.88 from 1983–94 in 157 first-class games. In 200 List A matches he took 219 wickets at 25.56.

Yorkshire v Derbyshire June 22–24 1983, Sheffield
Yorkshire first innings and second innings

Geoff Boycott c Anderson b Moir 23   not out 112
Richard Lumb lbw Mortensen 28   c Miller b Moir 0
Bill Athey c Taylor b Moir 0   st Taylor b Moir 12
Neil Hartley c Moir b Mortensen 2   lbw Mortensen 4
Jim Love c Taylor b Moir 3   c Hill b Mortensen 8
Simon Dennis c Taylor b Mortensen 0   (11) c Fowler b Mortensen 17
David Bairstow c Taylor b Moir 4   (6) b Moir 44
Graham Stevenson c Taylor b Mortensen 3   (9) c Fowler b Mortensen 1
Phil Carrick b Mortensen 15 (7) b Mortensen 1
Arnie Sidebottom c Taylor b Mortensen 7 (8) b Moir 19
Ray Illingworth not out 7 (10) b Moir 0
Bowling: First innings: Mortensen 16.4-5-27-6; Tunnicliffe 10-2-23-0; Moir 17-6-45-4; Fowler 3-0-12-0. Second innings: Mortensen 24.1-3-62-5; Tunnicliffe 11-2-37-0; Moir 34-7-114-5; Miller 1-0-7-0.

Derbyshire 1983

Barry Wood: Left Derbyshire in July 1983 after resigning the captaincy in May and joined Barnoldswick in the Ribblesdale League. He played his last three first-class matches in 1983 scoring 22 runs, plus six one-dayers with 89 runs and seven wickets. He played for Cheshire from 1986–89 and his son Nathan played for Lancashire from 1992–2000, then for Cheshire too. Barry Wood played for Yorkshire in 1964, then played for Lancashire from 1966–79, Derbyshire from 1980–83 and England from

1972–78 (12 Tests, 13 ODIs). From 1964–83 he played 357 first-class matches, scoring 17,453 runs at 33.82 and in 291 one-dayers scored 6,041 runs at 28.36. He took 298 first-class wickets at 30.73 and 332 one-day wickets at 21.30.

Iain Anderson: Opener scored 1,233 runs at 37.36 in 1983 plus 364 in 17 one-dayers. Derbyshire 1978–87 with 140 first-class matches and 4,726 runs at 23.86 and 81 one-dayers with 1,594 runs at 24.90. Later a coach, then an accountant.

Peter Kirsten: Did not play for Derbyshire after 1982. He debuted for the county in 1978 and scored 7,722 runs at 49.50 in 106 first-class matches for the county. The middle order batsman played 12 Tests and 40 ODIs for South Africa from 1991–94. Played 327 first-class matches with 22,635 runs at 44.46 and 358 one-dayers with 11,403 runs at 35.63. Later, he was a coach for Uganda, Zambia and Jersey. Brother Gary played 101 Tests for South Africa.

John Hampshire (1941–2017): He retired after the 1984 season and became an umpire from 1985–2005. In 1983 'Jack' Hampshire scored 485 Championship runs at 28.52 and 190 in six one-dayers. England 1969–75 (eight Tests, three ODIs). Yorkshire 1961–81, Derbyshire 1982–84. Played 577 first-class matches with 28,059 runs at 34.55 and 280 one-dayers with 7,314 runs at 31.12.

Alan Hill: Opener who played his last Derbyshire game in 1986 after debuting in 1972. He became an umpire for two years then a coach and worked in Derbyshire CCC administration as CEO, commercial manager and cricket development officer. 'Bud' Hill became Derbyshire CCC president in 2023. In 1983 the opener hit 1,311 Championship runs at 37.45 and 331 in 18 one-dayers. In 258 first-class matches he scored 12,356 runs at 30.89 and in 155 one-dayers 3,518 runs at 26.45.

Kim Barnett: Became Derbyshire captain in May 1983 until 1995. He played more games (813), scored more runs (36,212) and more hundreds (66) than any other player in the club's history. He then moved to Gloucestershire from 1999–2002 after being at Derbyshire from 1979–1998. In 1983 he topped the Derbyshire Championship averages with 1,423 runs at 38.45, plus 411 in 18 one-dayers. He played four Tests and one ODI for England between 1988 and 89. Played 479 first-class matches with 28,593 runs at 40.38 and 527 one-dayers with 15,564 runs at 34.89. Later a coach and Derbyshire president, then cricket director.

Geoff Miller: The all-rounder took 37 wickets at 34.54 and scored 699 runs at 30.39 in 1983, plus 322 runs and 14 wickets in 15 one-dayers. He played for Essex in 1987–89 but returned to Derbyshire for 1990 after debuting there in 1973. He later played for Cheshire and was an England selector from 2000–13 and president of Derbyshire in 2014. Played for England between 1976 and 84 (34 Tests, 25 ODIs). 'Dusty' Miller played 383 first-class matches, scoring 12,027 runs at 26.49 and taking 888 wickets at 27.98, and 334 one-dayers with 4,234 runs at 20.16 and 278 wickets at 29.44. Later an after-dinner speaker, he ran a sports shop in Chesterfield with footballer Ernie Moss. Appointed an OBE in 2014.

Bob Taylor: Played for Derbyshire and England until 1984 totalling 639 first-class matches. His 1,649 dismissals (1,473 caught, 176 stumped) remains a first-class record. He took 49 catches and made two stumpings in 1983 plus 12/1 in one-dayers. England 1971–84 (57 Tests, 27 ODIs). He played four Tests against New Zealand in 1983, scoring 63 runs and taking 11 catches. Also played 333 one-dayers with 345 catches and 75 stumpings. Later coached and worked for Mitre Sports. 'Chat' Taylor also promoted Dukes balls and worked as a cricket tour host. Awarded an MBE in 1981.

Bernie Maher: Maher played for Derbyshire as a wicketkeeper-batsman from 1981–93. In 1983 he scored 150 runs at 15. Played 133 first-class matches, scoring 3,689 runs at 21.82 and taking 289 catches/14 stumpings, and 111 one-dayers with 1,177 runs at 16.12 and 105 catches and 12 stumpings. He became a fly-fishing international.

Paul Newman: He played for Derbyshire from 1980–89. He took seven Championship wickets in 1983, plus 18 in one-dayers, struggling with form and fitness. In 135 first-class matches he took 315 wickets at 31.25 and in 177 one-dayers took 187 wickets at 29.94. Later played for Norfolk and played club cricket until he was 53.

Steve Oldham: He returned to Yorkshire for 1984–85 after being there from 1974–79, then coached at Yorkshire until 2011. He took 31 Championship wickets at 36.12 and 20 in one-dayers in 1983 for Derbyshire, where he played from 1980–83. In his career, he played 129 first-class matches with 273 wickets at 32.67 and 177 one-day matches with 240 wickets at 23.18.

Colin Tunnicliffe: His career ended after 1983, when he took 39 wickets at 35.17 plus 13 in one-dayers. He became Derbyshire commercial manager. Played 150 first-class matches with 319 wickets at 32.17 and 167 one-dayers with 190 wickets at 25.24.

Chapter 9

Essex: David Acfield and Derek Pringle

IN 1983, when Essex won the County Championship, the only Olympic fencer or Commonwealth gold medal winner to play first-class cricket was a crucial component of the team.

David Acfield, a thoughtful and skilled cricketer, spent more than 50 years serving Essex, and played an important part in the title win. Against Somerset in early June he took 4-105 and 6-34 against Somerset. This included five wickets in 13 balls to win the match with 55 minutes to spare, including Ian Botham twice. The slow left-armer also took 7-100 against Lancashire in early September in 49.2 overs after only bowling two overs in the first innings, such was the strength of the Essex attack. Lancashire held on for a draw, delaying Essex's title celebrations.

Edwardian era Essex fast bowler Claude Buckenham (football gold 1900 Olympics) played four Tests among his 307 first-class matches. Somerset and Cambridge

University opener Jack MacBryan (hockey gold 1920) played one Test and 210 first-class games while Brian Booth (hockey 1956) played 29 Tests for Australia. They were among the most successful Olympian cricketers. The best was Essex all-rounder J.W.H.T. Douglas (boxing gold 1908), who was England captain in 18 of his 23 Tests.

David Jackman of *Everything Essex Cricket*, who was my editor at the *Epping Guardian* 20 years before, suggested writing to Ackers. After all, Acfield studied history at Cambridge so, like Mike Brearley (classics and moral sciences), might appreciate a literary approach.

It worked. He emailed back two days after I posted my letter suggesting I send some questions so he can refresh his memory via Essex yearbooks.

'I will do my best, Matt … '

A bad start. He doesn't recall Panini: 'There seem to have been a number of stickers/cards in my time and I'm not sure I remember the ones you refer to. I still occasionally get asked to sign them.'

Being a full-time cricketer, world-class fencer and history teacher in the winters meant he had plenty of demands on his time beyond thinking about trivia like stickers. 'My fencing probably hindered my cricket career. Under Olympic rules at the time I was not allowed to earn money from cricket so between 1966 and 1972 I played as a voluntary amateur. In 1968 I played only three games before being selected for the Olympics and in 1972 I played only the first half of the season for the same reason. Trying to compete in two sports and earn a living in the winter was not easy. From a cricket point of view I should have retired from fencing in 1968, but then I would not have gone to the Commonwealth Games or the World Championships in 1970 and I would not have won four consecutive national titles from 1969 to 1972 which still has not been achieved since.

'Of course, cricket greatly hindered my fencing career for I only did it in the winter except in the big years and I should have won the individual gold in the Commonwealth Games but I came straight off the cricket field having not fenced for a few months. I flew back late at night and played against Yorkshire the next day when [Geoff] Boycott scored a double hundred.' He was 260 not out, his highest first-class score in England, at Colchester in July; Acfield 1-60 off 15 overs.

Why were Essex so good? 'The team spirit at Essex was exceptional. Many of us grew up together and we built a side over 12 years. That does not happen anymore because two divisions has exacerbated the transfer market and sides like Leicestershire lose their players to Nottinghamshire. In my time nine counties won the Championship but since 2000 only two non-Test match grounds have done so. We were variously described as mad or irresponsible as we had a lot of fun on and off the field but we took the game very seriously. One Middlesex player said they used to come to Chelmsford, laugh for three days and lose.'

One of the best-known matches of 1983 was Essex bowling out Surrey for 14, one of the lowest first-class scores ever. 'The ball swung in the Surrey match and every nick went to hand. If Sylvester Clarke had not tried to slog and nicked a four it would have been ten. We never looked like bowling them out a second time.' Acfield bowled 17 overs for 0-23 as Surrey drew the match with 185/2 in their second innings.

His best performance in 1983 was the 10-139 to force the win against Somerset. 'The first innings gave me a chance to bowl a long spell and that meant I was well prepared for the second innings when it turned a little. Of the four ten-wicket hauls I took, three were the result of a long first innings spell. In the first innings Ian Botham charged me, I lost control and the ball went down the leg side. He fell over and was stumped. In the second innings Keith Fletcher suggested I bowl and with the fourth ball of the over I tried to land it on his toe since he would try to reverse sweep. No pressure there then! He did, it worked, I felt good but the yearbook simply said he missed a full toss!'

Then there was the 7-100 against Lancashire in early September: 'The Lancashire match became a bit of a marathon. I took six wickets on the second day but a late order stand [Steve Jefferies with 75 not out and Paul Allott with 45 added 77 for the tenth wicket] held us up and turned what should have been an easy win into a rain-affected draw.' Securing the Championship remained elusive. Lancashire's next match saw Steve O'Shaughnessy's 35-minute century as Leicestershire sought a declaration and a result. Essex drew their next match too, against Yorkshire. But Middlesex's game at Trent Bridge against Nottinghamshire was rain-hit and Nottinghamshire captain Clive Rice was in no mood to give Middlesex the chance to win. So Essex won the Championship by 16 points, with the same number of wins (11) as Middlesex and one more loss (five to four), but nine more batting and seven more bowling points. This was the peak of Essex's run of success as they and Middlesex fought to be top dogs in English cricket. Essex won nine trophies between 1979 and 1986 including three Championships. Middlesex won eight, including three Schweppes/Britannic Assurance titles (Schweppes was inaugural sponsor from 1977–83 and Britannic Assurance from 1984–98).

In 1983, spinners Acfield and East only took 65 Championship wickets between them compared to 166 by opening bowlers John Lever and Norbert Phillip. Essex only used 15 players across 24 matches, and in 25 one-dayers. In contrast, champions Surrey used 23 in 16 Championship matches in 2022 and 19 in 2023. Spinners barely featured. They used 32 players in all competitions.

Acfield couldn't get into the team for the narrow Benson & Hedges Cup final loss to Middlesex. Fellow spinner Ray East did, and didn't bowl. 'I often felt under-bowled,' he said. 'Ray East and I used to call ourselves the Last Resort Bowlers or the Seamers' Sweater Carriers. What was difficult was not bowling much at all or even being left out of the side and then expected to bowl the opposition out when it turned having had no opportunity to find a rhythm. My biggest regret was never playing in a Lord's final or even being on the balcony. I played in the first five games of the B&H in 1979 when Ray East was injured, did very well but when Ray was fit I was left out of the quarter-final and we went on to win. Captains always favour the ball leaving the right-hander – no second line of defence when so many played with the pad and umpires gave few lbws, unlike today. I actually played 160 List A games including quarter and semi-finals but never in a final.'

Acfield's involvement in cricket after retiring from playing in 1986 saw him take senior roles in administration and influence the direction of the game.

He was a director of the TCCB and then the ECB for 12 years as chairman of the Cricket Committee: 'At that time it was felt any discussions should be cricket led so I chaired endless working parties into the structure of the game as well as bi-annual meetings of the cricket committee, captains, umpires, etc. and attended monthly board meetings. On my watch most of what you see today was brought in. I had to propose four-day cricket and two divisions but I'm not really in favour of either because both have been detrimental to the county game and I often say we have sacrificed the county game on the altar of the England team. The production of England players is one function of the counties but so too is providing a hub for the game in their region and to act as an inspiration for young people, just as I was inspired by watching Essex in the 1950s.

'Far fewer matches are played now which affects the membership and I have never subscribed to the mantra that we play too much cricket. I accept the fact that Test players, especially fast bowlers, need looking after and in the Acfield Report into the selection and management of England teams I suggested the coach/selectors should be allowed to rest certain players from county cricket if necessary. That was turned down by the counties. A couple of years later we had central contracts and few Test players play for their counties at all. That, combined with the unavailability of top-class overseas players, means the entertainment value and standard of county cricket has declined.

'Championship cricket is relegated to the start and end of the season but at least, so far, the idea of playing it while The Hundred is on has been resisted. That would turn the premier competition into a second-team game, just as the 50-over game is now with a hundred of the best players not available.

'Of all the changes I was heavily involved with, the most interesting was T20. Every few years it is necessary to revitalise county cricket – 60, 50, 40 overs, etc. T20 arose from a small working party I chaired. It was designed to be played between 5.15pm and 8.15pm on long summer evenings to attract women and children but now floodlights have changed the whole nature of the game. I only just managed to have it accepted 11-7 by the counties and there was much vociferous opposition. We had no idea it would be this successful or that it would threaten the longer formats. The players thought it was daft until they saw the crowds.'

After decades of service, Acfield's involvement ended on a sour note. In 2021, chairman John Faragher resigned following an allegation that he used racist language at a board meeting in 2017. Essex were later fined £50,000.

'Over the last 35 years I have held all the major offices at Essex – deputy chairman, chairman, treasurer and president. My presidency was marred first by Covid and then by allegations of racism directed against the then chairman and, later, others, including me, by disaffected board members. In order to purge the board it was agreed that all present at a meeting in 2021 should resign for not acting on the allegation of a racist comment which was allegedly made three years earlier which I did not hear. No one asked for action to be taken at the time. That included me as president. We still await the reports and it has been a difficult, long drawn-out process and rather a sad end to 57 years' continuous involvement with Essex.' [Essex CCC admitted it had made 'fundamental errors' after the report was published in December 2023].

Regrets? 'I should have worked harder on my batting but it was not done for tailenders to demand nets in those days. Not sure it would have made much difference with the battery of very quick, hostile bowlers around then, unlike the county cricket of today! And a Lord's final would have been good.'

Derek Pringle

Derek Pringle was always up my sleeve. I'd been to a book event for his autobiography *Pushing the Boundaries* in 2022 listening to one of my cricket hero's lugubrious and sanguine insights into the game.

We listened to a cricket hero of our youth reminiscing about the last days of fun on the county circuit when drinking, japery and skills meant more than coaching by data and shuttle runs.

Former Essex and England all-rounder turned writer, Pringle, now in his mid-60s, these days gives his opinion on today's game for *The Metro* and *The Cricket Paper*.

He liked Half Man Half Biscuit, never married and had an ear stud. In *Cricketers' Who's Who* 1983 Pringle says he likes phenomenology and modern music such as Talking Heads and Peter Gabriel, he wants more leniency on commercialism by the TCCB and for counties to play the others once (over three or four days).

On a table in the theatre where we meet for the event in Barnes, southwest London, are a pile of Pringle's entertaining and insightful book. He said that publisher Roddy Bloomfield, perhaps best known for editing *Fly Fishing by J.R. Hartley*, commissioned his book and recommended taking a few tales out, on grounds of taste. Pushed to give an example, we hear how Rodney Cass shat in a sink when rooming with prankster Ray East at the Grand Hotel, Scarborough. The Wakefield-born wicketkeeper used East's comb to push the turd down the plughole, gleefully relating his antics to the freshly coiffured slow left-armer at breakfast the next morning. You can understand why the anecdote was deleted.

East, the type who would use a double-sided bat for a laugh, told Pring he'd never write his own memoirs: 'The trouble is it will have to be the unvarnished truth and I will have no friends afterwards.' *Funny Turn, Confessions of a Cricketing Clown* was published in July 1983.

Ian Botham is never far from the chat. Pring was one of many who suffered in comparison to the great all-rounder, though he could keep up with Both's drinking, which made him a good team-mate and tourist. He breezes through his book/career. On the surprise England selection of the student Pringle in 1982, Botham commented, incredulously, 'Is he?' Then the fun starts: 'Botham made me feel very welcome.' After a team dinner of four courses, with wine, sherry and port, Botham got Pring in a headlock to take to the bar for a 'couple of relaxing pints'. This only led to a 'fitful night fretting and peeing'.

The dressing room had 'property rights'. Botham had a bench to kip on. Pring took up the Botham mantle. In 1982, in the Westmoreland Hotel (now the Danubius Regents Park) opposite Lord's, Geoff Cook, Pring and two Australian girls ('boy they could drink') downed a pint of lager standing on their heads one evening during the match, in full view of the public. England still won by seven wickets.

Aussies and Kiwi players (apart from Richard Hadlee) got up to similar. For the West Indies, it's 'not particularly in their culture to go to the pub for long sessions'. A 'generalisation' is Bajans like a drink, other islands like a smoke. Viv [Richards] didn't drink much but Joel Garner loved beer and rum, 'which he used to sweep up in those massive arms of his. "Man," he used to say, "those Aussie birds are sweet."'

Three quarters of every county team were drinkers. On the 1982/83 Australia tour Ian Gould was in a Brisbane bar where the happy hour was 11pm to midnight, so he started at 8pm to take advantage. Running 400-metre laps the next day he had to stop regularly to throw up. Wayne Larkins 'could knock spots off Gould'. He'd clear the mini bar every night when on the phone to his new woman. 'He did his tour fee on international calls.'

In those days there was a manager, assistant manager, physio and scorer with the team – no coach. Micky Stewart was the first professional coach in Pring's view. Norman Gifford knocked up catches and smoked his pipe.

Graham Gooch stopped the fun. 'He just wanted England to be better.' Fitness improved his game. Pring, a decent mimic, imitates Gooch's squeaky voice: '"If you fail to prepare you prepare to fail." I used to take it with a pinch of salt. He decided we had to get fitter for those three per cent gains.'

The revolution began as England were preparing to go to the West Indies. Playing the Nehru Cup in Delhi it was 'hot as Hades'. 'No nets today, boys,' said Gooch. 'We're running round that 400m track.' Larkins, Pring and Nick Cook collectively rolled their eyes. And that was it, the end of the amateur era.

England struggled nonetheless. Players that could have been selected 'in the late 1980s chaos' wouldn't have done much better. Peter Roebuck was 'unlucky not to have been given a go. I thought he was a better player than Tim Curtis,' said Pring.

Ahead of the 1982/83 Ashes tour 'the Aussie press did their usual trick saying it was the worst England side ever to come to these shores, though that might have been the case'. One excuse was the rebel tour to apartheid South Africa. Graham Gooch and Geoff Boycott were among those missing. Mike Gatting and Phil Edmonds weren't picked.

But Pring says there were still 'crazy selections' – he was surprised to play most of the Tests (three out of five) – thinking all along 'if we win this it'll be a miracle. I'm just a realist.'

Captain Bob Willis said England was a second XI with five decent players and the rest making up the numbers. Pring says drawing in Perth was a 'big event'.

At Melbourne, England won by three runs in the Boxing Day Test. Last pair Allan Border and Jeff Thomson were together for two hours, Pring at third man thought 'this is gone now, the grief we're going to get. Then a Botham long hop and, hey presto, Thomson nicked it.'

The Aussies didn't waste their breath sledging Pring. Derek Randall liked it. The chat calmed his nerves. Essex captain Keith Fletcher told his players not to speak to the jittery Nottinghamshire batsman. 'Alreet bigun.' Silence.

After the match, anything went. 'It came from county cricket – at Essex we had several, several beers afterwards. Fletch's rule was as long as you're ready to play at 11am I don't care, as long as it's legal. I was young, foolish and naive so of course I embraced touring life.' He speaks of a three women juggle. The players liked proper beer and you didn't get that in Australia. That's probably why Botham drank jugs of whisky and ice cream.

Geoff Boycott? He retired soon after the rebel tour so Pring's only dealings with him was during his gap year between Felsted School and Cambridge University. A B&H match was hit by rain – and was moved from Harrogate to Middlesbrough for a ten-over slog. Pring was 12th man. Essex were hammered by Yorkshire. Boycs' reaction: 'Never mind Essex, it's a shit game when the world's best opening batsman has to bat number 7.'

'Mike Denness, another boring blocker who never got on with Boycs, told him: "That's the nicest compliment you've ever paid me." Not you, you twat, me.' But Boycs was 'always alright with me'.

Pringle was born and brought up in Kenya – his Lancashire-born father Don played for East Africa and worked in Nairobi as a landscape consultant. But Pring did not feel much in common with Lusaka-born Phil Edmonds or South Africans Allan Lamb and Chris and Robin Smith. Edmonds used the term 'fellow African' and 'made a lot of it'. Pring's only observation is that Kenya's matting pitches did not hold him in good stead for playing in Australia.

He recalls racist abuse from an Essex member. This sort of thing happens less now as players are cocooned from the public. Back then, they could get close to cricketers – 'We welcomed it as long as they behaved'. West Indian Norbert Phillip bowled a few no balls during a tense one dayer. One guy gave abuse in a racist way. Pring stood up: 'He's trying his best, get off his case, no need for that.'

Supporter: 'You can shut your mouth. I pay your fucking wages.'

Pring: 'Tell you what, I'll take a sixpence cut. You can fuck off home.'

The supporter complained to the secretary 'and I got a bollocking'.

The 1981/82 rebel tour to South Africa, which left half the England team banned, gave Pring his chance: 'It was their choice. County cricket then was a very modest living. If you weren't playing for England, you were a free agent, so players thought, "Why not?"'

As a youngster, the only way to get better was 'self-determination'. You learnt in the bar with the senior players listening to the funny stories from John Lever and Ray East. The *Good Beer Guide* was in the kitbag. They didn't overdo it though, being in bed by midnight. Essex won six Championships, three John Player Leagues, a B&H, a NatWest, all without a coach.

It's not so good now. England can't improvise, or self-determine, according to Pring: 'Ben Stokes would have done well in any era. Jonny Bairstow is barrel-chested like his dad David. Gooch would love all the hard work of today. Mike Gatting wouldn't.

'Anyway, what does it matter? Who knows if you're any good at T20 or the Hundred? There's "No jeopardy". It's difficult to write about or get interested in. If you get hit, so what, you slog and get out – who cares?'

On the road in the 1980s, most people liked ELO on the cassette player. Botham had two tapes, Dire Straits and Dexys. Gooch was a Van Morrison obsessive, as was Graham Cowdrey. Another Pring eccentricity was his ear stud (a first for a male England player), the result of a bet with a medical student he met in Australia, some red wine, an ice cube and a hot needle. There's not much of that devil-may-care light-heartedness now, on or off the pitch.

Essex

Keith Fletcher: He captained Essex to three Championships, in 1979, 1983 and 1984. Essex managed the same number of wins and incurred more losses than Middlesex in the closest of these wins in 1983, but bonus points saw them clinch the title by 16 points. He scored 1,026 runs at 33.09 in 1983. 'The Gnome' played for England from 1968–82

(59 Tests and 24 ODIs). He scored 37,665 runs at 37.77 in 730 first-class games and 8,948 in 428 one-dayers at 29.96. Appointed an OBE in 1985, he played for Essex from 1962–88. The 1993–1995 England coach was then Essex coach until 2001 and president from 2023.

Graham Gooch: Gooch opened for Essex from 1973–97 and for England from 1975–95 (118 Test, 125 ODIs). In 1983 he scored 1,227 runs at 36.08. He also scored 1,048 one-day runs at 52.40 with a JPL record of 176 against Glamorgan at Southend. Gooch played 581 first-class games with 44,846 runs at 49.01 and 614 one-dayers with 22,211 runs at 40.16. He became a broadcaster and was Essex coach from 2001–05 and later an England batting coach. Awarded an OBE in 1991.

Brian Hardie: Hardie opened for Essex from 1970–90. In 1983 he scored 896 Championship runs at 28 and 515 in 18 one-dayers, with 18,103 in all in 378 first-class matches at 34.22. He also played 363 one-dayers with 8,606 runs at 29.55. 'Lager' Hardie won four Championships in eight seasons and three one-day titles from seven final appearances. Later, he taught cricket at Brentwood School in Essex.

Ken McEwan: The South African batsman scored 2,051 runs at 68.36 for Essex in 1983, topping the Championship averages. He also scored 533 one-day runs in 20 matches. In all he scored 26,628 runs at 41.73 in 428 first-class matches and 11,866 runs at 33.51 in 409 one-dayers. He retired from Essex after the 1985 season to return to farming in South Africa.

Keith Pont: All-rounder who played for Essex until 1986. In 1983 he scored 658 runs at 32.90 and took four wickets.

He played 16 one-dayers with 117 runs. He scored 6,558 runs in 198 first-class games and took 96 wickets at 33.21. In 249 one-dayers he took 146 wickets at 26.57 and scored 2,894 runs at 17.75. He was director of development at the ECB until 2005. Brother Ian Pont played for Essex from 1982–88.

Derek Pringle: All-rounder who played for Essex from 1978–93 and England from 1982–93 (30 Tests, 44 ODIs). In 1983 he scored 586 runs at 34.47 and took 41 wickets at 22.63 in 17 first-class matches plus 339 runs at 37.66 in 17 one-dayers with 22 wickets at 22.45 and an economy rate of 4.05. In 295 first-class matches he scored 9.243 runs at 28.26 and took 761 wickets at 26.58 and in 317 one-dayers scored 4,873 runs at 25.92 and took 383 wickets at 27.14. He became a cricket journalist for *The Telegraph* and *Metro*.

David East: Essex wicketkeeper until 1991, then commercial manager and CEO until 2012. In 1983 he took 63 catches and made five stumpings, the most dismissals in the Championship and 25 catches and four stumpings in one-dayers. From Essex from 1981–91 he played 180 first-class matches with 4,553 runs and 480 catches/53 stumpings and 171 one-dayers with 889 runs with 174/19.

Norbert Phillip: West Indian fast bowler played for Essex from 1978 until 1985, when he returned to live in Dominica. In 1983 he took 68 wickets at 19.67 with 6-4 against Surrey the highlight, plus 25 in one-dayers and 406 Championship runs. He played 230 first-class matches (7.013 runs at 23.61 and 688 wickets at 24.75) and 182 one-dayers (2,450 at 19.60 and 227 at 22.73) from 1969 including for the West Indies between 1978 and 79 (nine Tests, one ODI).

John Lever: Opened the bowling for Essex from 1967–89. He took 98 Championship wickets at 16.80 in 1983, topping the first-class averages. He took 106 in all first-class matches at 16.28. He also took 22 one-day wickets. At Essex from 1967–90, in 529 first-class matches JK took 1,722 wickets at 24.25 plus 674 in 481 one-dayers at 19.70. Played for England between 1976 and 86 (21 Tests, 22 ODIs). He was later a PE teacher and then a cricket tour host.

Stuart Turner: The all-rounder took 24 first-class wickets at 24.29 in 1983 and scored 161 runs at 10.06 plus 27 wickets in one-dayers. Played for Essex from 1965–86 then Cambridgeshire from 1987–95. Appeared in 361 first-class games with 9,411 runs at 22.84 and 821 wickets at 26.00 and 379 one-dayers with 4,333 runs at 18.67 and 470 wickets at 22.98. Later a schools coach.

Ray East: Played for Essex from 1965–84. In 1983 he took 22 wickets at 35.31 in the Championship plus 20 in one-dayers. In all he played 410 first-class matches with 1,019 wickets at 25.72 and 269 wickets in 280 one-dayers at 24.59. Later a schools coach.

David Acfield: Took 43 wickets at 27.93 (bowling 2,983 balls, less than half the number of Norman Gifford) and scored 66 runs at 7.33 in 21 Championship matches in 1983 and in one JPL match took 1-14 from eight overs. He played for Essex from 1966–86 taking 950 wickets at 28.21 in 420 first-class matches and 152 at 27.25 in 160 List A games. He was Essex president from 2017–23.

Chapter 10

Glamorgan: Mike Selvey

FORMER *Test Match Special* summariser Mike Selvey texted that he was available to talk. It was Good Friday. He was at Lord's watching Middlesex's first game of the season. He'd done his duty as Middlesex president but still had plenty to say. Selvey is perhaps the most rounded, thoughtful and intelligent cricket person of his generation, having won Championships, bowled for England and written and broadcast about the game.

Glamorgan president Ossie Wheatley, the Glamorgan captain in the 1960s, had recruited Selvey from Middlesex as captain for 1983. Aged 35, he had won the Gillette Cup (in 1977 and 1980) and three Championships (1976, 1980 and 1982). Middlesex would win trophies in each of the next three seasons, without him.

He believed Glamorgan had the makings of an improving team after finishing second last in the Championship in 1982. He'd helped turn South African all-rounder Rodney Ontong from a medium pacer into a more effective off-spinner. Homegrown players, like fast bowler Greg Thomas and opener Hugh Morris, were coming through, and Alan Lewis Jones, John Hopkins and Steve Barwick were maturing. Things were looking promising.

But in 1983, Glamorgan moved up just a single place, and Selvey was 'shell-shocked' by the setup, admitting he 'did not know what to do', despite a long career playing under great captains Micky Stewart at Surrey, Mike Brearley for a decade at Middlesex and Tony Greig for England in 1976 and 1977.

There were moments. Glamorgan won by seven wickets at Worcester, when medium pacer Barwick took 8-42. They beat Surrey by five wickets on 2 August for a second, and last, Championship win of the season.

Beating that season's champions Yorkshire in the JPL at Cardiff in June must have been good. Selvey bowled eight overs for 16. But in the NatWest Trophy second round Glamorgan were thrashed by Hampshire, who were inspired by a Gordon Greenidge century. There were a couple of no results in the B&H, then a big loss to Kent.

'We won a game quite early on against Worcestershire when Stephen Barwick bowled really well [actually in late July]. And it was fine. And then cases of champagne turned up in the dressing room, which was all very nice, but I thought, "We just won a cricket match. That's all we've done". And, yet that was how they saw it, a great victory. So that kind of gave me another clue to expectations. Selvey, who was said to have lost a stone and a half by dieting before the season started, thought this too much. Middlesex won regularly and didn't celebrate like that.

He'd seen it all before, but more often on the winning side for Surrey (1968–71), Cambridge University (1971) and Middlesex (1972–82). Mainly bowling into the wind, he took 90 first-class wickets in 1976 and 101 in 1978.

In 1974 he'd played in South Africa. 'I should have come straight home,' he says, airing his regrets louder than many of the dozens of professionals who spent winters playing in the apartheid nation in the 1970s and 1980s.

Were there politics in county cricket in 1983 when banned players such as John Lever and Derek Underwood dominated? Were they accepted? Apart from South Africa, the only other realistic paid playing options in the winter if you weren't on the England tour were Australia or New Zealand.

A player might earn £9,000 a year as an average county salary in 1983, and around £8,500 to tour with England. There was £1,500 a Test (£14,500 in 2023 or £4,500 for a white ball appearance). Benefits after ten years capped service for a county could be £40,000 tax-free, while the South Africa rebel tour of 1981/82 offered a similar amount or more.

Only a few players could make much from commercial contracts, for instance Ian Botham, promoting Saab, Shredded Wheat and Duncan Fearnley bats. The average national salary in 1983 was £8,500 (in 2023 it was £29,500, but cricketers could earn six-figure Hundred contracts, plus, if centrally contracted, £900,000 a year or £250,000-£350,000 for white ball cricket.

Selvey says: 'If I'd have been offered £100,000 or something to go and play cricket in South Africa in 1983,

I wouldn't have done it, because I went to South Africa naively in 1974 to play cricket in Bloemfontein. I really should have turned around and come home after a few days, with what I saw and what I heard, but I didn't. I saw it out for six months, but that six months were hugely influential in my life as it turned out, because they polarised my views entirely. What I saw meant I'd never go back to South Africa until apartheid had gone.

'I don't remember ever thinking, well I won't play against Graham Gooch. I don't know how that would have worked out [even if it had happened]. But the second rebel tour was the one that really should have resonated with people.'

Selvey made three Test appearances in 1976/77, playing with Lever, Underwood, Alan Knott, Bob Woolmer and Mike Hendrick, all banned by 1983, but was now down the fast-bowling pecking order at Middlesex, behind Wayne Daniel, Norman Cowans, Neil Williams and Simon Hughes.

'I'd just come to the end of my life at Middlesex. Glamorgan's chairman Ossie Wheatley [who was later a Test selector] approached me. I got the feeling they might have approached other people before me.' Moving was attractive 'because I probably wasn't going to be here [at Lord's] much longer and get the cricket I wanted. And there was a challenge there.'

But he felt alienated: 'I'd come from an environment where certainly for the previous six years since 1976 we'd got a winning culture and were used to winning games. I came down to a county where there was a lack of ambition or competence. I don't remember where they finished in the table in 1981 or 1982 but near the bottom anyway, and there was almost an element of, well, we've still got jobs.

'And it was a bit of a culture shock, I found it quite hard to know what to do. Middlesex just ran itself, but at Glamorgan you go there and suddenly you're in charge and it was very difficult. I was inexperienced in that kind of environment.'

He says even super-captain Brearley might have struggled: 'I played my entire career under four captains. Of course you learn a lot from Brearley, not in the way that people might think, but you do. But I suspect that if he came into that same environment, he would have looked around and thought there are things that I would say defied belief. There was a lot of internecine fighting going on. There's always this big battle between these two committees for a start, east and west, one Cardiff and one Swansea. We didn't have a grass practice pitch in the county. I find that astonishing, but that was a fact. There was nowhere to practice.

'There was an end goal area of an athletic stadium in Neath and an indoor school and that was our practice facility. How are you expected to compete with that? One thing that happened by the time I got there was Ossie Wheatley had gone and they got a new president and I didn't really get on with him or find him particularly supportive.'

The overseas pro situation was also fraught. When he signed, there was Ezra Moseley and Javed Miandad.

Moseley suffered a stress fracture in the back, so Glamorgan recruited another West Indian quick, Winston Davis.

Selvey didn't know about it: 'I've now got two overseas players but then we were told the TCCB had got a moratorium on the number of [new] overseas players you could have. So we found ourselves as the only county out of 17 who could only play one overseas player. When you play Somerset, you get Viv and Joel, you play Sussex and get Garth Le Roux and Imran Khan and at Hampshire there's Malcolm Marshall and Gordon Greenidge. And I've got to pick the side between one of the greatest batsmen who ever played and Winston Davis. And you try telling Miandad he's not gonna play. I said they could have issued a legal challenge but they wouldn't do it. So we were hampered like that and it was just very difficult.'

Both Miandad and Davis were at the World Cup too. Davis broke the World Cup best bowling figures record with his 7-51 for West Indies against Australia at Leeds.

Meanwhile, Selvey had started promisingly for Glamorgan with 6-47 against Oxford University. Later he took 5-37 against Yorkshire and 5-51 against Sussex. But both games ended in draws as Glamorgan lacked the bowling to take 20 wickets.

A telling match was when Glamorgan only beat Norfolk by 25 runs in the NatWest Trophy first round: 'I do remember that that was up Colman's ground in Norwich. We travelled from Cardiff to Norwich so you can imagine that journey. You're always on a hiding to nothing against a minor county because they're very good at playing on crap wickets and we got a bit of a bumpy ride.' He remembers a disputed decision with Norfolk's ex-Pakistan international Parvez Mir: 'We got out of jail. That was a bit too close for comfort.' All that travelling featured in an article in the 1984 Glamorgan yearbook titled 'On the Road'. He jokes that like the prime minister's son Mark Thatcher, who got lost on the Paris–Dakar rally in 1982, county cricketers clocked up mile after mile driving on their own safaris to matches. He played heavy and sometimes obscure rock music. His passengers either liked it or lumped it.

'We didn't get the best press. I fell out with a bloke who was the very long-standing cricket reporter for *Western Daily Mail*. We came out at the end of a game with a draw and Alan Lewis Jones batted nicely. He got about 80 [actually 62].

The journalist came up to Selvey and said he should give him his county cap. 'He'd been playing for five or six years and never scored a century [Jones ultimately scored five in his 1973–86 Glamorgan career]. I always remember that and that kind of tells you a little bit about how it was.'

Would things have been different if he'd been Welsh? 'It's possible. The players by and large were great, but I never felt completely part of it. When I go down there now and see them it's fine and they're very proud of the fact that I captained the side. But you know I never once got asked to a player's home so I felt a little bit on the periphery.

'Tom Cartwright was coach and that was quite tricky because Tom had two roles. He was the Glamorgan coach, but he was also the Welsh national coach. And it was kind of difficult to have somebody who was doing both those two things.' Cartwright had to choose and chose Wales. 'Tom was a guiding light, a really intelligent cricketer. He always told me to travel on your own. "You can't be too close to people and be their friends all the time."'

In 1983, Selvey took 56 Championship wickets, the most of Glamorgan's bowlers but there was a £100,000 loss. Opener Alan Jones retired at the end of 1983 after a 35-year career. His brother, wicketkeeper Eifion, was being pensioned off too, along with Malcolm Nash. There were other changes afoot: 'I felt later on in 1984 that a couple of people were trying to undermine me. Rodney Ontong was ambitious I remember. I made Rodney into an off-spinner. And he superseded Barry Lloyd, who was a good one-day bowler, in the team. We'd been able to persuade the groundsman Albert Francis to prepare some practice pitches on the square at Sophia Gardens and Barry was at practice one day and I said "well played" [about a second team performance] and he told me he'd been sacked. It was the first I'd heard of it.'

Long-serving left-armer Nash wrote in his 2018 autobiography *Not Only But Also – My Life in Cricket* that his non re-engagement in 1983 was a ruthless, painful and stressful experience. But it was typical of how many clubs operated in those days: 'The brutal truth is you reach a stage where you are no longer part of the plan.' The awful day came at a second XI game at St Helen's, a 'dagger in the heart'. Yachts were racing in Swansea Bay. His calm was disturbed by new Glamorgan secretary Philip Carling. It was bad news. Nash wished Ossie Wheatley had told him – someone he knew.

Nash packed his bag and drove to a favourite spot, Langlands Bay. The most significant change that year had been the arrival of Selvey. Nash said he was 'fit as a fiddle' approaching his 38th birthday but he wasn't bowling enough overs. It was announced that he had decided to retire and was to work for an insurance company. 'I hadn't retired,' he wrote.

Selvey says: 'That was a bit tricky. He was stuck on something like 999 first-class wickets but had three games without taking a wicket so I left him out and he never got back in again. You can see why he would not take it well. Maybe it was insensitive, but you try and move on.'

On the bright side, 'There were a few players that came on well. I showed Alan Lewis Jones something technical and I think he might have got five centuries so he was playing really, really well, as was John Hopkins. Rodney Ontong bowled spin well. Stephen Barwick, Greg Thomas came on. So we'd started to get some things together a bit but with hindsight Javed Miandad should have played every game. It was a strange experience.

'I don't remember the losses, I remember the wins. I'd come down from Lord's to an environment where if I wanted to speak to somebody in the office or get some expenses paid or whatever, you had to go out of Sophia Gardens, walk down by the River Taff over the bridge. That's where the Glamorgan office was, on the third floor above Laura Ashley in the High Street.'

Selvey left in mid-1984. He had a poor relationship with the club chairman and didn't need the hassle at the age of 36. It wasn't the way he'd have liked his career to end. The official reason was given as a knee injury. Glamorgan didn't have a selection process. Selvey picked the team, but the chairman said the selection committee decided he shouldn't play the next game and Selvey stopped battling. 'The situation would never have arisen with Ossie Wheatley or Tony Lewis as chairman. David Morgan and others on the committee were supportive too but it was finished and Ontong took over.

'I'd no idea then that I'd do journalism for the next 35 years. If I had carried on for a couple of years, maybe I would never have ended up doing the job, but who knows?'

Has the reporting of cricket changed between 1983 and today? 'Hugely. I'm under no illusions that my time at *The Guardian* from the mid-80s was unquestionably the best – a really good time. I travelled the world and enjoyed it so much. Now everything's so packed and of course *The Guardian* was at the vanguard of digital-first journalism, so there's just no time off because everything's going online in an instant.

'If I was a young journalist starting out now I'd have to be different. It's never been easier to get published but it's never been more difficult to get paid for it. Can you write for us? We can't pay you but it will give you profile. Well, last time I looked, they didn't take profile vouchers at Sainsbury's. But there's some really good young journalists and they work differently and they might be more diligent in their way.

'I was never a news journalist, I was always a match reporter really. My successor, Ali Martin, is a brilliant news reporter, and he's become a brilliant match reporter.

News stories weren't quite so crucial to cricket reporting as they have become. I never did a quotes story in my life and now you've got to get the quotes. I was paid by *The Guardian* to give my views on things, not other people's views on things. So I was happy. Ali and people before him like David Hopps and Andy Wilson did that role as news reporters.'

Does he think social media has been a good thing for cricket and cricketers or not? 'You're talking to somebody who until 2022 had 38k followers but when Elon Musk took over the platform I don't like the way it was going so I got rid of my accounts.

'Social media is a great tool for promotion of things. But it's also unbelievably vicious and then very rarely regulated, as it should be. It can be very cruel, and it's also exponential. Stuff gets out on Twitter that becomes fact before anybody's even verified it and people take it as fact.'

And the big cricketing differences between 1983 and now? 'There's more athleticism in the game. I think I took about 70 catches in my entire career and I didn't drop many. I just did not get many catches because people didn't slog. Now you put your gun fielders at deep midwicket. I don't believe batting and bowling has changed fundamentally. If I played white ball cricket now I'd need to learn new skills and a variety of different deliveries, no question about that. But line and length and the ability to hit the top of off stump doesn't change.'

Back to April 2023, Middlesex are about to bat against Kent. Openers Sam Robson and Mark Stoneman at Middlesex score ducks and the 'undroppable' England opener Zak Crawley hits 91 for Kent. But that doesn't prove anything.

'They can play how they want in the international matches but what it shows is a lack of acknowledgement about what county cricket is about. We play most of our red ball cricket before the middle of May or after August. That's not when they play international cricket. They play on better pitches and they're not playing for bonus points. They're not playing for promotion and relegation, things that really matter.'

I ask him about contacting Brearley. He says to write to Middlesex at Lord's. 'I hope it goes well, it's an interesting idea, the stickers. I'm still signing them today.'

Norfolk v Glamorgan, NatWest Trophy first round at Norwich, 29 June, 1983

Glamorgan 202/9 off 60 overs (Ontong 45, Parvez Mir 3-43), Norfolk 177 all out (Mir 37, David 3-26, Ontong 4-49, Lloyd 1-17, Selvey 1-20).

Glamorgan

Mike Selvey: RFM. The new captain took 56 Championship wickets at 34.17 in 1983 (62 at 32.30 in all first-class matches) plus 20 List A wickets in 19 matches at 28.00 with an economy rate of 3.97. In all cricket, he played 278 first-class matches (772 wickets at 26.66) and 267 one-dayers (332 wickets at 22.12). Surrey 1968–71, Middlesex 1972–82 (four Championships, two Gillette Cups). England 1976–77 (three Tests). Left Glamorgan in 1984 and became a *Guardian* journalist and BBC broadcaster. He was Middlesex president from 2019–23.

Alan Jones: Opener who played for Glamorgan from 1957–83. He scored 1,020 runs at 30 in 1983 and a record 34.056 first-class runs for the county. Played for England v Rest of the World in 1970. He was coach from 1983–98. He told me, speaking about 1983: 'It's such a long time ago. The only thing I remember was my last innings. I scored four and I was bowled by Malcolm Marshall. He was a great bowler, one of the best I ever played against.' On 10-13 September 1983, Jones's 27 years as a Glamorgan opener ended with nine and four against Hampshire at Southampton. Rain meant a draw. *Wisden* said he had given 'magnificent service' and that his loyalty and modesty made him much loved.

John Hopkins: An opener, 'Ponty' Hopkins scored 1,087 runs at 27.17 in 1983. He played for Glamorgan from 1970–88 scoring 13,742 runs at 27.32 in 305 first-class matches and 5,657 runs at 23.76 in 264 one-dayers. He debuted aged 17. In 1983 he hit 130 not out in the Sunday League fixture against Somerset at Bath, accumulating 510 runs in 20 one-day matches during the season. His 1986 benefit raised £35,230. An occasional wicketkeeper, his brother Jeff played for Middlesex from 1969–72.

Javed Miandad: Pakistan batsman (1975–96, 124 Tests, 233 ODIs), he played for Glamorgan from 1980–85. Scored 114 runs at 19.00 in four first-class games for Glamorgan in 1983. He scored 220 runs in six World Cup innings. In all he played 402 first-class matches with 28,563 runs at 53.37 and 439 one-dayers with 13,973 runs at 42.60. Later a broadcaster and coach.

Rodney Ontong: Glamorgan 1975–89. Played 367 first-class matches with 15,234 runs at 29.46 and 845 wickets at 31.34 and 293 one-dayers with 5,865 runs at 28.19 and 261 wickets at 32.50. In 1983 he scored 1,259 runs at 37.02 in 24 first-class games and took 54 wickets at 36.62. He also made 382 runs and took 28 wickets in 20 one-dayers. Later a coach.

Charles Rowe: Played for Glamorgan from 1982–84 after playing for Kent from 1974–81. In 175 first-class matches he scored 6,173 runs at 26.38 and took 128 wickets at 40.05 and in 118 one-dayers scored 1,563 runs at 20.29 and took 18 wickets at 29.33. In 1983 he scored 682 runs at 22.73 in 20 first-class matches and took 37 wickets at 41.29 plus 172 runs and seven wickets in 16 one-dayers. Later worked in the City.

Alan Lewis Jones: Glamorgan 1973–86. Played 160 first-class matches with 6.548 runs at 25.77 and in 112 one-dayers scored 2,047 at 20.47. Debuted aged just 16. In 1983, he scored 1,034 Championship runs in 22 matches at 32.31 and 485 in 21 one-dayers. Retired due to injury in 1986. His son Matthew played minor county cricket and for Glamorgan seconds.

Arthur Francis: Middle order batsman Francis played for Glamorgan from 1973–84 in 138 first-class matches with 4,938 runs at 24.56 and 100 one-dayers with 1,275 runs at 16,34. In 1983 he scored 903 Championship runs at 26.55

plus 129 runs in ten one-dayers. Could throw left or right-handed with equal prowess.

Terry Davies: Glamorgan 1979–86. He scored 1,775 runs in 100 first-class games at 20.88 and completed 165 catches with 27 stumpings, plus 75 one-dayers with 66 catches and 25 stumpings and 446 runs at 15.37. In 1983 he played 11 first-class matches with 260 runs at 23.63 plus 18 catches and two stumpings and another 9/4 in six one-dayers. Later a cricket and sports venue administrator in Australia and New Zealand.

Malcolm Nash (1945–2019): LM. Played 336 first-class matches from 1966–83 with 993 wickets at 25.87 and 271 one-dayers with 324 wickets at 21.27. In 1983, he took three first-class wickets in four matches, plus 13 one-day wickets. Later a coach in the USA.

Greg Thomas: Glamorgan 1979–88, then Northamptonshire until 1992. England 1986–87 (five Tests, three ODIs). Played 192 first-class games (525 wickets at 31.05) and 192 one-dayers (233 wickets at 27.32). In 1983 he took 15 Championship wickets at 31.46 in seven matches and 15 one-day wickets. Later a teacher and a legal industry company owner.

Barry Lloyd (1953–2016): OB. Glamorgan 1972–88. He played 147 first-class matches with 247 wickets at 41.02 and 64 one-day wickets in 95 matches at 38.06. In 1983 he took 18 wickets at 46.77 in 12 Championship matches plus 12 in one-dayers. His daughter Hannah played for England (1999–2003). He played club cricket with Pontarddulais until 2010.

Winston Davis was not included in Panini but took 52 Championship wickets in 15 matches for Glamorgan in 1983. He played for Glamorgan from 1982–84 and Northamptonshire from 1987–90 and West Indies 1983–88 (15 Tests and 35 ODIs). In the 1983 World Cup he took 7-51 against Australia at Headingley (eight wickets in five World Cup group matches in all). In 1998 he fell from a tree in St Vincent, becoming a tetraplegic. He later moved to Worcestershire.

Chapter 11

Gloucestershire: Jack Russell and David Graveney

OFF TO The Oval, but to Damien Hirst's Newport Street Gallery first. Brian Clarke's stained-glass exhibition *A Great Light* is a cool empty gallery experience next to the railway arches between Vauxhall and Waterloo.

Then back via the alpacas of Vauxhall City Farm to the cricket. Two minutes to four. At 4pm, they let me in. Surrey are losing to Lancashire, a rare defeat in a title-winning season. There are no former Lancashire players around to interview. I tube it to Green Park, then lurk around Jermyn St close to Fortnum & Mason, looking for old cricketers. I don't want to enter the Chris Beetles Gallery too early. Some sports-jacketed types show up and I follow them in. The Lord's Ashes Test starts tomorrow and Jack Russell has an exhibition at the gallery, 60 pictures to mark his 60th birthday. Sir Tim Rice is opening the show. Sir Elton John has just headlined Glastonbury, singing Rice's *Lion King* hit 'Can You Feel the Love Tonight'. This crowd is more MCC tie than tie-dye. Jack is over there charming an art lover.

I lurk round Jack, eventually introducing myself as the writer of the book on cricket stickers 1983: 'Thanks for inviting me. I like your Lake District pictures.' There's one called *Stickle Tarn, First Encounter* (£3,250) and another, *Haystacks* (£1,750). Later I see *Haystacks* is actually a haystack and not the Lakes fell. Jack is from the west. Stickle Tarn is in the Lake District, but Jack wouldn't know I'm from the north. It's great to be able to do this, he says. We shake hands. His are small and surprisingly soft.

He says in his launch speech that he hasn't got Oscar-winning lyricist's way with words like Rice. 'I'm haven't got your way with the gloves,' replies the lanky Rice, bending down to demonstrate a keeper's grab. Beetles jokes that pop star Harry Styles couldn't make it, so Tim, founder of the Chance to Shine charity with Mark Nicholas (Hampshire 1978–95), is there instead. Some ten per cent of sales go to the charity.

'Wicketkeepers are a special breed,' says Rice. He lauds Godfrey Evans as a great character, something keepers often are, perhaps because they dive around so much. He mentions Paul Gibb's 'ups and downs'. Cambridge-educated Gibb played as an amateur for Yorkshire and England in the 1930s, was an RAF pilot in the war, then resumed as a wicketkeeper-batsman for county and country before missing four seasons from 1947–50 to work for his father-in-law's tailoring company. He returned as a pro for Essex, became an umpire while living in a caravan and then drove a bus for a living, dying of a heart attack aged 64 as he clocked on at the station. Rice also cites as his favourite keepers Jim Parks, John Murray and, of course,

Jack, 'who perhaps almost unfairly is best remembered for saving us with Mike Atherton in support'. Set 479, England's Russell (29 not out) and Athers' (185 not out off 492 balls in 643 minutes) held up South Africa for four and a half hours to draw the 1995 Test in Johannesburg during England's first tour since South Africa's readmission after the apartheid era.

Jack says he is only good with words 'if there's an Aussie batsman about two yards in front of me'. He thanks Sir Tim, Chris Beetles and the gallery team. Chris has the wicketkeeper mentality, seeing things slightly differently. Chris has told Jack that he can paint what he likes, not just cricket. Lord's is the greatest stage. At Lord's he'd get there very early and pick his spot in the changing room, with Allan Lamb and Ian Botham arriving either side of him some time later.

That's a bit of a nightmare when there's a rain delay. They get so bored so quickly. The practical jokes start. He's lost count of the amount of times he's put his socks on and they come right up to his thigh, ends cut off. A new pair of trousers were a bit draughty round the kneecaps when he got changed at the end of play. He didn't mind that but you had to go to the sponsors lounge and Bob Taylor, one of his heroes, would be there and his knees would be sticking out. Botham and Lamb would be saying to people in the lounge, 'Don't worry about Jack. He's a little bit … he's had his pads on all day and he wants to give his knees a bit of air.' They were happy days: 'I wouldn't have missed them for the world.'

He salutes the crowd. 'Without you guys, this artist wouldn't be an artist.'

I walk past the Royal Academy, through crowds of tourists, past the National Portrait Gallery, across the river to Waterloo and home. Tomorrow is the Lord's Test. The England players are wearing bucket hats, like Jack did.

Two weeks later I'm asked back to the gallery. England have just won at Headingley to pull one back in the Ashes. It's now 1-2 to Australia but wicketkeeper/batsman Bairstow has struggled, dropping five catches and missing a stumping during the first three Tests. Surrey's Ben Foakes is a better keeper. The same happened with Russell and Surrey's Alec Stewart back in the 1990s.

I hang around in the Beetles gallery looking at the cricket paintings, jotting in my notebook. After my experience at The Oval when seeking out Roger Binny, I'm worried that I might be questioned about my activities again.

Jack's talking to the men with archipelagos of freckles on their bald heads. They are buying his paintings. He sells two while I'm there. One man tells Jack that Ted Dexter lived in Nice. I take my chance. 'My kid's first two names are Ted Dexter,' I say. Jack signs my catalogue and I take my picture with him. He'd be amazed if they drop Bairstow he says. Everyone's asking him that question but Jack's a people pleaser and answers happily. He agrees Bairstow's not as agile as some, but he's a very robust character. If the series goes to 2-2, he'll definitely be at The Oval.

He was at Lord's but didn't see much because he was meeting so many people. He'll be at the Cheltenham Festival, but not on the old players' day. The bucket hat's back in fashion. He's clutching a *Man and Superman* Penguin mug of tea. I can find no allusion between George

Bernard Shaw's sexual politics drama and events at Chris Beetles's gallery, though England women have just beaten Australia at Lord's and Jack has been painting women's matches. He'd like to paint in South Africa, scene of his rearguard action with Atherton, and speaks about doing more military works. I ask him about Graeme Fowler. 'The Brush Brothers' have bonded 40 years on through painting. It's good for mental health. Jack says he'll help me get Foxy on board with the book, which he generously adds is an original idea. I ask for tips for my son Ted Dexter Appleby, aged 11. He touches my elbow and wrist to show me the position of the arm from there to there. 'Never lose sight of the ball. Focus on the ball. Relax the thumbs. Enjoy it. If you miss one, forget it.'

Two months earlier, Jack Russell had replied to my email to his Chipping Sodbury art gallery address. I was pleasantly surprised. He had a reputation as an eccentric and even as a hermit or loner.

In 1983, Panini had Jack as a 'Face for the Future' alongside the likes of Neil Foster and Hugh Morris. He'd played for Young England and taken seven catches against Sri Lanka when still a 17-year-old schoolboy. In 1982 he replaced the injured Andy Brassington as Gloucestershire keeper.

The phone rings. A woman answers. Is Jack there? He was.

'You're making me feel old going back to 1983, it's a long time ago,' he says. It's 40 years; a whole generation.

'I know. It's amazing and that seems like yesterday.' He breaks the ice and thus begins a conversation with a cricket genius who is both a real charmer and who is one of only a few in Panini who has reached the top in another field outside sport.

As a Panini 'Face for the Future', did he feel he had a guaranteed cricket career?

'Oh, no, no, no. That was just my first full season after coming up a little bit in 82.' Russell had left a Bristol Tech accountancy course to go full-time in 1982. He got in the Gloucester first XI by July and then played the rest of the season. 'So, I sort of thought I was going to be a first-team choice but no guarantees until that following season. I never ever took my place for granted. I didn't want to get complacent. I spent my whole career thinking I need to play well, because I didn't want to get dropped. I was hoping I would never be dropped from Gloucester from 1982 till the day I finished, so I achieved that at least.'

But he was dropped by England. Russell debuted for his country in 1988, scoring 94 as nightwatchman against Sri Lanka at Lord's and winning the love of the British public forever. He played 54 Tests and 40 one-day internationals in the next decade, often in and out of the side. Better batter Alec Stewart was the usual replacement keeper.

'The first time I got dropped with England was in Adelaide [1990/91]. Angus Fraser had injured his hip. Phil DeFreitas played as an extra bowler and batter. I think we were getting smashed at the time as well [England were 2-0 down after three Tests]. So that was the first time I'd been dropped from any cricket team. That was a bit of a downer but the silver lining was I had 15 minutes on my own with Don Bradman. From then on I was always in and out but in terms of county cricket I never took it for granted.'

A quarter hour with Bradman was 'just like 15 minutes with whoever you want to think God is. It's like being with a Roman Emperor. It was in a dark room with quite a shy guy in Adelaide in one of the back offices. And it was just me and him together and just chatting about cricket and he was right up to date. We weren't chatting about the old days, we were chatting modern techniques and he was bright as a button and I think he was almost 90 then [Bradman died aged 92 in 2001]. He was razor-sharp and it was just magic.'

Russell wanted to thank Bradman for signing a load of prints of a sketch he'd drawn of the world's best-ever batsman, which Jack had shipped out to Australia. 'But when the England lads knew I was going to meet him they started loading me up with things to sign like books and bats and gloves and so I walked in with like a trolley load of stuff. He was good as gold. Absolutely. It was a magic, magic 15 minutes.'

I suggested he would be lucky to be on the tour these days: 'Well, I probably wouldn't be in because I wouldn't have hit enough sixes. I'd have to adapt my game but I think it would have helped me actually just to be more free and positive because when I played you had shackles on to not give your wicket away.

'I would have enjoyed the freedom, that would have been magic.'

There was one match in mid-July 1983 against Derbyshire and John Childs needed to take a hat-trick with the last three balls to win it. He took two but Ole Mortensen blocked the last one.

'I remember that game because I stumped John Hampshire [for 23 off Childs who took 6-81] and there's a photograph of me stumping him somewhere in my archives that some local photographer took. It was a hot day. And in the Sunday League game the day before, Bob Taylor, my hero, hit the last ball for six for them to win.'

Another remarkable game in 1983 was against Yorkshire when Boycott scored his famous 140 not out on the first day of the Cheltenham festival and skipper Ray Illingworth was deeply frustrated with Boycs' lack of urgency.

'There's a rule now where if you're a batsman and you're injured and don't field, you can't bat before number seven. Boycott was batting so slowly he was fined because they missed out on a bonus point on the Saturday. So on Monday morning he refused to field and then he came out in the second innings opening [scoring 97] and that caused a bit of a furore.

'With Yorkshire, we always said at every team meeting, let's just get on top because the crowd will get onto them. They'll start getting agitated with their own players and that's to our advantage.'

He remembers playing at Headingley for the first time, holding on for a draw at 196/9 chasing 266 in 185 minutes. 'There were bottles of beer for lunch. Can you believe that? I used to drink quite a lot, but then I realised after a couple of warnings that if I wanted to stay in the team, I'd have to knuckle down a bit more.'

What about sledging? 'Phil Edmonds gave you a bit when you were batting at the non-strikers' end, but Phil would abuse everybody, so that was fine.

'I was just a grubby little teenage upstart, wasn't I? So he picked on me because I couldn't bowl fast.'

New signing for 1984 Bill Athey was joined by Courtney Walsh (spelt Courteney in Gloucestershire's yearbook), yet to play for West Indies, who was registered with Northumberland and almost looked elsewhere when Gloucestershire only promised him second-team games. Things were looking up, and Jack, along with Jack Richards, Paul Downton, Bruce French and David Bairstow, was considered Taylor's replacement if he could get his attitude right.

Captain David Graveney took a risk dropping Brassington for Russell. In his book *Unleashed* Russell said Graveney 'blew his top' after a missed stumping of Northamptonshire's Tim Lamb in 1983 and told Russell he was drinking too much. John Shepherd was a critic, as was Phil Bainbridge. Spending winters playing in New Zealand in 1983/84 and 1984/85, instead of playing pool in a Stroud pub, and listening to Bill Athey and other outsiders were his wake-up call.

'Geoffrey Boycott would eat a big roast with two Yorkshire puddings for lunch and I asked him why. He said it was fuel if he was going to bat all day. "You've got to eat well and sleep well," he told me, and he was right. If you're concentrating all day you can't afford to be tired because that's when mistakes happen.

'It was a hard school and I probably deserved some of the abuse I got from my team-mates, but you weren't allowed an opinion on anything. I think I showed one or two up, to be honest and they didn't like it. And you know,

I got accused of not being a team man, when I was actually trying to be a team man by playing the best I could for the team. Mostly you were just told to shutup and get on with the job, but I loved every minute of county cricket.

'When I went on to play for England, basically nobody helped you and you had to get on with your own job. There was a coach for the first and second team but there was no keeping coach or batting coach. Now there's coaches for everything.

'You watched people and learned and did it yourself. I looked forward to the Kent and Derbyshire fixtures because I could speak to Bob Taylor, Alan Knott. I'd sit down for an hour and sometimes longer than that because he [Knott] was a slow changer and I'd try to learn from him.

'I was lucky because I had Andy Brassington, whose job I took. He used to help me quite a lot and supported me, even though I cost him his career, which says a lot about the guy. Without him I might not have progressed so quickly. But there was no coaching.'

Brassington was still at Gloucestershire in 2023, greeting former team-mates and opponents at the PCA old players' day at the Cheltenham festival.

Even with two keepers, Gloucestershire were a bit threadbare back in 1983. Sadiq Mohammad and four others left in 1982 and only Gary Sainsbury joined, although this wasn't uncommon in 1983 as several counties cut their staff to compensate for financial losses. Derbyshire, for instance, lost five players (and only brought in Ole Mortensen) and told members to expect a lower playing standard.

I was talking to my kid who's a wicketkeeper. He noticed the old players didn't wear helmets like the keepers do now.

Jack says: 'I never wore helmets to keep, just my floppy hat. I never felt the need. There might have been a few doing it towards the end of my career, but now even the academy kids have to wear helmets. I feel sorry for them because sometimes the helmets are heavier than the kids. I just don't know how they move. It would have affected my vision because you have to lift your head into a different position to see through the grille. You've got to have a strong neck.'

He replaced cricket with painting when his career ended, though he'd already become a keen artist while still playing. 'I'd go loopy without it. There's no question it kept me sane. I started in county cricket, sketching and drawing because we were sitting in the pavilion half the time watching the rain fall. I got fed up and I thought if Rembrandt can do it, why can't I?

'And then I had an exhibition that sold out and just snowballed. On days off on tour I would go painting rather than sunbathing or playing golf. It kept me sane and the only skill I've got left.'

I tell Jack about my Royal Academy Summer Exhibition painting in 2020. It was a Covid triptych painted on three pieces of slate. A Dutch princess bought it. Jack suggests I put RA after my name.

I ask him if his reputation for eccentricity was fair. He wore the same hat for decades and took tons of tinned beans and Weetabix on tour and used the same teabag endlessly. 'The problem we've got here. Matthew. is I don't see them [the eccentricities] as eccentric. It's like the alcoholic saying that he doesn't drink. I understand what people are saying but there was a logical reason for every single thing that I did.

'Was the hat superstition? Well, maybe, but it was comfort. The Weetabix at lunchtime? That was just because the carbohydrates get you through the afternoon. The beans were carbohydrate too. The tea is probably the one. I drink a lot of tea. I even had hot tea on the field occasionally if it was cold. Tea and biscuits are my addiction. The kit was comfortable and did the job, so I made it last. I didn't like change much, I'll admit that. Not with kit anyway.'

He taped his cuffs, an idea borrowed from Alan Knott, did up his top button and only had two pairs of gloves in 20-odd years. Most famously, he always wore the same bucket hat. That hat is now 'always in a safe place. I need to know where it is 24 hours a day otherwise I have a panic attack. I used to take it home or back to the hotel room, I never used to leave it in the changing room overnight. And if we were flying between venues on tour, it would be in my hand luggage, which used to annoy one or two because the smell wasn't great. I suppose calling for superglue in the middle of a Lord's Test was a little bit eccentric, but a piece of my bat was breaking. If it was said that was eccentric, I'd be struggling to argue with that.'

In his 23 years as a professional the game changed a lot: 'In my first pre-season we started on 1 April and during the first week we played football. The second week we were in the nets and then we played the season. My last pre-season 20-odd years started in October before the following season. That's a big change.

'I never used to catch a ball before January, even indoors.'

Russell never hit a Test six. Now, players lift weights, have heavy bats and range hitting programmes to make sure they do. Jonny Bairstow had hit 50 Test sixes by summer 2023 and Jos Buttler 33. Ben Stokes has hit 124, almost double the most by anyone playing before the 21st century. Ian Botham hit 67. 'When I started, I didn't do any gym work, not till the second half of my career anyway. I'd be looking like little Precious McKenzie wouldn't I? Like a little weightlifter. From a wicketkeeper point of view, I get a bit worried about that because sometimes they can look a bit bulky.'

Jack Russell progressed in 1983 so much he was spoken of in *Wisden* as 'certain Test candidate'.

John Barclay's *Life in the Long Grass* pens portraits of players. Jack Russell was 'widely regarded as eccentric', a word used to describe Barclay too. In fact, Russell was 'a man of rare insight, the most professional person I ever met, who coped well with pressure, was never flaky, and was a real patriot, getting Elgar and the national anthem played over the Tannoy in South Africa.' Russell was like a 'featherweight boxer' behind the stumps, weighing just 9st 6lb.

In 1983, Jack Russell scored 507 runs at 22.04 in 24 first-class games with 46 catches and 17 stumpings (the most in English first-class cricket that season). In 19 List A matches he scored 44 runs at 11 and took seven catches and made seven stumpings.

David Graveney

Having held many senior roles in the game and being from a renowned cricket family, it's good to see that David Graveney is humble enough to appear in a tent, interviewed by the broadcaster Dan Whiting in front of a couple of dozen fans. He's speaking at Cheltenham Cricket Festival about the Professional Cricketers' Trust, a charity which supports former players when they need it most.

After more than half a century in the game, the former slow left-armer and England selector now helps pick players for the under-19s, works for the charity and is also involved with the ECB Healthcare Trust. A gifted player, administrator and communicator, he has given a lot to the sport and remains committed to doing whatever he can to help cricket and cricketers.

'I was one of the 65 people who were made redundant [in 2017 when he was ECB national performance manager], understandably because of my age,' he says. 'Then they realised they had got rid of too many people. Mine is more of a consultative role, but you're a long time retired and I just love the game. I'm involved on the executive board at Gloucestershire and we have some challenges like a lack of money. You can't spend money you haven't got.'

In 1983, *Wisden* said Gloucestershire captain Graveney didn't make enough use of his own bowling. 'I think that is always a criticism of bowling captains.' The masterplan to solve this was, in 1985, to recruit Brian Davison (Leicestershire 1970–83) for a year. The 'frightening batsman' used to field on the boundary and his 'sole job was to tell me when to bowl'. He'd stick his finger in

Graveney's chest and say 'You bowl now.' Even when Grav had a 'logical' reason why he couldn't, 'Dav insisted and that worked.'

In 1983, 'you just got on with it,' despite the loss of leading batsman Zaheer Abbas to the World Cup and not having a replacement. Zaheer returned to play 12 matches for Gloucestershire, topping the averages. West Indian all-rounder Franklyn Stephenson appeared in just two matches before a back injury and Zaheer's return ended the future Nottinghamshire star's season.

'It was an era of multiple overseas players, and the ones you had stayed with the club for the whole year. I look at *Wisden,* and the lists of teams that an individual has played goes on for pages!' Sadiq Mohammad, Gloucestershire's other overseas batsman in the 1970s, alongside Zaheer (13 years from 1972) and South African all-rounder Mike Procter (Gloucestershire 1965–81) played for their teams in their respective home countries but when they came here it was just for one team.

He says being a leader in 2023 is not that different to 1983: 'Now, it's drifting back to old-fashioned captaincy. When I was captain [1982–88] Graham Wiltshire was coach – you only had one – and the senior players used to look after the junior players so the captain had a huge role. Tony Brown and Proccy controlled the team when they captained. You get the feeling with Ben Stokes it's exactly the same.'

We've met at the annual Cheltenham week rather than Gloucestershire HQ Bristol, but the festival matches which were a mainstay of the county circuit for more than a century have largely ended: 'If you drilled down into the arrangements of staging a festival, the local council supported it. I just look at the attendances and it's nothing to do with how Gloucestershire are doing or not doing.

'One thing I'm concerned about is whether people know when cricket is on. The three-day game was Wednesday, Thursday, Friday and another one started on Saturday and there might be Sunday League on Sunday. People could plan their lives but I just don't think that's possible these days because there's so many tournaments going on.'

Back in 1983, there was much less player movement between counties. One word sums that up for Graveney: 'Loyalty. That's very pertinent in my family because when my uncle [Tom, whose move to Worcestershire for the 1961 season after losing his job as Gloucestershire captain was blocked by Gloucestershire] played for Gloucester, and he had to stay out of the game for two years. That was an extraordinary scenario.

'I should have played for Somerset earlier [he left in 1990, two years after losing the Gloucestershire captaincy] because I used to get on with [Somerset coach] Jack Birkenshaw and welcomed his advice about bowling. I think when you lose the captaincy you've just got to move on. You either say nothing and people think you're sulking, or you get too involved and you're perceived to be taking control of it.'

He moved to Durham after a year at Somerset and says the impact of the 18th first-class county, and first new one for 70 years, was 'extraordinary'. He was working with his best friend in cricket, Geoff Cook, and took on the captaincy for their first two years, 1992/93.

Graveney, who was involved in the players' union PCA from 1975 and was chief executive from 1994–2003, says his biggest cricket achievements are working for the PCA to establish a proper pension fund and proper health cover for players, and helping players realise there's life after professional cricket.

He remains generous to his mentors: 'John Mortimore guided me when I knew absolutely nothing and Browny [Tony Brown 1936–2020, Gloucestershire all-rounder 1953–76] shaped me as an individual and a captain. I consider myself to be a very fortunate person.'

Gloucestershire

David Graveney: Gloucestershire 1972–90, Somerset 1991, Durham 1992–94. England Test selector chair from 1997–2008, replacing Ray Illingworth and replaced by Geoff Miller. Took 981 wickets in 457 first-class matches and 287 wickets in 382 one-dayers. The slow left-armer took 35 wickets at 33.14 in 1983 plus 427 runs at 21.35 and ten wickets at 36.10 with an economy rate of 4.34 in 18 List A games. Father Ken and uncle Tom played for Gloucestershire. Awarded the OBE for services to cricket in 2005. In 2008, Graveney became national performance manager, monitoring young players in domestic cricket.

Chris Broad: Opener who hit 1,061 runs at 42.44 in 1983. Left Gloucestershire after 1983 for Nottinghamshire, then returned for 1993–94. Debuted for England in 1984 and played 25 Tests (six hundreds) and 34 ODIs. Played 340 first-class games scoring 21,892 runs and 319 one-dayers scoring 10,386 runs. Scored 1,061 Championship runs at 42.44 in 1983 plus 381 in 11 one-dayers. In 2003 he became an ICC Test match referee. Son Stuart was a leading Test bowler from 2007–23.

Andrew Stovold: Gloucestershire 1973–90, a batsman and occasional wicketkeeper who played 354 first-class and 294 one-dayers, scoring 17,705 and 7,271 runs respectively. Scored 1,592 Championship runs at 43.02 in 1983 plus 486 in 16 one-dayers. Coached at Gloucestershire until 2008. Brother Martin played for Gloucestershire from 1978–82.

Zaheer Abbas: In 1983 his autobiography *Zed*, co-written with David Foot, was published. Pakistan 1969–85 (78 Tests, 62 ODIs). Gloucestershire 1972–85. First-class runs: 34,843 in 457 matches with 108 centuries. Scored 867 runs at 45.63 in 1983 and played in the World Cup, scoring 313 runs at 62.60. The 'Asian Bradman' was a sometime Pakistan manager and ICC match referee as well as ICC president in 2015.

Paul Romaines: Northamptonshire 1975/76 then Durham in minor counties before Gloucestershire 1982–91 scoring 8,120 runs in 173 first-class matches and 3,651 runs in 158 one-dayers. Scored 1,233 runs at 35.22 in 1983 plus 461 in 16 one-dayers. Became a teacher and cricket coach at Clifton College in Bristol.

Phil Bainbridge: All-rounder. Gloucestershire 1977–90, Durham 1991–96. Right-handed batsman and medium pacer with 15,707 runs and 349 wickets in 324 first-class matches and 5,559 runs and 293 wickets in 311 one-dayers.

Scored 1,068 Championship runs at 27.38 in 1983 and took 29 wickets plus 442 runs and 19 wickets in 19 one-dayers. Became an event management sales director.

Alastair Hignell: England rugby international 1975–79 and Gloucestershire batsman 1974–83. Cambridge University 1975–78. Scored 7.459 runs in 170 first-class matches and 2,454 in 136 one-dayers, with 1,034 at 35.65 in 1983 plus 377 in 17 one-dayers. He was a teacher in the winter and later a sports broadcaster and writer. Retired after being diagnosed with MS in 1999.

Andy Brassington: Gloucestershire wicketkeeper 1974–88. Played 128 first-class games with 882 runs and 128 catches and 47 stumpings as well as 57 one-day matches. In 1983 he did not play in the Championship, with Jack Russell taking over. Was later Gloucestershire's marketing executive and then a sports marketer.

John Shepherd: All-rounder for Kent 1966–81, Gloucestershire 1982–87. Five Tests for West Indies 1969–71. In 1983 he scored 1,025 runs at 36.60 and took 67 wickets at 30.55, plus 34 in one-dayers. Played 423 first-class games scoring 13,359 runs and taking 1,157 wickets and 328 one-dayers scoring 4,337 runs and taking 436 wickets. Later a school coach and Kent president (2011) and committee member.

Franklyn Stephenson: West Indian all-rounder who played for Gloucestershire 1982–83, Nottinghamshire 1988–91 and Sussex 1992–95. Played 219 first-class (8,622 runs and 792 wickets) and 282 one-dayers (4,717 runs and 448 wickets). Two Championship matches in 1983 taking 11 wickets at 12.72. Toured South Africa with the rebel West Indies team in 1982/83. Last to do the 1,000 runs/100 wickets in an English season, in 1988. Later a coach who ran a cricket academy in Barbados.

Richard Doughty (1960–2018): Gloucestershire 1981–84, Surrey 1985–87. Played 41 first-class (845 runs/89 wickets) and 49 List A matches (399/29). Six Championship games with five wickets and 123 runs in 1983 plus seven one-dayers. Became a counsellor.

John Childs: Gloucestershire 1975–84. Moved to Essex for 1985 (until 1996) and played two Tests for England aged 36 in 1988. Took 1,028 wickets in 381 first-class matches. In 1983 took 48 Championship wickets at 35.22 plus ten in one-dayers. Later a coach at Essex.

Chapter 12

Hampshire: Kevin Emery

KEVIN EMERY was easy to find. It's mid-March and the new cricket season is looming. There's an urgency to get going. He was the first cricketer I called. He has a website that features his Panini sticker in the centre of the home page.

In *Cricketers' Who's Who* 1983 he says his nicknames are Clint, Billy, Sinjon, Emmers. He has nine O levels and three A levels, from Swindon comprehensive St Joseph's and an honours degree in economics and history. He worked in the accounts department at Sydney University in the off-season of 1981/82, and in 1982/83 played for Mosman.

He admires Malcolm Marshall though Macca 'eats too much macaroni'. Interests include fitness ('needs to be!'). He'll watch international rugby on TV but he's more of a soccer man. Emery won the regional bowler competition in 1978. He played for England B in 1982 and was Commercial Union Under-23 bowler of the year 1982, taking 83 first-class wickets in his debut season.

The young fast bowler suspects he's not really qualified to have opinions, having only played one season, but believes over rates should take into account wides and no-balls.

'People used to give me one [a sticker] to sign on the PCA reunion days. So, I used it on the website when I had a beard and people would maybe think I hadn't changed for 20 years.'

He's worked in financial services for many years but is having some time out: 'I'm just sort of having a think about what I'm gonna do.'

In 1982 he had a brilliant year as Hampshire played positive cricket under captain Nick Pocock, who made lots of declarations and nearly won the Championship. Hampshire were third behind Leicestershire and winners Middlesex, the same place as in 1983 when they finished behind Middlesex and winners Essex.

Emery, a uniquely talented bowler who fought long, hard and often with success to prove himself after his first-class career ended, remembers: 'We were within touching distance. I was in my first season effectively in county cricket having gone down to Hampshire the summer before from university and done alright until I got a stress fracture of the spine.

'We were we in with a shout. I remember we played Middlesex at Uxbridge in September and we had a good seam attack and they produced a wicket, they had no grass, that was all mud. They won the toss and they flew in an extra spinner from Ireland [Dermott Monteith] and they beat us on a rolled mud surface that ripped square. So, who knows what might have happened? We had Malcolm Marshall and [Gordon] Greenidge and Tim Tremlett. Our spin attack probably wasn't as potent as some, but still ...'

John Southern took 8-85 in the match and fellow spinner Nigel Cowley 2-101. Middlesex's John Emburey took 4-80 and Phil Edmonds 10-107. World-leading fast bowler Marshall and his new ball partner Emery were blunted.

Wisden 1983 says bowling with Marshall was an obvious benefit to Emery, but his 83 wickets was nevertheless 'a splendid achievement'. Marshall took 134, the most in county cricket since 1964. Emery could have had 100 wickets too but he missed the early-season game with Oxford University. Steve 'Piggy' Malone took 7-55 and 5-55. 'If I'd played Oxford, which was just down the road from where I lived in Swindon, who knows?'

Emery shared a house with Marshall in Chandler's Ford in Hampshire. 'You get to know when either of you may have been a bit more tired than the other. Malcolm was skiddy quick. I nipped it a bit either way off the seam. Occasionally I may have swung it a bit and I think I surprised a few people.

'Malcolm was a great man. He could be very generous and he enjoyed the game and set himself high standards. He had targets against sides he'd not done as well against the previous year. I think I'm right that ours was the best partnership in terms of other new ball bowlers. We travelled to games together with Gordon [Greenidge] often. We'd chat a bit but often returning from games Malcolm would be straight in the back seat and fast asleep.'

He wasn't actually qualified to drive until the end of 1983. 'I didn't need to be, but a few players got sponsored cars.' Cowley organised sponsorship with a dealership in Southampton and, thriftily, organised the pool cars.

'In terms of earning capacity, it was nothing like it is today. But it was very enjoyable. Hampshire used to play at four venues: Southampton, Basingstoke, Portsmouth and Bournemouth. They had slightly different wickets although most of those were pretty flat. It was nice for me. It was all new stuff, travelling around the country. But a lot of the times as a seam bowler you're never really 100 per cent fit so you've got to manage your niggles.

'Bournemouth was a bit slower. We played Yorkshire there in 1982 and we got 300-odd declared and then they were at tea something like 150 for one or two in about 70 overs, Boycott blocking the crap out of it. Richard Lumb came up to me and he shook my hand and said, "Well done, you're the first bloke that got me out in the last six innings. That bloke," and he pointed to Boycott, "ran me out in the last four."' Emery removed Lumb in both innings that August bank holiday as Yorkshire ended eight down just ten runs short of chasing 227 in 53 overs.

'You know, there are cricketers who are very selfish,' he says. 'Usually, they're batsman. The bowlers are often the nicest people you meet off the cricket field away from the battle.'

In July 1982, in a innings win against Glamorgan at Portsmouth, Emery took ten wickets: 6-51 and 4-50. Marshall took 1-41 and 1-43: Emery remembers Glamorgan batsmen being distracted by noisy ships sailing to the Falklands. 'And next thing it's lbw, thank you!'

He adds: 'There were times when Nick Pocock would naturally turn to Malcolm more than he would give the ball to me to bowl at the tail, after you put in all the work at the top order. As a combination, if one is not firing, you want the other one to. And then if you both fire together then happy days.'

Emery started playing at 14 at Swindon Cricket Club (rather than at school), representing Wiltshire under-19s as an off-spinner aged just 15, then England Schoolboys at 16.

He took 6-36 on his Hampshire second-team debut in 1981 but suffered a stress fracture of the spine in July, rehabbing in Sydney that winter, then returning to Hampshire on a one-month trial. 'I took myself to Australia to get myself fit of my own accord. It wasn't in the contract, per se. I think they were saying, "We'll have a look."'

In 1982 his haul of wickets included 4-40 for England B v Pakistan at Leicester. Taking himself back to Sydney that winter he netted with England at the SCG before watching the Ashes Test, during which Eddie Hemmings's 95 as nightwatchman saved the game for England.

Returning to England, Emery was selected for the washed-out season opener for MCC against champion county Middlesex at Lord's but then he sustained severe ankle ligament damage in a second XI game against Sussex in May: 'Coming back from overseas I was quite tired as I'd bowled a bit in the winter. You're tired after the season in England too.'

It was to be almost 20 years before he played at HQ, for Optimists Cricket Club in the 1992 club knockout final against Kendal. 'We won and I got three for 20 or something and it was nice. I had a catch dropped too, so could have had a four-for.'

Back to 1983: 'The grounds were soft. I'd been sort of told by Pocock after the performance in 1982 I'd probably get my county cap, which means more money and security and you just feel settled. Malcolm wasn't back in 1983 because the West Indies were touring, and it was inferred that I needed to step up. But then there was rain, rain, rain. The first game was at Northampton [a rain-hit draw where Peter Willey scored 175 not out and Emery took 1-87, with Malone's figures 4-93] and we started late. It was wet and I slipped a bit on impact and bowled a few no-balls and I got dropped straightaway to the twos which I was unhappy about.'

He played in the first round Benson & Hedges Cup zonal game against Essex at Southampton on 7 May, bowling 8-0-32-0, opening the bowling with Malone (6-0-25-0). 'It was humid, it's swung a bit and there were a few wides, but all the bowlers bowled wides [21 in all], partly because they've not had enough time bowling out in the middle. I think I tried a bit too hard [Essex won by 113 runs]. So I got dropped to the twos, which again I wasn't particularly happy about and against Somerset rain affected the game. In the next game we played Sussex and I damaged my ankle ligaments badly on the soft ground twisting in soft foot holes and never really got it looked at properly so it just dragged on with a game off then I'd come back and play for the seconds and bowl like 40 overs and the ankle would be swelling up. That was the beginning of my ankle ligament damage. That was effectively why I didn't play much in 1983. I didn't get an X-ray. It was just "have a rest, just try and sort out yourself".

'That's not me saying "woe is me". Eventually, after 32 years, I got diagnosed that there was a bone spur and 32 staples were inserted into it. The doctor said to me "You have no ligaments. There's nothing there. That's why your ankle just rotates over and falls because of that damage you did." A batsman would have a broken arm or broken finger but with bowlers you can carry on, strap it up. But the left leg is your front leg. It affects your stride pattern when you're running and then, obviously, your delivery.

'I played in my old boots [team-mate Robin Smith nicknamed Emery 'Billy' after the comic character Billy's Boots]. I got a new pair of boots with new studs and the game at Portsmouth was the first time I've ever walked off a cricket pitch. I'd ripped the ankle more, the new studs sticking in the ground and pulling as I landed.'

He believes bowlers are looked after better now: 'You have your red ball and white ball and central contracts and people on the periphery. Take a guy like Olly Stone. Recently he's been injured for quite a few seasons. He's just moved county again [Northamptonshire to Warwickshire and then Nottinghamshire in 2023] but he's on a contract linked to England [pace bowling development contract from November 2022] so having the ability to have a large quantity of time off without your contract being at risk for the following season gives bowlers a little bit more security.'

Physiotherapists, strength and conditioning coaches, managed workloads and year-long rather than six-month contracts are all new too. He only remembers physios at Essex and Middlesex.

Having that support would have given him a longer career: 'One of the things with injury is early diagnosis. And there may have been a throwback to the 1970s where the old fast bowlers used to bowl themselves into form. But playing on uncovered wickets would have been slightly different in terms of impact on joints; softer, so easier.

'Hopefully, there are better programmes in place in terms of recovery and identification of niggles, which for fast bowlers will be in your lower back particularly. And there's more support in terms of what you need to do to keep fit and on the field of play. The best fitness for bowling is bowling, but you also need to have built-in rest periods as well.'

Player power has increased: 'Now your agent will tell you that you've got wickets in the bag. If they [the county] don't want to look after you then we'll get in another county. I just wanted to play and to get back out there in 1983.'

Emery played against Derbyshire at Portsmouth on 27 July, bowling nine overs and having Kim Barnett caught by Pocock for 16. He didn't bowl in the second innings and Malone replaced him for the next match. The young fast bowler played just five first-class games and took five wickets in 1983. He took 13 in seven matches for the seconds.

Hampshire reached the B&H Cup quarter-final and NatWest semi-final. Kent's Chris Cowdrey took 4-36 in the 72-run NatWest loss, but by then Emery was a long way from the first team.

In 1984, he did not feature at all in the firsts. In ten matches for the seconds he took 20 wickets at 22.60, just behind Keith Stevenson's 22 at 20.31. He and Malone left at the end of the year.

'It came as a bit of a shock, even though they had "signposted it" to a degree in July and August. I had a knee injury in 1984 and played through a good deal of pain in the twos, so I missed a few games and should really have had an operation in May, but the club wanted me to try and play through the pain.

'There wasn't much by way of medical help, for instance no X-rays or scans or physio support, so I guess from their perspective they had a player who had ankle ligaments in 1983, which continued to plague me, then a knee injury, all to my front leg over a couple of seasons and a loss of form, primarily due to playing injured! In relative terms I wasn't being paid that much, and despite being injured I still topped the second XI bowling averages in 1984.

'By way of comparison, people like Graham Dilley, Richard Ellison, Neil Foster and Paul Newman had had similar critical injuries and missed whole seasons but they were by contrast given more support. Fast bowlers – shock shock – get injured, especially given the workload back then. C'est la vie!'

Emery was at the Cheltenham PCA old players' day in July 2023. Inevitably, the differences between 1983 and now come up when the veterans meet: 'Without wanting me to sound like "it was always better in our day" in the early 1980s, the county sides had two overseas pros. And a lot of them were top of the tree. Nottinghamshire had Hadlee and Rice, Clive Lloyd and Michael Holding or Clive Lloyd and Colin Croft, or Patrick Patterson at

Lancashire. We had Malcolm Marshall and Greenidge. Derbyshire had John Wright and Peter Kirsten. I remember bowling at Lloyd and Viv Richards.

'Given central contracts and everything else and the way the Test schedule is, it isn't quite the case that all the top Test players play in the Championship now. It was top-level sport back then.'

India won the World Cup as Emery battled to regain form and fitness: 'That started the growth of India and maybe the throes of the IPL came from then. The IPL with the commercial rights and all of that has all been good for the players.'

He expands: 'They now can earn a handsome living in the winter. Back in the 1980s you had to go and find it yourself.

'The PCA has done a great job in bringing year-long contracts to the fore so you can concentrate on giving the body time off and strength and conditioning and investing in some training.'

An admirable part of Emery's character is the way he has kept playing for a range of clubs and trying to show his ability, taking more than 1,000 wickets in the last 40 years. 'I haven't bowled much in the last few years but I'm keen to help the bowlers. I just usually bat in the top three or four or open in the twos. I played about ten games last year [2022]. I'm 63 now so it's a bit harder on your body. There was an element of me trying, to prove to myself after the ankle injury.'

He's been toying with the idea of writing a book about his take on it: '1982 and then the drop off and then back playing a high level in cricket. I played Western Premier League till the age of 46, bowling and doing alright.'

Emery is justifiably proud of being one of the featured top Panini players of 1983: 'People now bring them to me and somebody sent me two or three so I kept one. So that's where that picture of mine [on my website] comes. I think in 1983 we had a competition to grow the biggest moustache and look a bit like old 1970s porn stars.

'I know from friends who follow sport that Panini stickers are synonymous with football and World Cup but I can say I've got my own Panini sticker.'

A column in *The Cricketer* called 'From The Inside', written anonymously by a county pro, said Emery's form had 'temporarily deserted him' and 'feverish' work was being done to rediscover the old rhythm and success rate, including using video equipment and psychological profiling.

Journalist David Foot, worrying about how the game was becoming less 'sentimental' than the one of his youth, wrote of unfounded doubts about Emery's action and echoed the concerns about his future.

After leaving Hampshire, Emery won the Southern League with Bournemouth CC. A trial at Northamptonshire in 1984 was curtailed by injury and in 1985 he played for Wiltshire but Buckinghamshire's Hartley Alleyne broke his jaw on a drying wicket at High Wycombe. He went back to Durban. There followed a year's contract with Warwickshire in 1986 but he suffered a lower back/rib cartilage injury. In his last game he took a five-for for Warwickshire seconds against Worcester City in a Birmingham League match.

Then it was Lansdown CC in Bath in the Western League Premier Championship and Western League and more Wiltshire honours from 1987–89. From 1991–96 he played for Optimists in the same league and won the National Club Championship at Lord's in 1992. From 1997–99, he played for Dumbleton in the Three Counties League and represented the league side. He captained Swindon and wrote for the *Swindon Evening Advertiser*.

He represented the West of England League representative side from 2000–03, and from 2000–06 was an MCC playing member on tours to Ireland, Italy and Sweden and tour manager to Spain and Gibraltar. Since 2009, he's played for Dumbleton and played and managed with the MCC. His website proudly reports: 'Kevin has taken over 1,600 league wickets and scored over 10,000 runs in his career to date.'

At the PCA old players' day at Cheltenham in July 2023, one of the dozens of former cricketers who met up was Tim Tremlett, Hampshire's leading all-rounder in the 1980s. His father Maurice and son Chris played for England and Tim came close too, at Headingley in 1983, when England lost to New Zealand.

He says he and Graham Monkhouse were in the frame after having their names mentioned in the press. 'It would have been horses for courses in those days and around about that time there were probably quite a few players who would have played once or twice for England but over the years there's become more constant selection. I think I would have been close at one time, about 1983/84/85.'

On Emery, he concurs with other players I spoke to in their sadness that his first-class career ended in 1983 amid form and fitness issues: 'In 1982 he burst on the scene and got 80-odd wickets and bowled with pace and was very close to getting selected for the Australian tour but he just missed out. Then he came back the following year and unfortunately in a match situation he got the yips and had trouble with his radar, which was a great shame because he was a real prospect.'

Hampshire

Nick Pocock: Venezuela-born batsman for Hampshire between 1976 and 84, scoring 3,790 in 127 first-class games and 1,346 runs in 105 one-dayers and was captain from 1980–84. In 1983 he scored 681 Championship runs at 27.24, plus 174 in 22 one-dayers. He moved into insurance for HBI, then helped set up the Sporting Index spread betting firm and worked in sports insurance.

Gordon Greenidge: West Indies opener who played for Hampshire from 1970–87 and played 108 Tests from 1974–91 and 128 ODIs. Scored 37,354 runs in 523 first-class matches and 16,349 in 440 List A games. In 1983 he scored 1,438 at 64.36 in the Championship and was a World Cup finalist scoring 250 runs at 41.66, after helping West Indies win in 1975 and 1979. In all he scored 1,208 one-day runs in 27 matches in 1983. He became an international coach and selector. His son Carl played county cricket.

Chris Smith: Opener who debuted for England in 1983, playing eight Tests in total. 'Kippy' scored 1,831 runs for Hampshire at 61.03 in 1983, where he played from 1980–91. Also scored 703 runs in 19 one-dayers. He scored 18,028 first-class runs in 269 matches and 6.700 in 214 one-dayers. Younger brother Robin topped the 1983 Hampshire averages with 401 runs at 66.83. Chris became marketing manager at the Western Australian Cricket Association.

Mark Nicholas: Hampshire 1978–95. In 1983 he scored 1,192 runs and took 23 wickets in 24 Championship matches and made 388 runs and took 22 wickets in 24 one-dayers. In 377 first-class matches he scored 18,262 runs at 34.39 and took 72 wickets. In 359 List A games he scored 7,334 runs and took 101 wickets. He was Hampshire captain from 1985–95, winning four trophies. He was then a broadcaster and became MCC president in 2023.

Trevor Jesty: All-rounder. Jesty played 490 first-class matches, scoring 21,916 runs at 32.71 and taking 585 wickets at 27.47 between 1966 and 1991. Hampshire 1966–84, Surrey 1985–87, then Lancashire to 1991. Played ten ODIs in January/February 1983. In 1983 he scored 1,019 runs at 44.30 and took 21 wickets, plus 854 runs and 20 wickets in 23 one-dayers. Became an umpire until 2013.

Nigel Cowley: Off-spinning all-rounder who played 271 first-class (7,309 runs at 23.05/437 wickets at 34.04) and 305 one-day (3,022/248) matches. In 1983 he took 38 wickets at 25.39 and scored 302 runs in 21 Championship games at 18.87 plus 26 wickets in one-dayers. Was with

Hampshire from 1974–89 and Glamorgan in 1990 before becoming an umpire.

David Turner: Played 426 first-class games between 1966 and 1989, making 19,005 runs at 30.55 plus 9,904 in 381 one-dayers. In 1983 he scored 425 Championship runs at 32.69 plus 237 in 12 one-dayers. Later took over the family shoe business in Wiltshire.

Tim Tremlett: Hampshire all-rounder from 1976–91 scoring 3,864 runs at 21.00 and taking 450 wickets at 23.99 in 207 first-class matches and 266 wickets in 213 one-dayers, plus 870 runs at 14.03. In 1983, he took 58 Championship wickets at 22.15 and scored 229 runs at 19.08 in 22 matches. In 24 List A games he took 29 wickets at 26.13 with an economy rate of 3.82. He also scored 57 runs at 7.12. Later Hampshire's coach and director of cricket.

Bobby Parks: WK Hampshire 1980–92. Grandson and son of England and Sussex players Jim Parks senior and junior. Played 256 first-class and 251 List A matches with 642 catches and 72 stumpings and 3,957 runs at 19.58 in first-class games and 266/47 and 972 runs at 16.20 in one-day matches. In 1983 he took 51 first-class catches and made nine stumpings, scoring 180 Championship runs at 13.84. He scored 46 runs and took 33 catches with six stumpings in 24 one-day matches in 1983. Later an accountant then coach at Hampshire.

Malcolm Marshall (1958–99): West Indies fast bowler from 1978–91. Played 408 first-class matches (11,004 runs at 24.83 and 1,651 wickets at 19.10) and 440 one-dayers (3,795 at 16.86, 521 at 23.71). In 1983 he took 80 Championship wickets at 16.58 in 16 games, scored 563 runs at 46.91 and played in the World Cup final, taking 12 wickets at 14.58 (second in the averages behind Richard Hadlee) in the competition with a tournament-best economy rate of 2.50. He took 38 one-day wickets in 1983. Later a Hampshire and West Indies coach, he died of cancer aged 41 in 1999.

Kevin Emery: Took five wickets in five Championship matches in 1983 and 0-32 in a single one-dayer. In his career between 1982 and 84 he took 88 wickets at 25.35 in 30 first-class matches and 27 at 26.03 in 21 List A games. Later worked in finance.

John Southern: Played for Hampshire between 1975 and 83 taking 412 wickets in 164 first-class matches at 29.81 including 24 at 35.33 in the 1983 County Championship. He also took 14 wickets in 25 one-dayers. Took 5-75 in his penultimate appearance, an eight-wicket win against Nottinghamshire at Bournemouth, then retired at the end of the season aged 31. Later moved to New Zealand.

Chapter 13

Kent: Chris Cowdrey

AT THE Chelsea Flower Show in May 2023, I bump into George Plumptre, cricket writer turned National Gardens Scheme CEO, who was raised at Goodnestone Park in Dover, Kent. How about Chris Cowdrey?

The name Cowdrey is synonymous with Kent cricket. Chris Cowdrey has been steeped in cricket all his life and continues to serve Kent, having won trophies with the county, tested himself for his country and for half a century used his all-round talents to play and promote the game. He's a speaker so has a website. 'Just rushing to The Oval but let's talk about it soon – next week good. All the best, Chris.'

Surrey are playing Kent in a T20 in late May 2023. Sean Abbott hits an English record 34-ball century. Cowdrey says Abbott's innings was one of the best he's ever seen. But T20 is under threat from The Hundred. Crowds are down and Lord's was half full for Middlesex-Surrey the day before.

A generation before The Hundred the game was simpler. Cowdrey was offered a Kent contract in 1976 which he has said was probably because of the name and his good eye. The advantages come early because of the name, but not later when you lose form, and at least ten people a day says 'I saw your old man play.'

Michael Colin Cowdrey (MCC were his initials) captained England 27 times in Tests and was the first England cricketer to play 100 Tests and the first to be given a life peerage (in 1997 as Baron Cowdrey of Tonbridge, though West Indian Learie Constantine became a life peer in 1969). He died of a heart attack aged 67 in 2000. I spoke to his son Chris as he drove over the dips and peaks of what I imagined were the Kent Downs. It was a rollercoaster conversation, interrupted by poor phone reception.

Chris Cowdrey captained Kent 290 times between 1982 and 90 and was officially club captain from 1985–1990. In 1984/85 he toured India with England when Ian Botham wouldn't. India spinner Laxman Sivaramakrishnan took 12 wickets on Cowdrey's Test debut, at Wankhede. Cowdrey bowled Kapil Dev but England lost by eight wickets.

In 1988, he was appointed England captain against West Indies, for one match, the third Test at Headingley. England were having a disaster against the best side in the world. Mike Gatting, John Emburey and, after Cowdrey, Graham Gooch also captained that series. England lost 4-0. His godfather Peter May appointed him as the second 'son of' to captain England, after F.G. Mann. This was with a view to taking the side to India. He was a better player of spin than pace. But he got injured and missed The Oval Test and never played for England again. They changed their mind.

Allan Lamb pulled a calf at 183/4 and that was the turning point. England were all out for 201. Cowdrey was lbw to Malcolm Marshall for a duck. Derek Pringle took 5-95 as West Indies only made 275 but England collapsed again, after Tim Curtis had battled for 90 minutes for the second time in the match. Cowdrey was bowled by Courtney Walsh for five and England lost by ten wickets, with the captain's last international action to have the winning runs hit off his bowling.

Kent lost John Shepherd, Charles Rowe and Nicky Kemp before the 1983 season. Richard Ellison was at university. Eldine Baptiste had been preferred to Abdul Qadir as overseas player and Asif Iqbal, aged 40, had finished. Graham Dilley and Chris Tavare were likely to play for England, but the ageing team still had the stalwarts Derek Underwood, Alan Knott and Bob Woolmer available, as well as the promising Cowdrey, Derek Aslett, Mark Benson and Neil Taylor.

'I started the [1983] season well. Chris Tavare was captain and he was pretty hard on me at the start of the season saying it was about time I started to achieve the things he suggested I could do. It was good. It went well, I had two good years and it got me on an England tour [India 1984/85].

'I remember it [his top score of the season of 123, one of five centuries] was down at Folkestone, where I tended to get runs. Every batsman has a ground where they always seem to get runs and mine was Folkestone. I don't know why. It was a turning pitch normally and I quite liked the ball when it was turning. I remember that day well.

'In 83 we had a good side. We had one or two who were coming to the end of their careers and we just didn't quite seem to put together the results we should have. I don't quite know why. Or even remember where we came in the Championship, but we weren't competing to win it.'

The 1983 NatWest final should have been a career highlight: 'We were going well and bowled Somerset out for about 190 so we had a good chance. They had a good attack of course. It was a very disappointing day in the end.'

He'd been playing as well as he'd ever played, made runs in knockout rounds with 122 not out in a narrow second-round four-run win against Essex, 56 in the 105-run quarter-final beating of Warwickshire and 4/36 in the 71-run semi-final win against Hampshire at Canterbury. He whacked 103 not out (Vic Marks 5-134) against Somerset at Taunton in the Championship game after the final but the final went wrong.

'It was a typical Lord's pitch, a good one for the final. It was one of those days where they should have made 240. It always helps when you get Viv Richards out for under 100. I remember he was caught by Alan Knott off Graham Dilley [for 51] and we were in the game big time then.'

Viv Richards's wife had given birth to a son the night before and Viv would have loved to have celebrated with a century, Ian Botham said after the match, but a half-century and a win would do. With Richards and Botham out before lunch, Kent were on top but Somerset's Garner, Botham, Marks and Richards himself were hard to get away.

Tavare top-scored with 39 off 80 balls and his side continued in bad light, with Dilley and Richard Ellison taking them to 160, but Garner, Botham and finally Colin Dredge finished them off. Somerset were regulars at Lord's finals. Kent had not been there since 1978, but returned in 1984 and 1986, losing both times. Somerset were off to Worcester to try and stay in the race for the Sunday League the next day. The weary side lost by 55 runs and Garner's 8-0-41-0 contrasted with the previous day's 9-2-15-2. The robust Botham backed up his 2-29 with 3-29 at New Road.

'He's a good friend of mine, Ian Botham, and he wanted to hit me out of St John's Wood, somewhere into Park Lane. He got a bit excited and was caught on the fence trying to pull it out of the park. It wasn't a particularly good ball.' Cowdrey had a strong day in the field and came into the game in the form of his life. Kent were chasing 190 but he was stumped third ball off Vic Marks for nought. Marks had lobbed one up and it drifted down the leg side. Cowdrey had set off for a single before he'd hit the ball.

'I wasn't attacking. I'd only been in three balls and was just trying to work him round the corner. We didn't need to attack. We were only chasing a low score. It was disappointing when in the form of my life I got myself out. That's the way cricket goes.

'In limited overs cricket, Chris Tavare was one of the most savage strikers of the ball of all time. Of course, he went into defence mode in longer formats and sure, he played Boycott-like cricket in Test matches. He was a very organised captain. He led us to a couple of cup finals. Everything was planned to the last jot and he was a top guy.'

The NatWest showpiece typically concluded the season on a high: 'The end of season cup final was always a fantastic day, the big showpiece of the year. Everybody was desperate to get into that final at Lord's. It was so good for the club and great for all the supporters. It was a massive day.'

Kent won the 50-over cup in 2022 'but it doesn't quite mean the same, because there are so many different formats of the game. It's not quite such a big deal, which is sad.'

Cowdrey's all-round attacking style meant he was quite a modern player in many ways: 'I would have loved to play T20. It wouldn't have suited everyone, but it would have suited me because I bowled a bit. I was an attacking batsman, I loved fielding and if you look around the IPL and Big Bash, most of the guys who do well do a bit of both and love fielding.

Wisden said Cowdrey was a 'revelation' in 1983. Cowdrey says it's quite a long time ago to work out why it was such a breakthrough year. He'd begun with a century against Cambridge University then made four in the Championship, with a top score of 123 against Leicestershire at Folkestone in late August. His century came in 152 minutes with one six and 12 fours against a fair attack of George Ferris, Gordon Parsons, Paddy Clift, Jonathan Agnew and John Steele.

Kent won by ten wickets but only came seventh in the Championship with seven wins and 13 draws in 24 matches.

Derek Underwood took 100 wickets and Bob Woolmer averaged 51 in the Championship. Wicketkeeper Alan Knott averaged over 40 and kept to the high standard the fans 'took for granted', said *Wisden*. All were banned from playing for England after touring South Africa in 1981/82, though Underwood was 38, Alan Knott 37 and Woolmer

35, so were getting on a bit. 'Certainly, when you're looking at people like Graham Gooch, it would be twice the side with him than without him. I don't remember that making a big difference to results.' Tavare was unavailable for much of the year because he was playing Tests and one-dayers for England, including the World Cup semi-final.

Cowdrey's autobiography was called *Good Enough?* because of an article written by *Wisden* editor John Woodcock: 'And he put something like "Chris Cowdrey will never be as good as his father, but as long as he's good enough" and I thought, "exactly, that's all it's about, isn't it?"

'People used to say you'll never be as good as your father and that's the most ridiculous question because not many have ever been in the history of the game. An unusual title for the book but it seemed to work.'

I ask about that modesty and whether it was something Cowdrey had to carry over his career and beyond: 'Yes, maybe. My father was a modest man and always taught our family not to be too showy and just get on with it. But it was very much a case of me just enjoying it and doing as well as I could and having fun. I got a lot of pressure early on with people comparing me and every time I played a shot through extra cover people said, "There we are, he's got the Cowdrey cover drive," and I did consciously change the way I played. I became a leg side player because he wasn't a leg side player. That turned me into a good one-day player, but I lost a lot of stuff I might have had in the longer game. People stopped comparing me then and said, "Who is this bit-part slogger?" I'd be alright today!'

And the weekly regime of travelling and playing on the circuit? 'It was very much more so than today, but when you look back you think how did we do it? How did the bowlers stay fit with all this travelling? The fast bowlers bowled 30 overs in a day and then had to get in a car and drive four hours and then you're bowling again the next morning at 11am. It's incredible really but it was the fun of the game. We had weeks when you had two three-day matches and a Sunday League game so it was fantastic because you had three different matches to look forward to. They haven't got that now. They spend more time practising than we ever did.'

Cowdrey had a heart attack in 2011 (as did Geoff Cook, also featured in this book, in 2013). Now, players have to be super-fit and can't socialise like they used to. 'We didn't always even have a physio. There were times when you got a knock and you had to stick some ice on it yourself. You had to run it off or ask someone, "what do I do with this injury?"'

What is CC asked most? 'I'm always asked about the old man, that's the first question. What's it like to have a famous father and all that. The other one nowadays is what do you think of Bazball? People who are obsessed with Test cricket do not understand the part T20 has in world cricket. I love Test cricket and the longer game as well.'

I talk about how my kid's team has just lost three games in a tournament at Esher. Chris is sympathetic and says plenty of people will have lost there and there's always another game coming. He wishes me good luck.

Kent

Chris Tavare: Opener or middle order batsman who played for England (31 Tests, 29 ODIs) from 1980–89 and Kent from 1974–88, then Somerset from 1989–93. Played in the World Cup semi-final and captained Kent in the NatWest final in 1983. Scored 683 runs at 45.21 in 1983 in the Championship. He also scored 1,120 runs in 26 List A matches at 50.90, the most by any English player, with 212 at 30.28 in the World Cup. In his career, he played 431 first-class matches with 24,906 runs at 38.79 and 399 one-dayers with 11,407 runs at 33.45. Became a teacher.

Neil Taylor: Kent opener from 1979–96 and for Sussex from 1997–98. Played in 325 first-class matches, scoring 19,031 runs at an average of 39.56 and 248 one-dayers scoring 7,041 runs. Scored 1,161 Championship runs at 36.28 in 1983 plus 432 in 15 one-dayers. Later became a teacher.

Laurie Potter: Potter played for Kent (1981–85) then Leicestershire (1986–93) with 223 first-class matches (9,027 runs at 28.93, 177 wickets at 38.86) and 207 one-dayers (4,218 at 24.24/81 at 32.29). In 1983 he scored 258 runs in six Championship matches at 23.45. Later he became Leicestershire's cricket development officer and a PE and cricket teacher.

Bob Woolmer (1948–2007): All-rounder for Kent (1968–84) and England 1975–81. In 350 first-class games he scored 15,772 runs at 33.55 and took 420 wickets at 25.87 and in 290 one-dayers scored 4.078 at 20.39 and took 374 wickets at 20.64. In 1983 he scored 969 runs at 51.00 in

13 Championship games and took seven wickets. Later a coach for South Africa, Kent, Warwickshire and Pakistan. He died suddenly in Jamaica, the day after Pakistan were knocked out of the 2007 World Cup.

Mark Benson: Kent opener 1980–95. One Test and one ODI in 1986. Played 292 first-class matches (18,387 runs at 40.23) and 268 one-dayers (7,814 runs at 31.86). In 1983 he scored 1,410 at 42.72 plus 463 in 25 one-dayers. Later became an umpire.

Christopher Cowdrey: All-rounder. Kent 1976–91, Glamorgan 1992, England 1984–88 (six Tests, three ODIs). Scored 1,364 first-class runs at 56.83 in 1983 in 22 first-class matches with five centuries and took 12 wickets at 61.03. In 25 List A matches Chris took 11 wickets at 27.63 with an economy rate of 4.00 and scored 689 runs at 38.27. Played 333 first-class matches with 12,252 runs at 31.90 and took 200 wickets at 39.81 and 6,846 in one-dayers at 27.05 with 204 wickets at 29.30. Later a broadcaster and speaker. Father Colin, brother Graham and son Fabian all played for Kent. He was Kent president in 2023.

Derek Aslett: Kent middle order batsman between 1981 and 1987, scoring 6.218 runs at 34.23 in 119 first-class matches and 2,161 in 95 one-dayers at 27.35. In 1983 'Dazzler' scored 1,437 runs at 43.54 plus 472 in 16 one-dayers. Later an antiques dealer in Western Australia.

Alan Knott: Kent wicketkeeper from 1964–85 who played 511 first-class matches scoring 18,105 first-class runs at 29.63 and taking 1,211 catches and 133 stumpings. He also played in 317 List A games with 343 catches, 54 stumpings and 3,260 runs at 16.13. Played 95 Tests from 1967–81 taking 250/19 and scoring 4,389 runs, as well as 20 ODIs. In 1983 he scored 806 runs at 38.38 and took 39 catches and eight stumpings as well as 252 runs in 25 one-dayers with 26 catches and three stumpings. Later a coach, he moved to Cyprus.

Graham Dilley (1959–2011): RF. Kent fast bowler 1977–86, Worcestershire 1987–92 and England 1979–89 with 41 Tests and 36 ODIs. Took 648 first-class wickets in 234 matches at 26.84 and 279 in 237 one-dayers at 22.92. Played in the 1983 World Cup semi-final before a neck injury sidelined him for a year. Took 28 wickets at 21.46 for Kent in the 1983 Championship season and 29 wickets in 24 one-dayers for Kent and England (seven in six internationals). Later a coach.

Kevin Jarvis: Kent seamer from 1975–87 then Gloucestershire to 1990, taking 674 wickets in 260 first-class games at 29.67 and 344 in 262 List A matches at 23.52. In 1983 he took 29 wickets at 53.27 plus 21 in one-dayers. Later worked for a bat maker and a charity.

Richard Ellison: Swing bowler who played 11 Test and 14 ODIs for England from 1984–86. From 1981–93 he took 475 wickets in 207 first-class matches at 28.99 and 188 in 175 one-dayers at 28.29. Took 49 wickets at 26.69 in 1983 plus 31 in one-dayers. Later a teacher in charge of cricket at Millfield School.

Derek Underwood: Kent slow left-armer from 1963–87 and England from 1966–82. Took 297 wickets in 86 Tests and 2,465 in 676 first-class matches at 20.28. 'Deadly' also played 411 one-dayers with 572 wickets taken at 19.40. In 1983, he took 106 first-class wickets at 19.28 and 37 at 16.67 in one-dayers, to be the country's leading wicket-taker. With Kent colleagues Alan Knott and Bob Woolmer, he was part of Kerry Packer's World Series Cricket (1977–79) and the 1981/82 South Africa rebel tour. Became a sports turf consultant and MCC president in 2009.

Eldine Baptiste. He took 50 Championship and 25 one-day wickets and scored 755 Championship and 245 one-day runs in 1983 (17 matches in each format) but was not included in Panini. The Antiguan right-arm fast bowler played for Kent from 1981–87 and West Indies from October 1983–1990 (ten Tests and 43 ODIs). He also played for Northamptonshire in 1991. Later a coach.

Chapter 14

Lancashire: Graeme Fowler

I HAVE to thank Jack Russell for helping me hunt down Graeme 'Foxy' Fowler. He set up two easels at the bottom of Foxy's Durham garden in September 2021. Fowler paints expressionist portraits and landscapes. There are no realist cricket pictures like Jack's.

'I wouldn't be painting without Jack,' he says. 'I hadn't painted since I was at primary school. Anyway, we did it. My wife couldn't believe that I'd painted and I enjoyed the process so much I went out the next day and bought a load of paints and I've been doing it ever since.'

He's also been folk singer Roy Harper's drummer. Harper's 1975 song 'When an Old Cricketer Leaves the Crease' refers to John Snow and Geoff Boycott and is an elegy to games gone by.

In 1983 Fowler topped Lancashire's averages with 1,253 Championship runs at 54.47. Back then, he rocks a bit of football casual styling in his Panini sticker, with flick hair and designer-label sportswear that was fashionable in the eighties. As an opener, he scored a century for England against New Zealand at The Oval (105 off 303 balls opening with fellow century-maker Chris Tavare in a 189-run win) and was the first to hit four consecutive World Cup half-centuries. In the semi-final against India, he was bowled by Roger Binny for 33, after adding 69 with Tavare.

What a year. *Wisden* said Fowler had learnt from being in Australia the previous year. He'd top-scored with 65 in the second innings in the three-run win at Melbourne when Norman Cowans took 6-77 and Australia's last two (Allan Border and Jeff Thomson) added 70 before Botham had Thomson caught at slip. Fowler recalls in his autobiography *Absolutely Foxed* a dinner with pop star Elton John and Ian Botham, who put Fowler in a headlock to try and get him to drink whisky and was impressed that he resisted. As a youngster, he told Lancashire veteran Barry Wood that he was a better player than the England man, earning Wood's respect.

Against Leicestershire in 1983 he hit ten sixes in successive scoring shots, although Leicestershire were employing non-specialist bowlers. This was a 100 that took just 46 minutes, when Steve O'Shaughnessy's came in 35 (54 balls). They added 200 off 119 balls in 43 minutes.

'It was a complete farce. Roger Tolchard batted too long in the first innings which meant we didn't have enough time to set them a total which would allow us time to bowl them out. For about four or five overs me and Steve O'Shaughnessy just blocked. Then I walked down the wicket and said to Shauny, "Make sure you capitalise because at the end of the season when somebody votes on your contract they won't remember if one of your hundreds was done in these circumstances so get some runs. You could get the fastest hundred of the season here."

'It worked out I was on 98 facing David Gower and Steve was at the non-striker's end and he was on 92 I think. And he said, "Fow, I thought you said I could have the fastest hundred." I just patted the next ball to long off and we walked a single and the next two balls Shauny hit for four and he'd equalled the fastest hundred of all time with Percy Fender. I am very glad I didn't get it because it was just farcical. Shauny could have beaten that record by at least ten minutes because we blocked the first five overs.'

Fowler had debuted for England in August 1982, scoring 86 in a seven-wicket win against Pakistan at Leeds. A rotund replacement seamer, Ehteshamuddin, plucked from Daisy Hill in the Bolton Association League to fill a hole in Pakistan's injury-hit attack, bowled Fowler in the first innings.

'I played against him the week before for Lancashire. He bowled the perfect ball. It pitched on off and came back a long, long way. I think that was probably his last wicket. Then he came in number 11 and Beefy broke his jaw so that was the end of him.' Fowler made 86 in the second innings and looked set for a long England career.

Just two and a half years later, at Kanpur, he hit 69 in his last Test. In the previous Test he had made 201 in a nine-wicket win at Chennai, the first Test double century by an England player in India. India's attack included World Cup winners Kapil Dev, Ravi Shastri and Mohinder Amarnath. Fowler put on 178 with Tim Robinson, at the time England's second-biggest opening stand of the 1980s, after Fowler's with Tavare against New Zealand at The Oval in 1983. Mike Gatting came in at No 3 and hit 221.

Graham Gooch returned from his rebel tour ban and Fowler didn't play a Test for England again. A neck injury suffered in a car crash seven years earlier left him with trapped nerves.

This meant 1983–85 were his peak years, with the World Cup a highlight: 'I averaged 72. I didn't think I played well at first but I got four consecutive fifties and apparently no English player's ever done that. The semi-final at Old Trafford was also the biggest disappointment I ever had. They were really horrible wickets at that time, slow and dead. I knew because it was my home ground that I had to get the runs because I didn't think anybody else would be able to bat on it. I got 30 then got out. If I'd have got runs we'd have won the semi-final. Other people disagreed with me, but you just know sometimes.

'I averaged 72 in the World Cup then I got a hundred in the first Test then I only got 30 I think in the next Test [9 and 19 caught behind off Ewen Chatfield in both innings as England lost by five wickets at Headingley] and then I was dropped. Can you imagine that happening these days? Hundred, 30-odd, dropped.

'It was terrible. We'd say goodbye after a domestic Test match and you had not a clue whether you'd see anybody again. There was only Botham, Bob Willis, Gower, Allan Lamb and Bob Taylor that knew they were going to be playing. You'd find out from a local journalist whether you were playing or been dropped. The three selectors were Peter May, Phil Sharpe and Alec Bedser and I met all three of them and each of them said they'd voted for me! You'd no idea what was going on.'

As well as central contracts, which help continuity of selection, fitness and training has come a long way since 1983: 'I'd left Bede College [in Durham] in 1978 and I'd been playing for the second team for three years. I walked through the gates at Old Trafford as a qualified PE teacher and they put me in charge of training! At the start of the season, I could run five miles in 27 minutes but after a day's fielding I was knackered. At the end of the season, I couldn't run five miles in 27 minutes but I could field every day and never got tired. I knew inherently there was something wrong with our training but I didn't know how to fix it. All we had was a physio who wouldn't even give Ian Botham a massage. It was dreadful really.'

Gooch was banned but Fowler says the Essex opener's return should not be linked with the end of his England career. 'It's not true because in 1986 I opened in two one-day internationals with him and by then I found out I had a broken neck. It's one of those things that sticks.' In his autobiography, Fowler says that after Gooch and Boycott were banned England didn't have a settled opening pair for the 1982 season.

His opening partner in 1983 was Chris Tavare: 'Tav was absolutely brilliant. Obviously, he was a very quiet bloke. Before our first Test together at Headingley he asked if I liked to just leave the ball early on or play shots and then calm down. I'd never ever thought about it so I just said 'merit' and he said, "what?" And I said, "I play it on merit. If it's a bad ball I hit it and if it's a good ball I block it." I liked batting with Tav. I knew where he was looking for his runs and he knew where I was and we had a really good understanding.

'Tav could bat as quickly as anybody, he just took it upon himself. There was a lot of shot players like [Mike] Gatting, Gower and Beefy so he just tried to play the anchor and let the other lads play around him and it worked. He did a good job for England.

'I did play on merit. Early on you'd look to leave it and be cautious, but it was natural for me to hit the ball. But I changed my technique between 1982 and 1984 completely. In 1982 I used to play and miss outside the off stump. By 1984 I hardly did that because I'd moved across my stumps. But I did get on with it.'

Touring Australia in the winter before helped set Fowler up for 1983: 'The 1982/83 tour didn't start off very well because once you play for England everybody wants to coach you. I tried to bat like an England opener for the first six weeks and my highest score was 27 and I just couldn't do it so I didn't play in the first Test. Then we got to Brisbane and I'm not playing again and then I got a knock on the door at 8am from Bob Willis.' The England captain told him he was playing because Ian Botham had broken Geoff Cook's wrist bowling bouncers at him in the nets. I think I got six [actually seven, c Yardley, b Lawson] in the first innings and then I just thought fuck it, if I'm not good enough to play for England, I'm going to fail doing it my way. I'm either going to live by my sword or die by my sword. I batted a bloody long time and I got 83. In the third Test at Adelaide I didn't get many [11 and 37 in an eight-wicket defeat] but in the fourth Test at Melbourne I just got past 50 and then Jeff Thomson bowled me a yorker which jammed between the bottom of my bat and my big toe and my big toe to this day is still in pieces, so that was the end of my tour.

'They took me to hospital and Derek Randall pushed me round in a wheelchair. The following morning Bernard Thomas the physio knocked on my door and said it was going to be too hard to get me to the ground so they left me there. I watched the rest of the Test on TV in my room, even though the ground was only about 400 yards away! Can you imagine that happening now? I could hear all the roars but I was watching it on the telly!'

He recovered to play on the way home in the first one-day international in Sharjah, against Pakistan, and hit a century. But the match was later downgraded to a friendly.

Fowler played for Durham after leaving Lancashire, then set up a Cricket School of Excellence in 1996. Fowler has been open about his struggles with depression, writing about them in his 2016 book *Absolutely Foxed*.

He was at Durham from 1993–94 then went to Durham University (where he studied 20 years earlier – he and Paul Allott were the first Durham ex-students to play for England since Frank Tyson in 1954) from 1996 and coached at the university's Centre of Cricketing Excellence from 2001. Future Test players Andrew Strauss and James Foster graduated and Will Smith and Tom Westley are among other alumni.

'I came up with the idea of a centre of excellence with the very simple premise to help lads complete their education and progress their cricket at the same time. When I went to university only about 12 per cent of people went to university and when I started the centre of excellence it was just over 50 per cent so simple maths tells you that 50 per cent per cent of your best cricketers are at university. I organised proper training and seminars on how to make yourself a better player. They were physically tested three times a year and had these fantastic training programmes. I was there just under 18 years and Durham alone sent over 60 players into first-class cricket. Andrew Strauss said it was more professional than Middlesex's setup. Five went on to play for England. We had five county captains and three or four women also played for England. When I set up the other five centres in 2010, 24 per cent of English county cricketers had been to one of the six. Now the centres of excellence don't exist. I'd left a good legacy, but they've just thrown it away. Can you imagine any other sport doing that?

'My friend Dave Belshaw and I designed an interactive lecture about mental health, and we had the results independently verified which were way better than we could ever have imagined. We asked, "how likely are you to talk about mental health to somebody?" And it went from 20 per cent to 80 per cent after respondents did the lecture. We took these results to the ECB who said they'd love to take this further but they never got back. I also put together a scheme that could have been taught by ECB's regional coaches and delivered to every club cricketer in three years for £100,000, but they didn't take it up. That's just ridiculous.'

Fowler would still like his experiences to be used by English cricket: 'I'm basically retired, I have a granddaughter I take to school and bring home. I walk the dog and I paint. I'm trying to deliver the mental health sessions to young offenders or recovering addicts but that's not come off just yet. But I'm still hopeful it might.'

Lancashire

Clive Lloyd: West Indies captain 1974–85, winning the World Cup in 1975 and 1979. Lancashire 1968–86. Played 490 first-class matches (31,232 runs) including 110 Tests and 378 List A games (10,915 runs) including 87 ODIs. In 1983 he scored 447 runs at 29.80 in 11 Championship matches and 112 runs in the World Cup at 28.00. He was later West Indies manager, a referee, commentator and coach.

Graeme Fowler: Lancashire opener from 1979–82 and Durham 1992–94. England (1982–86) 21 Tests, with a century against New Zealand at The Oval in 1983, and 26 ODIs with four fifties in the 1983 World Cup. Scored 16,663 runs in 292 first-class matches and 8,927 in 315 one-dayers. In 1983, he scored 880 List A runs at 44.00 in 22 matches, with 360 at 72.00 in seven World Cup matches with a strike rate of 62.82, seven runs behind second-placed Viv Richards and 24 behind David Gower, who played the same number of innings. Scored 1,403 first-class runs at 51.95 with five centuries in 1983. Later a coach and commentator.

Ian Cockbain (1958–2022}: In 1983, the right-handed middle order batsman scored 291 runs in eight matches.

Scored 1,483 runs in 47 first-class matches from 1979–83 and 887 in 59 List A games. Left Lancashire after 1983 and played for Cheshire until 2001 scoring 8,496 runs in Minor Counties Championship matches. Son Ian played for Gloucestershire. Ian Cockbain senior died in 2022 aged 64.

David Lloyd: Left-handed batsman and left a spinner, he retired after 1983 to play for Cumberland, then umpire and coached England before becoming a writer and commentator. 'Bumble' played nine Championship matches in 1983, scoring 485 runs at 40.41 and taking 16 wickets. He played 407 first-class matches (including eight Tests) with 19.269 runs and 237 wickets, and 288 one-day games with 7,761 runs and 39 wickets. Son Graham played for Lancashire and is an umpire.

Chris Maynard: He took 27 catches and made two stumpings in 21 Championship matches in 1983. Later played for Warwickshire until 1986. Played 117 first-class matches and scored 2,541 runs and held 186 catches with 28 stumpings. Also played 126 one-dayers (95/14). Scored 190 runs and took 13 catches with five stumpings in 20 one-dayers in 1983. His career was ended by a knee injury; he was later a publican in Wales.

John Abrahams: Middle order left-handed batsman who scored 1,261 runs at 39.40 in 23 Championship matches in 1983 plus 421 in 22 one-dayers. Scored 10,059 runs in 252 first-class matches and 3,759 in 215 one-dayers. Captained Lancashire in 1983 when Clive Lloyd was unavailable, then from 1984–85. Lancashire won the Asda Challenge in 1983 against Hampshire at Scarborough and Benson & Hedges Cup in 1984. Played for Lancashire from 1973-88. Wife Debbie Abrahams is an MP. Later Cheshire's coach, he also worked for the ECB.

David Hughes: In 1983 scored 522 runs at 20.02 after a career-best 153 against Glamorgan on 30 April. 'Yozzer' also scored 452 one-day runs in 18 matches. Played 447 first-class matches (10,419 runs/655 wickets) and 458 one-dayers (4,993/248) from 1967-91, latterly as captain. He was later Lancashire manager.

Steve O'Shaughnessy: All-rounder who scored 685 runs at 27.40 in 22 Championship matches in 1983, including a 35-minute century against Leicestershire in September. Also scored 210 runs in 22 one-dayers. In his career (Lancashire 1980–87, Worcestershire 1988–89) he played 112 first-class matches with 3,720 runs and 2,999 in 77 one-dayers, with 114 and 115 wickets respectively. Later a Cumberland player (1994–2003), and an umpire.

Jack Simmons: Off-spinner who took 68 wickets at 26.57 and made 679 runs at 23.41 in 23 Championship matches in 1983 plus 122 runs and 16 wickets in 22 one-dayers. From 1968–89 'Flat Jack' played 450 first-class matches (9,417 runs/1,033 wickets) and 471 one-dayers (3.421/498). Later Lancashire and ECB chairman.

Paul Allott: Right-arm quick bowler, he took 38 wickets at 30.36 in 1983. Played for England between 1981 and 85 including 13 Tests and 13 ODIs. From 1978–92 he took 652 first-class wickets at 25.55 in 245 matches and also took 321 wickets in 291 one-dayers. 'Walt' took eight wickets at 41.87 in the World Cup and 30 in one-dayers in the 1983 season. Later became a TV commentator and Lancashire's cricket director.

Colin Croft: West Indies fast bowler. Did not play for Lancashire or West Indies post-1982 after going on the rebel tour to South Africa in 1982. Later a commentator, having been an airline pilot. Took 428 wickets at 24.59 in 121 first-class matches and 102 in 81 limited overs. Played 27 Tests and 19 ODIs from 1977–82.

Ian Folley (1963–93): Left a medium pacer turned slow left armer for Lancashire between 1982 and 90 and Derbyshire in 1991. Played 140 first-class matches, taking 287 wickets at 32.60 and 35 in 43 one-dayers at 32.14. He died in 1993 aged 30 after being hit in the eye playing for Whitehaven. Took seven wickets in 12 Championship games in 1983, plus ten in one-dayers.

Chapter 15

Leicestershire: Nick Cook

NICK COOK was a breakthrough player, taking 90 wickets in 1982, the second best in the country after Malcolm Marshall's 134. The slow left-armer made his England debut the following season and was an immediate success. I emailed him at the ECB. He retired as an umpire in 2022. A couple of hours later I started a conversation with one of the most convivial and popular cricketers and umpires of the last half-century.

Born in Leicester, his father was a butcher. A grammar schoolboy, he made his county debut in August 1978, aged 22. Five years later, he carved through Test match opposition at the first time of asking. 'I do remember that sticker album, very much so,' he says. 'I remember signing a few autographs for people who had it. And I remember 1983 very well.'

The upward curve began the year before: 'We were so close to winning the Championship. By about June I'd hardly got any wickets and Leicestershire played Derbyshire at the colliery ground in Coalville for the first time in donkey's years. It was a pretty poor surface and it turned and I got one wicket in the game, their number 11

Steve Oldham [1-60 then 0-55 as Derbyshire won by five wickets]. Geoff Miller took about 12 for Derbyshire. And I thought CIR, career in ruins. I was having a pint at the bar on my own and Geoff Miller [8-70 and 4-68] came in. He was the last person I wanted to speak to but we had a good chat for ten minutes and after that I got on a roll and took a truckload of wickets.'

Cook had done well in two 1982 Championship games against Essex, where Keith Fletcher was captain, taking 6-35 in a 25-run win at Leicester in July and 6-17 and 6-113 in a six-wicket win at Colchester in August.

In early 1983 Cook 'wasn't pulling up any trees but was bowling okay, steady away, nothing brilliant in terms of wickets'. Leicestershire were playing Essex at Chelmsford when England slow left-armer Phil Edmonds hurt his back getting out of his car. Spinners Derek Underwood, John Emburey and Peter Willey were all banned after the rebel tour of South Africa.

The TCCB's Donald Carr phoned Leicestershire captain Roger Tolchard at teatime. Tolly told Cooky, 'I've got good news and bad news. You've got to go to Lord's but you're only on standby for Phil Edmonds, who doesn't know whether he'd be fit or not.

'I got into a fairly excited state. I was batting with Brian Davison and nearly ran him out twice.' Davison brought him back to reality. 'That dressing room was tough, old school. I'm not sure how people would get on in today's woke society.'

Cook had travelled with Chris Balderstone to Essex so had no transport to get to Lord's for the third Test against

New Zealand. A supporter gave him a lift, dropping him off at the team hotel by the ground.

A natural raconteur, Cook asks me if this is the sort of stuff I want to hear. It is. The players were having their pre-match meal. He'd never met Bob Willis before, but there was one spare seat and it was next to him. 'Beefy said there was no point having a team talk. He just said, "I'll get a hundred and we'll win the game."'

The next morning Botham gave him a lift because he was the only one with a car, 'one of his Saabs that he used to write off on a regular basis. So we drove 60mph down the terraced back roads and I walked into the dressing room with my coffin at 9.50am. I should have been there at 9.30. Bob Willis was sat in the corner and said, "Hello, Cooky, you might as well have a game."'

A nervous Cook fielded at the unfamiliar position to him of cover. He was usually short leg. But New Zealand openers John Wright and Bruce Edgar didn't risk any singles 'and it dawned on me they were as nervous and apprehensive as I was. When I came on the first two balls were shin high and a toe-high full toss before I put it in the right spot. I got a wicket in my third over and it went well after that.' He took 5-35 and 3-90, helping England win by 127 runs. 'The irony was after we won the game it was straight back to the county side and guess who we were playing? New Zealand.' He took one wicket in the match.

'At Trent Bridge for the fourth Test I bowled brilliantly, the best I've ever bowled. It was one of those games when you have the ball on a string. If I wanted to bowl half a yard quicker or slower or pitch half a yard shorter or fuller, I could do everything I wanted.'

He took 5-63 and 4-87, bowling 82 overs in all. England won by 165 runs: 'I was pretty naive about everything and just treated it like a county game. I tried to change as little as possible how I went about the game before, during and after so my routines and habits were similar to county cricket. That was very important because when the enormity dropped on me about playing Test cricket I changed too many things. When I was selected on the odd occasion later, specifically in 1989 in Australia, I changed so many things and it didn't work for me.

'If only I could have carried on like 1983, but in six years you lose your naiveté and you think more about what might go wrong than right. After play I liked to have a couple of beers, which would be almost shunned these days. Then I could go to bed and relax and get a good night's kip and not worry too much about the enormity of the next day's play.

'There were extroverts and introverts who don't say a lot and those that do the crossword or listen to music and there were the wheeler-dealers of the team. I always say that the game's different but the characters are the same.

'On the pitch it's a misnomer to say people were not fit in the 1980s but they are specifically fitter today. Strength and conditioning coaches keep players on the field for a lot longer and rehab is better when you get an injury. There's more science to playing the game. Everyone can look the opposition up as a batter or a bowler but back then you only knew if you'd played against them. At a game a couple of years ago I walked past the analysis room, and they were watching this lad bowl his variations and he was making his debut! That sort of information was just not available in the 1980s or 1990s.

'There's very little interaction between the teams at the close of play, which I always thought was such an important part when I played. They'd say, "What happened to your action?" or "I've not seen you do that before."'

It was like the chat he'd had with Geoff Miller: 'Those conversations were gold dust and I think in the modern day they work out different ways, but in my day it was a beer. With [Yorkshire's] Phil Carrick it was "let's talk cricket for an hour and then we'll talk about wine, women and song after that".'

David Gower has memories of hairy extra-curricular activities playing Cambridge University for Leicestershire in 1983. Punting with Cook and two companions, Gower fell in, but still made 72 a few hours later. He was dared to get his first ten runs on the leg side. The boys were pissing themselves as Chris 'Baldy' Balderstone kept getting sent back.

Gower hit back-to-back centuries against New Zealand as England won the Test series 3-1, all live on the BBC. Back at Leicestershire, the dressing room was full of characters. 'Birky [Jack Birkenshaw] and Barry Dudleston were working on the next way to make a bit of money. Brian Davison was larger than life. Les Taylor would tell stories about when he was a miner and about boxing. John Steele was a man of few words with a dry sense of humour. It was a strong dressing room. Players were digging you out.

There was no mollycoddling. Us junior ones sometimes got roasted even when we'd done nothing wrong.'

From Balderstone, who also played professional football for 20 years, Cook learnt how to keep himself fit and prepare for the game: 'He was seminal in turning me from a bit of a jack the lad into someone with a bit of focus and professionalism.'

Cook played then umpired for more than 40 seasons. He retired aged 65 in 2022: 'I miss the game but I don't miss umpiring, and I'm not even missing the game at the moment. It's almost become too bloody difficult. There's so much politics.

'Umpires and players would be in the bar together so you'd be stupid not to listen. Now there are cameras coming out of every orifice. They're supposed to be coaching aids but players all look at the footage and see what they want. A lot of the fun and enjoyment has gone out of umpiring for the lads doing it now.'

Cook has always been his own man. 'I got in trouble because I talked too much or had my hands in my pockets or moved around too much. But if you stand for six or seven hours in the middle you have to be yourself. If you try to do something different you never succeed.'

Now he's doing 'bugger all really'. Racecourses need ticking off. He might pop down to Wantage Road and Grace Road and say hello to a few people. 'I'd like to own the winner of the Champion Hurdle but that's not going to happen.

'I've done nicely out of the game. I never particularly thought about making money. It was just a fantastic lifestyle and it took me all around the world. It's given me a great life.'

England v New Zealand at Lord's, August 11–15 1983: England 326 (David Gower 108), New Zealand 191 all out (Nick Cook 26-11-35-5, Norman Cowans 4-50), England 211 (Ian Botham 61), New Zealand 219 all out (Cook 27.2-3-90-3).

Leicestershire

Roger Tolchard: Batsman/wicketkeeper who played 483 first-class games from 1965–83 (captain 1981–83) with 15,288 runs and 914 catches/127 stumpings and 310 one-dayers with 6,055 runs and 248 catches/34 stumpings. Played four Tests in 1976/77. In 1983 he took 44 catches and made nine stumpings and scored 671 runs at 25.80 in 24 Championship matches plus 307 runs in 17 one-dayers. Later a coach at Malvern College, his brother Jeff played for Leicestershire and nephew Roger Twose for Warwickshire and New Zealand.

Chris Balderstone (1940–2000): Opener and left a spinner. Yorkshire 1961–70, Leicestershire 1971–86. Played 390 first-class matches with 19.034 runs and 310 wickets. Also 238 one-dayers with 5,664 runs and 28 wickets. In 1983 he scored 1,443 Championship runs at 42.44 and took six wickets, plus 167 runs in six one-dayers. Professional footballer from 1958–78, notably as a classy midfielder for Carlisle United. He played two Tests in 1976. Later an umpire, he died of cancer in 2000 aged 59.

John Steele: Played 379 first-class matches with 15,054 runs and 584 wickets and 302 one-dayers with 3,532 runs and 293 wickets. In 1983 Steele scored 284 runs at 17.75 and took 39 wickets at 29.92 plus 16 in 13 one-dayers and 133 runs. Leicestershire 1970–83, Glamorgan 1984–86. Brother of David Steele (England/Northamptonshire/Derbyshire). Later an umpire from 1988 until 2011. He told me, about the 1983 season: 'I was obviously disappointed when Leicestershire said they were going to sign Peter Willey and my place was in jeopardy. It was my benefit season [£33,470] and spectators think "he's taken the money and ran" but I wanted to stay, then Glamorgan made an enquiry. The big difference between then and now? T20 has come in; other than that nothing really.'

Nigel Briers: Right-handed opener for Leicestershire from 1971–95 with 381 first-class matches and 18,726 runs and 8,216 in 338 one-dayers. Captain 1990–95. In 1983 he scored 1,265 runs at 38.33 plus 444 in 17 one-dayers. Later a cricket director at Marlborough College.

Brian Davison: Leicestershire 1970–83 and Gloucestershire 1985. Played 467 first-class matches with 27.453 runs at 39.96 and 334 one-dayers with 8,343 runs at 31.24. In 1983 the Zimbabwean scored 1,265 Championship runs at 38.33 plus 330 runs in 14 one-dayers. Davison asked for a 30 per cent pay rise and a consortium of local businesses had come up with a short-term fix for 1983, but Davison left after the season finished for a job in Tasmanian cricket. Secretary Mike Turner said the club cost £400,000 to run and only £200,000 came in from cricket revenue. As a smaller county Leicestershire struggle with cash to this day, especially as they have no

Hundred team or a Test match ground. Davison was later a politician in Tasmania.

David Gower: Leicestershire 1975–89, Hampshire 1990–93. He played 448 first-class matches scoring 26,339 runs and 430 one-dayers with 12,255 runs. In 1983 he scored 702 runs in 13 Championship matches at 41.29 and played in the World Cup semi-final, topping the tournament averages with 384 runs at 76.80 with a 84.95 strike rate, the highest of anyone with more than 200 runs. 'Lubo' scored 819 runs in 19 one-dayers in the 1983 season. Played 117 Test matches and 114 ODIs from 1978–92, scoring 8,231 and 3,170 runs, respectively. Later a broadcaster.

Tim Boon: Right-handed opener from 1980–97 scoring 11,821 runs in 248 first-class matches and 3,602 in 173 one-dayers. In 1983, he hit 18 runs in four Championship matches. Later a coach.

Mike Garnham: Wicketkeeper for Gloucestershire 1978–79, Leicestershire from 1980–88 and Essex 1989–95. In 207 first-class matches he took 429 catches and made 41 stumpings and scored 6,240 runs. Also played in 256 one-dayers with 2,640 runs and 217/37. In 1983 he made no Championship appearances but in 12 one-dayers took seven catches and made two stumpings. He replaced Roger Tolchard as Leicestershire wicketkeeper in 1984. Later worked in planning in Essex.

Andy Roberts: West Indies fast bowler from 1974–83. Hampshire 1973–78 and Leicestershire 1981–84. Took 202 wickets in 47 Tests and 87 in 56 ODIs. He took 889 first-class wickets in 228 matches and 274 in 195 one-dayers.

In 1983 he played in the World Cup final (he won in 1975 and 1979) and took 11 wickets at 21.63 in the tournament. He took 16 wickets in four Championship matches for Leicestershire in 1983 and 23 in one-dayers. Later a cricket administrator and coach.

Les Taylor: Seam bowler for Leicestershire from 1977–90. Took 581 wickets in 218 first-class matches at 25.21 and 302 in 210 one-dayers at 21.41. In 1983 took 69 wickets at 19.39 plus 18 in one-dayers. Played two Tests in 1985. Later a postman.

Gordon Parsons: Seamer for Leicestershire from 1978–97 with Warwickshire (1986–88) in between. 'Bullhead' took 26 wickets and scored 207 runs in 13 Championship games in 1983 plus ten in one-dayers and 809 wickets (and 6,763 runs) in 338 first-class matches in total at 30.29 and 356 (plus 1,941 runs) in 351 one-dayers at 30.75. Brother-in-law of the late South Africa captain Hansie Cronje and later a coach in South Africa.

Nick Cook: Slow left-armer for Leicestershire 1978–85, Northamptonshire 1986–94 and England 1983–89. Played 356 first-class matches taking 879 wickets at 29.01 and 223 one-dayers with 200 wickets at 34.06. In 1983, took 73 first-class wickets at 25.46 with a best of 5-35 for England v New Zealand at Lord's on debut. He bowled 321 maidens, the fourth-highest in 1983, behind Derek Underwood's 358, Norman Gifford's 346 and John Emburey's 328. He also took nine wickets in one-dayers in 1983. Later an umpire.

Paddy Clift (1953–96) was not included in Panini. The Zimbabwean all-rounder won the 1983 Cricket Society

Wetherall Award for the Leading All-Rounder in English First-Class Cricket for his 843 runs at 32.42 and 83 wickets at 19.18. He also played 15 one-dayers, scoring 227 runs and taking 14 wickets. One of his two first-class centuries, an unbeaten 100 against Sussex at Hove, was made in a county-record 50 minutes in a rain-hit draw in September. He was later a banker and coach in Durban, where he died of bone marrow cancer aged 43.

George Ferris who played for Leicestershire from 1983–90 was also not included. The West Indian fast bowler took 53 Championship wickets in 13 matches in 1983. He achieved his best figures in his fourth match for Leicestershire, when he took 7-42 and 3-62 in a win against Glamorgan at Hinckley where seven of his victims were lbw. The Antiguan later lived in Orlando, Florida. After working in insurance he ran a pet supplies business and was also a careers consultant.

Chapter 16

Middlesex: John Emburey

I'M AT The Oval in June 2023 for Surrey v Middlesex. Surrey hit 252 in 20 overs (unthinkable in 1983) and Middlesex won for the first time that season. Sixes everywhere. I see Paul Allott, bag on his shoulder, walking through the exit next to the pavilion just before the end and try and pursue him, but I dither and he's gone.

The kids disappear to collect refundable beer cups and I rue missing my chance to tick off Lancashire. We leave and I spot a familiar figure, being willingly stopped by cheery fans for a chat.

We wait a minute and I fall into step on the warm and merry night with the former England off-spinner. We're close to where I was nearly arrested a fortnight before at the World Test Championship. Since then, England have lost the first Ashes Test and that day Enid Bakewell had rung the Trent Bridge bell and waved to me.

I give Emburey my 1983 spiel: 'I had a good year that year,' says Emburey. 'First to 100 wickets. You don't forget that. I do remember the stickers.' He makes a rectangle shape with his fingers: 'They were about two inches square and two and a half inches down.' We stop at the traffic lights. 'I don't suppose I could give you a call?'

I'd spoken to him before, at the Chelsea Flower Show in 2018 when industrialist Swati Piramal sponsored an Indian cricket garden, marking 70 years of the British Council in India. The garden featured Himalayan blue poppies, some giant stumps and the ICC World Cup, which England won in 2019.

Emburey, with florist daughter Clare, a Chelsea exhibitor, was looking at the garden and I asked them about it for a *Wisden* article I was writing. He is one of the best analysers of the game past and present, having played and coached professionally for 50 years.

At The Oval match there were 24 sixes and 52 fours hit in 39.2 overs, which produced 506 runs at 12.5 an over. Being that expensive was unthinkable to Emburey, who had a List A economy rate of 3.82 runs an over and went for 2.20 an over in his Test career from 1987–95.

He texts back that he's available after finishing some notes for an Ashes Q&A event with Ian Botham and Jason Gillespie.

Emburey left Surrey and moved to Middlesex in 1971, eventually replacing veteran Fred Titmus, before making his debut for England in 1978.

By 1983 Emburey was unavailable for international selection because he had toured with the England rebels in 1981–82. He and the rest of the team were banned for three years by the TCCB for breaking a moratorium on touring the country, imposed by the ICC because of the South African government's apartheid policy.

In his 1987 autobiography Emburey wrote about being a 'rebel without applause', adding: 'More has been written and spoken over the SA question than any other topic which has directly affected my career. There's been a significant bearing on my life.'

The punishing blow was far more severe than he expected. The money helped to pay for a mortgage of a 'decent but hardly palatial home' in Brondesbury Park. The ban cost him three overseas tours worth £10,000–£12.000 each and 15 home Tests worth £1,500 each.

Emburey played for Western Province for the next two seasons instead of England, alongside Gooch. They did impressions of each other, Ern's round-arm action amusing Gooch who put a cushion up his jumper to ape his mate. Back in England, his first daughter with wife Susie, Clare, was born in March 1983.

The Middlesex vice captaincy was withdrawn after the South African tour. Mike Gatting got it instead and became Mike Brearley's successor for the 1983 season. But Emburey stood in for eight games while Gatting played for England. Middlesex had five of their 12 Championship victories under the spinner's guidance. The 1983 season presented a new challenge – life after Brearley, rather than playing for England, and playing under Gatting. 'Gatt was a bulldog breed, not like Brears.' But the mild-mannered Embers was assertive with Gatt when it came to field placings and admitted he was jealous.

Middlesex couldn't play at Lord's for seven weeks at the height of the season. They led the table for two and a half months, then Roland Butcher and Wilf Slack got injured in the run in. June's six wins in a row, with Embers taking 6-13 at Dartford against Kent, and four wins in succession while Gatting was at the World Cup were the highlights, but the wins dried up as August went on. There was just one victory, over Warwickshire, when Emburey took seven in the match and scored 61. Opposition spinner Norman Gifford bowled 34 overs but only took 3-113.

When I call, John is looking after his grandson and is getting ready to pick up Botham. He remembers 1983 as his 100-wicket year. 'I got banned in 82, 83, 84 so I played a full season. Before that I'd not really had the opportunity to try for 100 wickets because you didn't play enough cricket. The pitches would have been in my favour to some extent, particularly at Lord's.'

The one-day finals were the biggest matches of the county season, and Emburey was at home at HQ. The B&H final was one of the most thrilling games, he recalls. Essex captain Keith Fletcher won the toss and put Middlesex in. At a damp and overcast Lord's, it was seaming all over.

Clive Radley scored 89, putting on 49 with Emburey for the sixth wicket as Middlesex struggled to just 196/8. Essex were 127/1 before Edmonds and Emburey squeezed the run rate: 'We bowled either side of tea to rush through a few overs. I was speaking to Graham [Gooch] because they were only two or three wickets down not requiring too many with lots of overs to go and, all of a sudden, they lost a few wickets very quickly. Then they got themselves into trouble and we ended up winning the game. I do remember getting Fletch out caught at silly mid-off and it made a massive difference.' Norman Cowans cleaned up last man Neil Foster at 8.48pm to win the match by five runs.

In mid-August came the NatWest semi-final at Lord's with 15,000 watching. 'With Ian Botham! He hit me for six very early on. I came on and he swept me for six into the Mound stand and then Gatt took me off immediately.' Part-time bowler Wilf Slack replaced Emburey and bowled nine overs.

Botham scored 96 not out, rescuing Somerset from 52/5, chasing Middlesex's 222/9. 'I bowled the last over to Botham when the scores were level and he just had to block it out because if he'd got out, we would have won because the scores were level so he just blocked it. Amazing really.' Somerset then beat Kent in the final, which Middlesex should really have been in.

In the Championship, Emburey showed his true worth. Against Leicestershire at Lord's in mid-July he scored 47 and 73 not out and took 8-22 in the match. He was as pleased with his batting as much as bowling, especially as George Ferris's short ball had badly injured Roland Butcher to bring Embers in.

Another Emburey triumph was against Essex in early August at Chelmsford. Middlesex scored 83 on a grassy pitch, Essex replied with 289, then Middlesex hit 634/7. Essex bowled 57 overs in 82 minutes after tea to boost the over rate and avoid fines. Gooch bowled 56 overs and took 1-173. Emburey scored 133. The 551-run difference between the two innings was a world record.

Spin partner Edmonds played for England in 1983 but took just four wickets in two Tests before Nick Cook replaced him: 'We helped each other. I helped him bowl an arm ball because he didn't really have one. If we'd bowled 35 overs the day before we didn't really need to go in the nets and have a practice in the morning, so we used to go in front of the pavilion and bowl half a dozen balls to each other and then go back upstairs and have a cup of tea.

'During matches we didn't help each other. We complemented each other. If the number four batsman was in with a number 11 batsman, I would try and keep the number four on strike, so Philippe had an opportunity bowl at number 11. With Philip Tufnell it was the total opposite. He wouldn't try to squeeze the number four and didn't mind if, off the last ball of the over, the guy got a single because it meant he might have a chance of getting the number 11 out next time. With Philip, I complemented him, but he didn't complement me!'

Emburey says when he stepped in for Gatting 'there wasn't a lot of captaining to do. It was just a matter of "okay, have a break" and someone else would come on.' Emburey contained and Edmonds attacked, spinning it harder: 'We didn't begrudge another person's success. There would often be times when Philippe would get a seven-for and I'd get one or two. Philippe would get the wickets but that didn't mean to say I didn't bowl well.'

They had been competing for a Test place. England rarely played two spinners in a Test at home. That wasn't an issue in 1982–84. Middlesex only had Emburey on the England banned list, compared to Kent, who had Bob Woolmer, Alan Knott and Derek Underwood, and Essex with Gooch and John Lever. 'Obviously it made a difference to Middlesex because I was the first to 100 wickets in the country. Lord's pitches when they were dry were very helpful for the spinners. They didn't get the water on the pitch like they do now. The pitches are emerald green now. If I was a spinner now, I wouldn't play for Middlesex. I'd have gone somewhere else.'

Emburey recalls the last Championship match of the season, at Nottinghamshire, when Middlesex required a victory if they were going to pip Essex to the title. '[Nottinghamshire captain] Clive Rice was monitoring what was happening at Chelmsford but he really ruined our chances of having an opportunity to win. They could have made a game of it but didn't. Ultimately, they stopped us having a chance of winning the Championship.'

The match was abandoned because of rain. The news came as Yorkshire's last second innings wicket fell at Chelmsford. The end of the Nottinghamshire match meant it was irrelevant that rain came to Chelmsford too, preventing Essex from chasing 137 for victory in 30 minutes plus 20 overs against Yorkshire. Lever, another 100 wicket-taker in 1983, took 11 wickets.

They were halcyon days, as Emburey reflects: 'The 1970s and 80s were a great time to play cricket because all counties had two overseas players. Everyone had a good fast bowler. But at the end of the day what made a big difference was we had two crackerjack spinners.'

Nevertheless, the dressing room was volatile, according to Emburey, 'We'd often have arguments over the cricket. If we felt someone wasn't pulling their weight during a session, when we came off the field during lunch or tea we'd have an opinion, Mike Brearley would have encouraged it and Gatt continued that.

'We'd have a blazing argument and most of them would revolve around Philippe because Philippe disagreed with everything. If we felt someone wasn't making any effort then something would be said. We'd have a barney about it. All the aggression we built up in the dressing room, when we got on the field was taken out on the opposition. Once we got things off our chest, it was forgotten. That was another one of our strengths.'

He gives a flavour of life after a day's play: 'We didn't socialise a lot. There'd be a couple of us that got on well and we'd have dinner together but it wasn't a close-knit dressing room. We had five West Indian players or players of a Caribbean heritage [Wayne Daniel, Cowans, Neil Williams, Butcher and Slack]. It wasn't a divided dressing room or anything like that. We'd go out together during away matches but when we were at home everyone went home.

'The West Indian boys didn't really drink or socialise because it wasn't their thing and everyone understood that. We'd go down the Tavern after the game and have a drink with the opposition and the same would happen away.'

He recognises a move away from any socialising in the last 15–20 years but says England one-day captain Eoin Morgan (2015–22) encouraged players to go out for a drink together: 'He felt that was a good part of the game where he got the players together. You're not going back to your room on your own and not communicating with anyone. Eoin changed all that.

'Playing county cricket in the eighties was good but playing international cricket was crap because you don't know whether you were going to be selected or not, so lots of players played in fear of being left out. You only had to have an ordinary game and they'd pick somebody else who was not necessarily a better cricketer than you. Selection was bloody awful and it's only since central contracts that you're recognised as the best in the country for the particular thing you do.'

He gives the example of England opener Zak Crawley, who was averaging 28 in Tests at the start of 2023. 'I don't think there's been too many international players who played as many Tests as him with such a low average. Back in our day it wouldn't have happened but what a great feeling to play like that now, knowing you're probably going to play in the next Test match, and you can play with a bit of freedom and abandon. It takes a heck of a lot of pressure off you. England won't change and I don't blame them.'

He regrets not getting the chance to captain England more often. He captained twice in the 1988 'bloody shambles' series against the West Indies, which England lost 4-0.

His tight wicket-to-wicket line and aggressive batting might have suited the modern game: 'I'd have got on alright in T20. Some of the current players talk out of their arse when they say cricketers of our generation wouldn't have been any good at T20 but there were a lot of players when T20 started who were shit as well. Players adapt and practice and if we'd had T20 we'd have done the same thing. You can't tell me the likes of Gooch, Lamb,

Botham and Gatting wouldn't have been good in that form of the game.

'I was probably the first spinner that bowled at the death and bowled yorkers, you work out a way of playing. The only difference is it's more difficult controlling a game with the slightly shorter boundaries because people want to see sixes and fours hit and that's one reason you don't get a lot of off-spinners being successful in T20. It's mostly left-arm spinners darting the ball into the pads and leg spinners that bowl back of a length and much flatter when you've got to guess which way the ball's going. I see some very ordinary players playing Twenty20 cricket and I'm watching them play Test cricket as well.'

Emburey excelled in all formats in 1983, playing 47 first-class and List A matches, taking 126 wickets in 6,507 balls and scoring 1,035 runs, the modern double.

Wisden made Emburey one of its five Cricketers of the Year (with Armanath, Jeremy Coney, Chris Smith and Gatting), saying he would have traded his 100 wickets for the Championship. Middlesex fell 17 points short of retaining the trophy. Perhaps the difference, according to Emburey, was the loss of Brearley. 'What was missing was his captaincy, ability and his tactical astuteness and awareness. We had the same side, literally a team of Test players.'

In July 2023 I visit Lord's for Middlesex against Surrey. Rory Burns makes 79 and retires to the Tavern afterwards with a group of internationals including Jamie Overton, Tom Latham and Mark Stoneman. It's like 1983 all over again.

Benson & Hedges Cup final at Lord's – 23 July 1983

Middlesex v Essex

Middlesex

Graham Barlow b Foster 14
Wilf Slack c Gooch b Foster 1
Clive Radley not out 89
Mike Gatting run out 22
Keith Tomlins lbw Gooch 0
John Emburey c D East b Lever 17
Paul Downton c Fletcher b Foster 10
Phil Edmonds b Pringle 9
Neil Williams c & b Pringle 13
Wayne Daniel not out 2
Norman Cowans did not bat
Extras 19. Total: 196/9 (55 overs)
Bowling: Lever 11-1-52-1; Foster 11-2-26-3; Pringle 11-0-54-2; Turner 11-1-24-0; Gooch 11-2-21-1.

Essex

Graham Gooch c Downton b Williams 46
Brian Hardie c Downton b Cowans 49
Ken McEwan c Cowans b Edmonds 34
Keith Fletcher c Radley b Edmonds 3
Keith Pont hit wicket b Williams 7
Derek Pringle lbw Daniel 16
Stuart Turner c sub (Carr) b Cowans 9
David East c Gatting b Cowans 5
Ray East run out 0
Neil Foster b Cowans 0

Extras 23. Total: 192 all out (54.1 overs)
Bowling: Daniel 11-2-34-1; Cowans 10.1-0-39-4; Williams 11-0-45-2; Emburey 11-3-17-0; Edmonds 11-3-34-2.

Middlesex

Mike Gatting: Middlesex 1975–98. England 1977–95 (79 Tests, 92 ODIs). Played 551 first-class matches with 36,549 runs at 49.52 and 551 one-dayers with 14,476 runs at 33.74. Scored 83 runs at 20.75 in the 1983 World Cup and 121 at 30.25 in two Tests. Altogether he hit 1,494 at 64.95 in 18 first-class matches, leading the English averages. He scored 651 at 31.00 in 27 one-dayers in all competitions. He worked in his sports shop in 1982/83 after missing selection for the Ashes tour. Later a coach, commentator and 2013 MCC president.

Wilf Slack (1954–89): Left-handed Middlesex opener from 1977–88 who played 237 first-class with 13,950 runs at 38.96 and 183 one-day matches with 4,639 runs at 30.32. England 1986 (three Tests, two ODIs). In 1983, Slack scored 874 Championship runs at 38.00 plus 459 and 13 wickets in 19 one-dayers. Died of a heart attack while playing in Gambia.

Keith Tomlins: Right-hand bat at Middlesex from 1977–85, then Gloucestershire 1986–87. Played 108 first-class matches with 3,880 runs at 27.13 and 82 List A games with 1,257 runs at 20.95. In 1983 he scored 606 Championship runs at 28.85. Later a coach.

Graham Barlow: Left-handed opener from 1969–86, England 1976–77 (three Tests, six ODIs). Played 251 first-class matches with 12,387 runs at 35.90 and 257 one-dayers with 6,006 runs at 27.55. In 1983, he scored 1,519 Championship runs at 49.00 plus 513 in 18 one-dayers. Later a coach and teacher in New Zealand.

Roland Butcher: Middlesex 1974–90. England 1981 (three Tests three ODIs). Played 277 first-class matches with 12,021 runs at 31.22 and 273 one-dayers with 4,899 runs at 22.26. In 1983, he scored 646 Championship runs at 43.06 plus 324 in 12 one-dayers. His cheekbone was broken by a ball from Leicestershire's George Ferris at Lord's in mid-July, ending his season. Later a coach in West Indies.

Clive Radley: Middlesex 1962–90. Played 559 first-class matches with 26,441 runs at 35.44 and 409 one-dayers with 10,476 runs at 30.54. England 1978 (eight Tests, four ODIs). Scored 748 Championship runs at 24.93 in 1983 plus 608 in 23 one-dayers. Later Middlesex and MCC coach.

Paul Downton: Wicketkeeper for Kent 1977–79, Middlesex 1980–91 and England 1977–88 (30 Tests, 28 ODIs). Played 314 first-class matches (690 catches and 89 stumpings) and scored 8.270 runs at 25.13 and 297 one-dayers with 3,349 runs at 22.62 (281/64). In 1983 he scored 508 Championship runs at 22.61 and took 54 catches and five stumpings in first-class matches, plus 238 runs with 30 catches and six stumpings in 22 one-dayers. Downton was ECB Managing Director from 2013–15 after a career in the City before becoming Kent's director of cricket from 2018–23.

Phil Edmonds: Slow left-armer for Middlesex from 1971–92 and England from 1975–87 (51 Tests, 29 ODIs). Played 391 first-class matches with 1,246 wickets at 25.66

and 301 one-dayers with 323 wickets at 25.11. Took 72 Championship wickets at 20.70 in 1983, plus ten in one-dayers. Later a corporate executive.

John Emburey: Off-spinner who played 513 first-class games from 1973–97 taking 1,608 wickets at 26.09. He also took 647 wickets in 538 List A games and played 64 Tests (1978–95) and 61 ODIs. He scored 12,021 first-class runs, including 1,713 for England, to add to his 147 wickets (plus 501 runs and 76 wickets in ODIs). In 1983, he scored 782 first-class runs at 27.92 in 25 matches and took 103 wickets at 17.88. Also played 22 List As with 253 runs at 25.30 and 23 wickets at 20.78 with an economy rate of 3.19. Only Malcolm Nash (2.78), Ian Folley (3.07) and Ray Illingworth (3.10) had lower among players with ten or more wickets. Later a coach.

Wayne Daniel: Middlesex 1977–88 and West Indies 1976–84 (ten Tests, 18 ODIs). Played 266 first-class matches with 867 wickets at 22.47 and 362 one-day wickets at 19.16 in 241 one-dayers. 'Diamond' took 29 one-day and 47 Championship wickets in 1983. Later a coach and commentator.

Norman Cowans: Middlesex 1980–93 and Hampshire 1993–95. Played 239 first-class matches and 224 one-dayers with 662 wickets at 24.86 and 263 at 27.33 respectively. England 1982–85 (Tests 19, ODIs 23). In 1983, he took 18 Championship wickets at 25.27 plus 22 in one-dayers. Played four Tests in 1983 and took 12 wickets at 37.25. Also took 2-31 in a single World Cup appearance. Later worked in sports promotion and as a DJ.

Simon Hughes: Medium-fast right-armer for Middlesex 1980–91 and Durham 1992–93. 'Yozzer' played 205 first-class matches with 466 wickets at 32.48 and 202 one-dayers with 272 wickets at 25.47. In 1983 took 33 Championship wickets at 25.33 plus six in one-dayers. Later a commentator and writer.

Chapter 17

Northamptonshire: Geoff Cook

FOR A book I wrote about Durham cricket in 2002, their then coach Geoff Cook very kindly wrote the introduction. Cook was pleased to have helped; he's a man who has helped many in the game over the years.

For 20 years Northamptonshire's opener (1971–90) and a successful captain from 1981–88, the former England batsman (1981–83) is perhaps better known as Durham coach, from 1991–2018. Under Cook, they went from being a minor county to winning three County Championships and the Friends Provident Trophy as well as reaching Twenty20 finals day for the only time.

Cook had been made number one entry in Durham's new hall of fame in March 2023. 'It's a pretty good initiative by the club. It was nice to be involved in it and to get together,' he told me.

Going back to 1983, Cook started off the year in the England team in Australia. He cracked a rib in the nets (facing Ian Botham) just before the second Test at Brisbane in November 1982, giving Graeme Fowler his chance. Cook had scored 99 and 77 in the previous match against New South Wales. Cook describes the trip as 'that infamous tour'.

The rib injury meant he was out for three weeks before returning with 73 not out against Tasmania. Back in the Test team, he scored 10, 26, 8 and 2 in back-to-back Tests at Melbourne and Sydney (a draw in January 1983, Cook's last Test), dismissed by a mix of Jeff Thomson, Rodney Hogg and Geoff Lawson. This was the first Test series since England's 3-1 home triumph in 1981 and Australia regained the Ashes 2-1, with England's only win a three-run victory at Melbourne.

There was a B&H one-day series with Australia and New Zealand in January 1983, where Cook played a bit part as England came third, then three ODIs in New Zealand in February, which Cook was not involved in, his England career over.

'I didn't think I'd get back in, not really. I was doing okay, when I first got in. I played poorly in Australia in two or three Tests out there and then other people got a go so my prospects were diminishing by the hour.'

One of the reasons Cook got more chances was because of the South African tour and players getting banned, Graham Gooch for instance.

There were lots of clandestine talks on the India 1981/82 tour about joining the rebels but Cook did not go in the end, though many of his team-mates who lost 1-0 to India that winter, including Geoff Boycott, Gooch, Derek Underwood, John Emburey and John Lever, did, as did his Northamptonshire colleagues Peter Willey and Wayne Larkins.

'It was really very divisive. You know, the whole planning for the tour was very much undercover stuff and lots of whispering was going on. There was a lot of hearsay. I felt eventually it was a bit of a threat to the English game. But everybody made their own personal decision and went on the rebel tour for their own reasons, so good luck to them.'

Back in November 1981, in his debut ODI, England beat India by five wickets. Roger Binny removed Cook for 13, caught by Gundappa Viswanath: 'He was just a steady bowler, like Madan Lal and Amarnath that wouldn't fill you full of fear, but they were very efficient at what they did.'

India's star all-rounder Kapil Dev signed for Northamptonshire in 1981 after touring England. He didn't take many wickets (six in three matches, plus 175 runs), or in 1982 (nine in the Championship in six games, though he was player of the series in the Test and one-day series against England, both lost by India). In 1983 Kapil took 16 wickets and scored 349 runs in seven matches.

Cook said, 'Kapil Dev was obviously a terrific coup for the county to get him to play. I went up to Cumbria to sign him. Jimmy Amarnath's wife was working in a hospital up there and he was staying with them. It was tremendous for Northamptonshire to have a top all-rounder, but his influence soon disappeared.'

After India's World Cup triumph their inspirational captain went home: 'He didn't quite return to England on time. I imagine he was being feted enormously back in India so we were just living day to day waiting for him to return back. I think Kapil had run out of energy when he came back. He still had lots of supporters but in terms of being able to contribute I think English cricket didn't really turn him on. He was a quality performer and obviously world-class. So India had a bit of the ingredients, but collectively they probably overshot themselves.

'On that tour of India it was apparent that sort of shift of power was starting to materialise. It was evident to everybody what a massive commercial potential India had.'

Northamptonshire roped in a replacement for Kapil in James Carse, father of Durham and England's Brydon Carse, who was recommended by team-mate Larkins. But the South African fast bowler was not a success, with just 22 Championship wickets at 32.68 in ten matches.

Another problem for Northamptonshire was a dispute with Willey, who left after 18 years for Leicestershire at the end of 1983: 'There was a bit of internal politics going on with the groundsman and Pete sided with the groundsman in a legal issue. Obviously, that didn't go down too well with the club, so there was a running rift, and it was a tricky one to be in the middle of. There were some strong-minded people involved in it all, which is always a good thing. But when you're trying to balance things and doing the best for the team at the same time it was tricky.'

Willey, player of the season for a second successive year, and Larkins had given evidence for dismissed groundsman Les Bentley, and according to *Wisden* gave 'no assurances about his future attitude'. Willey was restored to the England team in 1985, as was Larkins in 1989/90.

Cook says: 'It was an interesting team. We had a pretty strong batting line-up with Allan Lamb and Larkins and Willey and Richard Williams as well. We had a couple of very efficient medium pacers, which sort of reflected how the Indian team was. It was widely thought that all we were short on was some real firepower, which we tried to correct with a couple of signings, but that never really materialised. It wasn't until later on in the 80s that we did, with Curtly Ambrose.'

In 1983, there were few outstanding moments but one game was memorable for a great bit of captaincy by Ray Illingworth. In the NatWest at Headingley on 20 July, Northamptonshire had lost a couple of wickets. Illingworth went to field at silly point, 'just to put pressure on, which was a tactic rarely used then', according to Cook. 'It showed his attacking qualities and I think Kapil was out caught [for 0] off Phil Carrick, which was a brilliant bit of captaincy that stood out for me.' Northamptonshire scored 211/7 before Jim Griffiths took 5-33, bowling Yorkshire out of 165.

In the quarter-finals they lost to Middlesex by seven wickets: 'That was more true to form I think.'

Cook recalls Larkins's entertainment value and ability being second to none and David Steele returning in 1982 from three years at Derbyshire for 'a whiff of oxygen. He left as a batsman and came back a spinner. And he did a wonderful job too.'

Middlesbrough-born Cook was one of many north-easterners to play for Northamptonshire, including popular England opener Colin Milburn, footballer/slow left-armer Malcolm Scott and Cook's contemporaries Willey, wicketkeeper George Sharp and seamer Alan Hodgson. Later came left-arm opening bowler Simon Brown, who won an England cap after moving to join Cook at Durham.

Cook had moved from Northamptonshire back north to become Durham coach in 1991 ahead of the county going onto the first-class circuit in 1992.

'It was that exodus that was part of the push behind Durham to get first-class. We were losing a lot of players at the time. The Weston brothers, Phil and Robin, and the Roseberrys, Michael and Andrew, were moving south, as well as the Northamptonshire connection. So the local administrators really used that as a leverage to get first-class.

'It was whispered as a possibility back then [in 1983]. Durham was always high on that list or a combination of them with Northumberland was seen as a possibility. And Durham was the leading minor county by a long way, in terms of players produced and in terms of trophies won. There was a massive objection to increasing the number of counties but eventually the case was strong enough for them to be admitted.'

He was with Durham from 1991–2018. Cook says: 'It's been an absolute privilege to be involved and be given the opportunity to be there at day one to try and develop teams, cricketers and philosophies. I've had a fantastic time culminating in three or four years of perhaps the most successful of the counties on the pitch. That was great fun to watch. A lot of youngsters went on to play for England and that has been a source of great pride.'

Another great contribution by Cook was his involvement in the Professional Cricketers' Association from the mid-1970s. He rose to be joint secretary with Durham's 1992/93 captain David Graveney, from 1989–94. 'Each county would have a representative and I was quite happy to put a case for the players within the dressing room. And it just went on from there. The players' union started to become a little bit disillusioned, and it almost disappeared but thankfully two or three people were marvellous and they kept it going. And now the PCA is one of the best professional sporting institutions that there is.'

Tory peer Ian Botham thought of Cook as very left wing. Broadcaster John Arlott said there were no more than six left wingers in the county game. Middlesex's Simon Hughes suggested about three – the fingers of one hand with a couple removed. Arlott was PCA president from its foundation in 1967 to his death in 1991. The PCA helped capped players' wages rise to £7,665 by 1985, up from a minimum wage of £4,500, established in 1979 in an inflationary economy which meant average county wage bills rose from £700,000 in 1978 to £2m by 1985.

Botham wrote in his 2007 autobiography that he was offered the Durham captaincy for 1992 but Cook's dream was a 'socialist cricket republic', wanting all players to be equal. He had promised that David Graveney could be skipper. Cook says: 'That's where my politics is and was. It wasn't the case of right or wrong. In that sense we were able to support the players right across the board, and I had a good time and made some good friends and did one or two things that we were pretty proud of. I didn't go around wearing any sort of revolutionary hat. It was just a question of trying to see fairness. [Being left wing was] very much the minority.'

He believes that's still the case, given the money involved: 'I can see the reason that people want to make every day count in terms of promoting themselves and trying to maximise what they can do.'

The big political issue affecting world cricket in 1983 was South Africa, but Cook says race wasn't much talked about at the time: 'I think it was not accepted but it wasn't massively a topic within the game, I think people just got on with the team that was around them, and that was a very healthy situation.

'The philosophy of old-fashioned county cricket was changing emphasis. It was a very slow evolution to the worldwide force that cricket is now. Coaching generally started to have a new emphasis around that time.' The ECB/TCCB revamped old MCC coaching philosophies and, consequently, coaches became more influential in professional as opposed to just youth cricket.

'It's a totally different game now. The demands of the players are far greater, quite correctly as well. We used to be pretty self-sufficient. You would have a strong captain, a group of senior professionals who ran the team themselves and it wasn't until people like Micky Stewart and Ray Illingworth came in to oversee county teams as coaches or managers that things started to take a different direction. I think it was for the good as long as the captain had the final say, but that was always going to be a tricky balance to get initially, as managers and coaches tried to justify the role in the group.'

Northamptonshire

Geoff Cook: Northamptonshire opener 1971–90, England 1982–83. Hit 1,496 runs at 40.43 in 23 Championship matches in 1983 and 1,510 at 39.73 in all (24 matches) with one century and 11 fifties. He scored 465 runs in 22 one-dayers at 27.35. In his career he played 460 first-class matches with 23,277 runs at 31.97 and 377 one-dayers, scoring 8,705 runs at 26.78. Northamptonshire won the Tilcon Trophy in 1983 against Yorkshire at Harrogate on 8 July. Later a coach with Durham.

Wayne Larkins: Northamptonshire opener from 1972–91, Durham 1992–95 and England 1980–91 (13 Tests, 25 ODIs). 'Ned' played 492 first-class matches with 27,142 runs at 34.44 and 485 one-dayers In 1983, he hit 1,774 first-class runs at 42.33 in 25 games (fourth-most after Ken McEwan, Geoff Boycott and Chris Smith) and 683 one-day runs at 34.15 in 22 matches, so 2,457 in all. He hit 236 v Derbyshire at Derby, passing Peter Willey's county record 227 from 1976 then 252 v Glamorgan including 100 before lunch and between lunch and tea. His 172 in the John Player League at Luton against Warwickshire was shown live on BBC. Later had various jobs including as a milkman.

Richard Williams: Northamptonshire 1974–92, he appeared in 284 first-class matches and scored 11,817 runs at 30.93 and took 376 wickets at 33.83. Also played 266 one-dayers and scored 4,263 runs at 24.36 and took 159 wickets at 29.27. In 1983, he scored 1,161 runs and took 42 wickets in 24 Championship matches plus ten one-day wickets and 286 runs in 22 matches. Later an electrician in Buckinghamshire.

Allan Lamb: Northamptonshire 1978–95, England 1982–92 (79 Tests, 122 ODIs). Played 467 first-class matches with 32,502 runs at 48.94 and 15,658 runs in 484 one-dayers at 39.14. In 1983 hit 1,232 first-class runs at 56.00 including 392 at 65.33 in four Tests v New Zealand with 137 not out to help win the last one, at Nottingham, plus 789 one-day runs including 278 at 69.50 in the World Cup with 102 against New Zealand at The Oval. Later a TV analyst, he also set up an events/travel company.

Peter Willey: Right-hand bat and off-spinner for Northamptonshire 1966–83, Leicestershire 1984–91 and England 1976–86 (26 Tests, 26 ODIs). Played 559 first-class matches with 24,361 runs at 30.56 and 756 wickets at 30.95 and 458 limited overs with 11,105 runs at 26.25 and 347 wickets at 32.11. In 1983, took 31 Championship wickets at 30.83 and scored 1,483 runs at 47.83. Also scored 624 one-day runs in 22 matches and took 13 wickets. Later an umpire.

Robin Boyd-Moss: Right-hand batsman for Northamptonshire from 1980–87. Played 153 first-class matches and scored 7,171 runs at 30.25 and 83 one-dayers with 1,602 runs at 22.88. In 1983, he played 25 first-class matches and scored 1,437 runs at 35.04 with two of his three centuries in the varsity match, when he also took seven of his nine wickets for the season. Later a coach in Kenya where he also ran a garage, a car hire business and a farm.

David Steele: Batsman and slow left-armer from 1963–78 Northamptonshire, 1979–81 Derbyshire, 1982–84 Northamptonshire and England 1975–76 (eight Tests, one ODI). Played 500 first-class matches and scored 22,346 runs at 32,47 and 260 one-dayers with 4,381 runs at 23.05. Also took 623 first-class wickets at 24.89 and 81 in one-dayers at 28.27. In 1983, he took 66 Championship wickets at 21.43 in 24 games and scored 506 runs at 22.00, plus six wickets and 59 runs in four one-dayers. A printer by trade, he became a coach.

Kapil Dev: Northamptonshire 1981–83, Worcestershire 1984–85. India 1978–94 (131 Tests, 225 ODIs). Played 275 first-class games with 11,356 runs at 32.91 and 835 wickets at 27.09, plus 309 one-dayers with 5,461 runs at 24.59 and 335 wickets at 27.34. In 1983 he took 16 wickets at 24.06 and scored 349 runs at 43.62 in seven Championship games. In the World Cup, he hit 303 runs at 60.60 and took 12 wickets at 20.41, captaining India to victory. Later India coach and a cricket administrator as well as a Sports University of Haryana chancellor.

George Sharp: Northamptonshire wicketkeeper from 1968–85. He played 306 first-class games with 565 catches and 90 stumpings and 285 one-dayers with 242/50. In 1983, he scored 447 runs at 29.80 and made 41 catches and five stumpings plus 250 runs and 16 catches/three stumpings in 21 one-dayers. Later an umpire.

Neil Mallender: Medium-fast bowler with spells at Northamptonshire in 1980–86 and 1995–96 and Somerset 1987–94. Played for England in 1992 (two Tests). He played in 345 first-class games and 325 one-dayers with 937 wickets at 26.31 and 387 at 25.44 respectively. In 1983 'Ghostie' took 48 wickets at 31.27 in 21 Championship games, plus 27 in one-dayers. Later became an umpire.

Jim Griffiths: Right-armer for Northamptonshire between 1974–86. He played 177 first-class games and took 444 wickets at 29.05 and in 165 one-dayers took 183 wickets at 27.09. In 1983, he took 50 wickets at 28.48 in 22 Championship games plus 21 in one-dayers. Later a driver for Carlsberg Breweries and then a local haulage contractor.

Tim Lamb: Middlesex 1974–77, Northamptonshire 1978–84. Played 160 first-class matches taking 361 wickets at 28.97 and 160 one-dayers with 190 wickets at 25.70. In 1983 he took 11 Championship wickets at 23.72 in seven games plus 16 in one-dayers. He became Middlesex secretary, then TCCB secretary, then chief executive. He left the ECB in 2004 and was chief executive of the Sport and Recreation Alliance until retiring.

Chapter 18

Nottinghamshire: Peter Such

I'M IN my hometown of Keswick for Easter 2023 and it's hailing. The bleak day picks up when Peter Such calls.

The former England off-spinner joined the ECB in 2009, going full-time in 2012 to work with bowlers in the England Performance Pathway as the National Lead Spin Bowling Coach. After leaving the role in November 2019, Such became a match referee ahead of the 2020 County Championship season.

Such provides insight about how he broke into county cricket as a teenager. He was 18 in 1983 and is the youngest player in the Panini album: 'I remember the rather unflattering photo! Now and again, you get one sort of dropped in your lap and they say can you sign please?'

He's also a thinker about spin bowling, coaching and match refereeing, the future of spin. Such still runs a spin academy, which is where I found how to contact him.

Born in Helensburgh, Such is one of nine Scottish-born players who played for England along with Mike Denness, Gavin Hamilton, Alec Kennedy, David Larter, Gregor MacGregor, Ian Peebles, Eric Russell and Dougie

Brown. The son of a Royal Navy chief petty officer, his mother was a midwife. The family moved to the Midlands when he was young and his father became a teacher.

Such is now a coach, in both cricket and life. He retrained following a career which went from potentially being unfulfilled to finding international success and winning a host of trophies at his third county, Essex.

Wisden said Nottinghamshire's 1983 season will not be remembered but that was not unexpected because of Test calls and injuries, as well as 'financial stringencies necessitating a cut-back to the playing strength'. Such cites Richard Hadlee's absence playing for New Zealand as particularly significant. The next year he did the double. 'We just didn't perform particularly well during that year.'

Captain Clive Rice, the other overseas pro, had an ongoing neck injury so he wasn't bowling. 'He was just playing as a batter. We were a little bit short-handed shall we say, but it gave opportunities for younger players like myself and Andy Pick and Paul Johnson.'

Bob White, who'd been a county off-spinning all-rounder since the 1950s, had been captain of the seconds and a mentor to Such but had left to become an umpire at the end of 1982. The current Test off-spinner Eddie Hemmings kept Such out of the Notts team: 'I used to chat quite a bit to Eddie, who obviously was a very fine bowler. He'd say try this or how about the other end? Next time you encounter this situation, you'll be a bit wiser perhaps.'

Hemmings had been a hero in his last Test, at Sydney as New Year 1983 dawned, reaching 95 as nightwatchman to save the match for England. He also took six wickets but didn't play another Test for almost five years. England tried several spinners in that era. Slow left-armer Nick Cook took 17 wickets in two Tests against New Zealand in 1983. John Emburey was banned so Vic Marks and Phil Edmonds played in the series as spinners too.

In 1983, Hemmings, despite suffering from a shoulder complaint, bowled 710 overs and conceded 2,000 runs in the Championship for Nottinghamshire, who had just three fast bowlers, Mike Hendrick, Mark Saxelby and Kevin Cooper, to fall back on.

So Rice was able to give Such a few chances. 'He was very, very positive. It was all about winning games and taking wickets so from a young spin bowler's point of view that was absolutely brilliant. He kept giving you opportunities, even if it didn't work out for a game or so. That type of captaincy is no longer in existence for us spinners. As a consequence, spin bowling is a challenge. Other people might get more opportunity, whether they were batters or pace bowlers.'

Back in 1983, Such still lived at home. 'I was 18 years old. The club had a deal with the local Ford dealership, and I got a Ford Fiesta. Then we also used to have a kit van as well. So for five months [of the season] you had a Ford Fiesta, and for one month you drove the kit van. So that was different, but it is what it is. There were five cars with two or three people in each car travelling to away matches. You might play two or three weeks without a day off. You were tired by the end of the season, but it was fine.'

A big change since 1983 is turnover of players from match to match. Nottinghamshire had 11 core players, plus Mike Bore and Such as spare spinners. Other than that, Andy Pick was breaking through, Hadlee played infrequently and Nigel Illingworth and Mark Fell were fringe players. Now there might be six or seven changes from game to game as one-day specialists come in.

Nottinghamshire played 13 three-day second-team games too, winning two and losing three, with Such topping the bowling averages. There were 34 players used: 'If you won the second-team Championship that told you one of two things: you either had some very, very talented young players that would be pushing to move into the first team or you had too many experienced players who might need to move on.'

Leicestershire won the Second XI Championship and Under-25s Cup, helped by future first-team regulars James Whitaker, Tim Boon, Russell Cobb, Mike Garnham, Gordon Parsons and Jonathan Agnew. Nottinghamshire players who made it were Johnson, Pick, Such and Mick Newell.

Opportunity knocked: 'I wanted to go as far as I could so I approached the game on a day-to-day basis. I didn't plan anything out. I had the chance to go to university, but I chose to give cricket a go with the view if it didn't work out for me, then maybe I could slip back into education. But I felt that I made good progress in my first year in 1982 and wanted to keep pushing.'

His first-team breakthrough came against Kent in late June 1983 at Trent Bridge: 'It was a turning pitch. I think in cricket in those days you have more variety of pitches.'

Kent played aggressively. 'That kept us in the game. There were a few poor shots and perhaps also a few balls that disappeared as well.'

Off his longish run for a spinner, Such took 6-123 in the first innings, which was to remain his best for the county, but he finished on the losing side. Derek Underwood took 13-161 for Kent.

There were some gnarly old pros in that Kent team. 'Their main players were Underwood and Alan Knott and what a combination they were as a spin bowler and a wicketkeeper. To be on the same field as those guys was fantastic. There was always a little bit of chat. You'd always go to the pub or the bar on the ground and chat to the opposition.

'Invariably, you'd gravitate towards someone who did what you did. I really enjoyed talking to them. They were pretty much at the back end of their careers but they were also moving into the coaching side of the game.'

Late in the season, Such starred for Young England against Australia Young Cricketers in three Under-19 Tests and a one-day international, alongside team-mates Pick and Johnson. He took 16 wickets in the three Tests, including 7-72 in the final match at Chelmsford, a record until beaten by Graeme Swann a decade later.

But for Nottinghamshire, after his haul against Kent, Hemmings took 11 wickets in a win against Lancashire and Such bowled just six overs. Then in the next, a heavy loss to future champions Essex, the season's leading run scorer South African Ken McEwan hit a swift 81 not out as Such went for 101 in 12 overs.

'I think you had better overseas players,' says Such. 'Guys of that stature wouldn't play a whole season these days.'

It took a decade from 1983 for Such to play for England: 'Spin bowlers probably take longer to develop. There's always that element to it and I wasn't good enough before. I played for three different counties because I was seeking opportunities to play so that I could further my career. I just wanted to play games of cricket. I left Nottinghamshire because Eddie Hemmings was the main spin bowler and I wasn't playing all that much. Then Andy Afford came on the scene and the left-arm spinner, right-arm off-spinner was the combination that they wanted, and I didn't really feature. So I went to Leicestershire and then it got to the back end of the 1980s and we played on green pitches with the high seam ball so after a year or so I didn't feature there and I heard Essex were looking and things took off from there.'

Among Nottinghamshire's 12 stickers of 1983, only Mike Hendrick had played for another county (Derbyshire 1969–81), though Hemmings subsequently played for Warwickshire and Sussex and Mark Fell moved to Derbyshire for 1985. In 2023, a full XI and more at Notts have played at other counties, including Stuart Broad, Joe Clarke, Ben Duckett, Haseeb Hameed, Alex Hales, Olly Stone, Ben Slater, Brett Hutton, Toby Pettman and Colin Munro. Hales has played for 16 professional teams worldwide.

'Maybe there's less loyalty in the game these days,' observes Such. 'Back in the 1980s having a testimonial or benefit year was a really big thing for a player. You would stay for longer, whereas now, perhaps it's not as relevant. When I played, players moved for an opportunity rather than a better deal.' Counties could be stubborn about changing registrations too, but Such faced none of those barriers to his development.

The off spin/left-arm spin partnership worked for Such at Essex alongside John Childs in the 1990s. They won the Championship in 1991 and 1992 and the NatWest Trophy in 1997 (Such hit the winning boundary in the semi-final) and they won the Benson & Hedges Cup in 1998. In 1993, he took a season-best of 76 first-class wickets and bowled more first-class overs than anyone else.

He says he wasn't good enough until 1993 to play for England. In his last Test, in 1999, he batted 72 minutes for a duck (the second-longest ever in Tests) and then took 4-114 in 41 overs, outbowling the more flamboyant Phil Tufnell. In Such's first Test, six years earlier and also at Manchester, this time against Australia, he again outdid Tuffers, taking a career-best 6-67, then a second innings 2-78, but England lost by 179 runs. In all he batted 97 minutes for once out against Shane Warne, Merv Hughes and Craig McDermott. Warne (4-51 and 4-86) bowled the 'ball of the century', turning the perfect leg break past a bemused Mike Gatting, overshadowing Such's efforts.

Perhaps the more understated Such, who would be an unlikely *I'm A Celebrity* TV camp-mate of Tuffers (who won the TV gameshow in 2003), suffered in comparison to his fellow England spinner too. He was also eschewed by the selectors' keenness to play leggies to try and match

Warne (England had Ian Salisbury) or spinners who batted (John Emburey, Vic Marks, then Robert Croft and Ashley Giles) or slow left-armers (Phil Edmonds, Nick Cook).

Warne-style mystery balls 'weren't really my strength. I spun the ball as hard as I could and tried to get as many in the right area as I could. So no, no real magic.'

But he'd have liked to have known the rev count, a measure spin bowlers use today: 'You weren't able to count revs until you had radar devices there are now. The way that you worked out whether or not someone's spinning it hard is that if two spin bowlers bowled on the same pitch and one got more out of it and the opposition found it harder. You can always work it out from the ball in the air and what he does off the surface. But if you've got a definitive measure, then you've got something that you can work as a coach and a player. Can I increase the revolutions I get on the ball?'

Another change is there's more opportunities for spinners in white ball cricket now: 'That's where you can earn good money for not working as hard. But I think the real opportunities are in long-form cricket.'

Why is that, when you won't get as much money? 'Central contracts. T20 gigs are where the big bucks are, but it's all about what you want to do. I've always been a longer format man. Not that I didn't enjoy one-day cricket. I just felt long form was more of a challenge and a more skilful game.'

But aren't Test cricket's days numbered with the advance of shorter formats? 'I don't think Tests are under threat in England because we fill the ground out with the way [Brendon] McCullum and [Ben] Stokes have adopted a more positive philosophy. That's been really exciting. And if you want to have Test match cricket, you've got to have Championship cricket. If you're going to develop the spin bowler in longer format cricket, you have to get some miles on the clock to be good and to do that you're going to need to play more cricket.'

But he agrees the game has changed immensely. White ball cricket has become more dominant; shorter formats more prevalent; and 'yes, spin bowlers have a big role to play in those. There are so many more leg-spinners around and white ball cricket has had a lot to do with their ascent.'

Such believes he could have adapted to have played now: 'I always believe that if you are good enough to play in one era, you will be good enough to play in another era. You just might have to do things differently.'

The core skills are still the same; spin the ball and land it in good areas. In shorter formats there's less emphasis on the stock ball. 'In T20s if you bowl the same ball too often, you end up in the stands.'

Such is proud of his post-playing appointments: 'I was national spin coach for ten years or so with the ECB and I loved that. I'd say I was involved in Moeen Ali's early development, Jack Leach, Dom Bess, Matthew Parkinson, Mason Crane. Ultimately, it's down to them and you just try and help them and give them what you can when you can.'

His main jobs now are as a match referee supporting umpires and working as a spin bowling coach in the winters. Refereeing is a cricket job that didn't exist 40 years ago: 'It's a relatively new role, but it is an important role in terms of the stuff that you have to do. You're there to support the umpires and provide developmental feedback. You're there to ensure the smooth running of the game and do all the liaison with the authorities.'

He muses: 'I've always been involved in the game as a coach or player. At elite level at some point your time ends so you reinvent yourself and go again. Things have moved forward. There's an awful lot more technology involved and again, there's lots of video footage. All of those sorts of things they weren't around in 1983. If you were on television once a year, then that was a lot. Everybody sees everything now.'

Such has few disappointments: 'You think there's always a little bit of regret over a game or a decision or a choice that you make over the period of time that I've been privileged enough to be in the game. I count myself lucky that I'm still involved in the game.'

Nottinghamshire

Clive Rice (1949–2015): All-rounder who played for Nottinghamshire from 1975–87. Played 482 first-class matches with 26,331 runs at 40.95 and 930 wickets at 22.49 and 479 one-dayers with 13,474 runs at 37.32 and 517 wickets at 22.63. South Africa 1991 (three ODIs). Captain for Nottinghamshire's Championship titles in 1981 and 1987. Scored 1,026 Championship runs at 36.64 in 19 Championship matches in 1983 plus 576 in 16 one-dayers. Later a coach.

Tim Robinson: Opener. England 1984–89 (24 Tests, 26 ODIs) and Nottinghamshire 1978–99. In 1983 he scored

1,464 runs in 24 Championship matches plus 431 in 20 one-dayers. Played 426 first-class games with 27,571 runs at 42.15 and 398 one-dayers with 11,889 at 34.36. Later an umpire.

Basharat Hassan: Right-hander who played for Nottinghamshire from 1966–85. Played 332 first-class matches with 14,394 runs at 29.07 and 285 one-dayers with 6,842 runs at 28.04. 'Basher' scored 890 Championship runs at 26.96 in 1983 plus 321 in 18 one-dayers. Later an umpire.

Derek Randall: Nottinghamshire 1971–93 and England 1977–85 (47 Tests, 49 ODIs). Played 488 first-class matches with 28,456 runs at 38.14 and 12,300 runs in 467 one-dayers at 32.28. In 1983 he scored 583 Championship runs at 27.76 and 390 in 16 one-dayers. 'Arkle' scored 194 runs at 38.80 in three Tests against New Zealand in 1983. Later a coach.

Mark Fell: Nottinghamshire 1981–83, Derbyshire 1985. Fell played 20 first-class matches with 506 runs at 14.45 and 35 List A games with 703 runs at 18.50. In 1983 he scored 46 runs at 6.57 in four Championship matches. Later a coach.

John Birch: Right-hander for Nottinghamshire from 1973–88. Played 250 first-class games with 8,673 runs at 27.53 and 234 one-dayers with 3,793 runs at 24.95. In 1983, he scored 1,007 Championship runs at 29.61 plus 350 in 19 one-dayers. Son Dan played for Derbyshire.

Bruce French: Nottinghamshire 1976–95 and England (1985–88, 16 Tests, 13 ODIs) wicketkeeper. He played 360 first-class (817 catches, 100 stumpings) and 296 one-dayers

(275/36). In 1983 French scored 589 runs at 18.40 and took 49 catches and made three stumpings. Later a coach.

Mike Hendrick (1948–2021): Nottinghamshire 1982–84, Derbyshire 1969–81, England 1974–81 (30 Tests, 22 ODIs). Took 66 Championship wickets at 17.00 in 1983, plus 12 one-day wickets. In 267 first-class matches he took 770 wickets at 20.50 and 297 wickets in 226 one-dayers at 19.59. Later a coach for Ireland, Scotland, Derbyshire and Nottinghamshire.

Kevin Cooper: Nottinghamshire 1976–92 and Gloucestershire 1993–96. Played 305 first-class games with 817 wickets at 26.94 and 283 one-dayers with 271 wickets at 33.00 plus 17 one-day wickets. In 1983 he took 50 Championship wickets at 30.60. Later a coach and groundsman.

Kevin Saxelby: Nottinghamshire 1978–90. Played 136 first-class matches with 300 wickets at 32.35 and 161 one-dayers with 224 wickets at 25.90. In 1983 he took 47 Championship wickets at 26.91 plus 25 one-day wickets. In 2018 he worked with the PCA to launch the 'You Do Matter' campaign to help prevent suicide, in memory of his late brother, Mark.

Eddie Hemmings: Off-spinner for Warwickshire 1966–78, Nottinghamshire 1979–92 and Sussex 1993–1995. Played 518 first-class games with 1,515 wickets at 29.30 and 455 List A matches with 453 wickets at 31.89. England 1982–91 (16 Tests, 33 ODIs). Tore a muscle in his bowling shoulder on the 1982/83 Australia tour, but still took 7-23 for Nottinghamshire against Lancashire at Old Trafford in

June 1983. Hemmings bowled through 710 Championship overs hoping to play for England. He took 59 wickets at 33.89 plus 21 one-day wickets. Later ran a village shop.

Peter Such: Nottinghamshire 1982–86, Leicestershire 1987–89, Essex 1990–2001 and England 1993–99 (11 Tests) off-spinner. Such played 306 first-class matches with 849 wickets at 30.54. In 211 one-dayers he took 212 wickets at 31.25. In 1983, in ten first-class games, he scored 13 runs at 1.18 coming bottom of the batting averages and took 20 wickets at 38.35. Also took 0-66 in one List A match when Essex's Graham Gooch and Ken McEwan hit a JPL second wicket partnership record of 273. Later a coach.

Chapter 19

Somerset: Nigel Popplewell

HAVING REACHED an impasse in collecting players, midway through writing the book I went to the MCC Library to get a flavour of 1983 in a silent, empty (of people, it's full of books) Victorian room behind the pavilion, where no one has ever hit a cricket ball.

In *Wisden Cricket Monthly* David Foot tells of how Ian Botham, who left his Yeovil comprehensive aged 16, trains in the 1983 off-season at unglamorous Glanford Park with Scunthorpe United FC manager Allan Clarke.

In contrast, fellow Somerset all-rounder Nigel Popplewell has a 2:1 in natural science from Selwyn College, Cambridge University. His father was a Cambridge University cricketer and judge, and younger brother Andrew is a judge too. *Cricketers' Who's Who* 1983 reveals Nigel boxed for Cambridge in a single bout at middleweight. He competed at athletics 'in a very incompetent and amateur manner'. It's almost, but not quite, *Chariots of Fire*. His reading matter is English social history of the 20th century.

But for the purposes of this book, the most important fact is that Popplewell had a breakthrough cricket year in

1983. He's a top tax lawyer and I spoke to him an hour after Jack Russell. I was excited by the chance to hear two unforgettable figures from my childhood. And it turns out, both are great communicators, with a lot to give to cricket.

I'd seen Popplewell play at Weston-super-Mare in 1980, when Yorkshire's Simon Dennis (also featured in this book) took his first wicket, and the name stuck with me, just like with Arnie Sidebottom's. He's not in Panini but, with hindsight, should have been, given the 1983 he had.

The all-rounder played at Radley and Cambridge and then roomed with future Somerset captain Peter Roebuck in Taunton after his fellow Cambridge graduate invited him to play for the county. They lived two doors down from West Indian fast bowler Joel Garner. In the NatWest Trophy semi-final against Middlesex, Popplewell took 3-34 with his medium pace, and he scored 46, adding 104 in 33 overs with Ian Botham, then he made another 35 in the final, against Kent, helping Botham, Viv Richards, Garner and Vic Marks win Somerset the cup. Botham inspired him, said *Wisden*, and when Botham was at the World Cup, he had more opportunities.

That was quite a dressing room with liberals Vic Marks and Roebuck and future Tory Lord Botham in it. Popplewell retired at the top of his game aged 28 to move into a legal career. He wrote a eulogy for Roebuck when his old friend died in 2011.

'He [Roebuck] bought a house in 1980 and I shared it with him for probably a year and a half. Joel bought a house a couple of doors down. I don't remember socialising much with Joel. He kept slightly different hours. But playing with those people like Viv and Joel and other overseas players like Martin Crowe in 1984 and Sunil Gavaskar in 1980 was just fantastic. And they were so nice. And they contributed so much both on and off.'

Marks and Roebuck shared a dressing room with the alpha male, Botham. This created 'occasional' debates about politics: 'Botham was slightly more right wing than a lot of people. But he argued his corner and actually we got on very well even though people came from all sorts of backgrounds. So, you've had the sort of people like myself and Vic and Peter who've been to Cambridge or Oxford and Peter Denning and Brian Rose have both been to college. They're people who actually had a tertiary education, then you have those sort of superstars and then you had people like Colin Dredge and Trevor Gard, who would be farming in the winters or driving lorries or something like that.

'But somehow the cricket and the common interest of doing well for Somerset bound us together, and that actually was glue enough and everybody got on really, really well. But there was a certain amount of chatter about most things in the dressing room, and also we would drive in cars to away games. And if you've got billeted with people in the cars, you would chat about anything and everything. As I say it was an eclectic group. But it worked very well. And the conversations ranged far and wide.'

Popplewell wrote in Somerset's 1983 yearbook about 'Musical Youths'. Denning and Gard liked the Wurzels, Garner soul, Richards reggae, Botham Dire Straits 'painfully' loud, Marks Carole King and Carly Simon ballads and Roebuck Radio 4 quizzes, Bob Dylan, Rod Stewart and Elvis Costello, listened to in the garden.

So was 1983 a breakthrough year? 'I don't know. I mean, I tried to improve my bowling action in the winter of 1982/83. And that seemed to work so I became I suppose a better all-rounder in 1983, and I had a good season.'

Somerset lost Richards, Garner, Marks and Botham to the World Cup. Popplewell stepped up and was capped halfway through the season at Bath. 'And I think that was justifiable actually because we'd had a long season up to then.'

In June, Somerset played back-to-back Championship matches on 4–7 June versus Essex, then 8–10 v Gloucestershire, then 11–14 v Sussex, 16–17 v Glamorgan, 18–21 v Derbyshire and 22-24 v Gloucestershire at Bath, with three Sunday League matches in between the weekend games.

Somerset had a great one-day victory against Glamorgan at Bath on the first Sunday of the festival, scoring 237/5 with Popplewell hitting 84. And then on the Friday he hit a century in 40 minutes against Gloucestershire, finishing with 143 not out in 62 minutes with 40 scoring strokes including nine sixes and 17 fours.

Popplewell says he'll check *Wisden* to justify his claim that Somerset only had a day off on World Cup final day, Saturday, 25 June. He went to a wedding. Somerset had a one-day game that Sunday and all the superstars came back: 'So I suppose during that season I did sort of slightly come of age. And, you know, for that month or so, I was punching above my weight.'

Somerset had won the Benson & Hedges Cup in 1982. 'Then the next season it was just plodding on and it was refreshed in a way by the World Cup. The younger players actually did well so that when the World Cup players came back the team was in really good shape. We had a good season, one reason being that we had had that rejuvenation during that month.'

Somerset finished the season well too, winning the NatWest Trophy in September. Popplewell had a big influence getting there with the bat and ball in the semi-final on 17 August.

The players were tiring: 'We'd been up to Derbyshire straight after Weston-super-Mare. The Weston festival was always a hard time, and everybody was absolutely exhausted.' Peter Roebuck's 1983 season diary *It Never Rains* recalls everybody else was asleep apart from the next man due in.

Somerset travelled down to the semi-final on Tuesday night, having been beaten by Derbyshire in a one-day game at Heanor on 14 August by eight wickets.

'We were all shattered. We were completely unprepared for this semi-final against Middlesex, who were one of the great sides in those days. We did okay in the morning. And so I went off and had a huge lunch thinking I wasn't going to be needed to bowl. And then Both said, "we'll have a few overs from this end." Again, I was totally unprepared and then people kept slogging it up in the air. They always thought they could slog me around and they did most of the time but that day they just chucked it straight up and I took some wickets [3-34, Wilf Slack, Mike Gatting and John Emburey].

'And we went in and it was just chaos. We lost five wickets and Viv smashed it around before he was caught brilliantly by Wayne Daniel at mid-off, off Neil Williams. Both was standing at the other end and we were 50 for five and completely dead in the water. But we've got that 50 in about ten overs. Now in those days if you've got four an over for 60 overs and you had to chase down 240, that was a big total.

'I went in, and I was with Both and I'd never heard him when he was so relaxed. He just took all the pressure off me. He was completely in the zone. He told me to "just play" and because we weren't under pressure from the scoreboard we could play out a couple of overs without putting pressure back on ourselves. It's a complete anathema doing that in today's game. And I think I outscored him. He just sat at one end, and I shifted around a bit and scored reasonably quickly and he'd block a bit and then hit a four and we just kept pace with each other and it was just good. Neither of us felt that the other needed to play a different way from our normal game. He played a wonderful shot when John Emburey came on. Both hit him out of the ground over the Tavern Stand. And that was it. He got knocked out of the attack because of a fantastic shot. And in a way that changed the complexion of the game because it meant that Emburey, who was one of the great one-day bowlers, wasn't going to bowl anymore.'

Popplewell got out to a 'stupid shot' but Vic Marks came out and knocked it around with Botham. 'He played a really sensible measured innings and the scores were level and all we had to do was not lose a wicket [in the last over] so Both padded up to virtually every ball. He was very, very close to being out last ball because he simply padded away a straight ball. He was never going to be given so he kicked the ball away and just turned around and rushed into the pavilion. But I think he was probably pretty close to being lbw.'

The YouTube video of the match shows Botham, in a sunhat, slashing Norman Cowans and Williams to the boundary and, indeed, hitting Emburey into the very top of the old Tavern Stand, in front of a full house. The lbw shout does look close though.

In the final, Popplewell scored a crucial 35 as Somerset won a low-scoring match against Kent: 'Again, that was an odd game because we played Hampshire [at Taunton] before and the weather was absolutely appalling. The sightscreens had blown over. We drove up to London that Friday night thinking, "Well if we get a game, it's going to be miraculous." And they decided very sensibly that we could get a game but it was going to be rain-affected.'

The match was reduced to 50 overs a side from 60. 'We weren't quite sure how a 50-over game was going to look. Graham Dilley bowled with three slips and two gullies, and it was green and overcast. Derek Underwood did not bowl, so you had the best one-day bowler in the world who didn't bowl at all. And then I came out and I got a few but they were all fairly flighty runs.

'We took crucial wickets at crucial times. Vic bowled really well. I think it was probably a fairly comfortable win. But again, we only made 190 which in today's game over 50 overs is light relief.'

The weary Somerset team lost to Worcestershire at Worcester the following day which, combined with the defeat to Derbyshire at Heanor, meant Popplewell's side failed to win the Sunday League. Yorkshire's final match was rained off, giving the Tykes the title on more away matches won: 'We should have won both trophies. Collis King at Worcestershire lapped it around. But, you know, we were pretty exhausted from the day before, and also just drained because it's a long season.'

We talked on the first day of the county season in 2023. How would you have got on with the schedule and the opportunities today? 'I think we'd have coped. We had three one-day competitions, which is the same as it is now. Now there's only two one-day competitions, unless you're playing The Hundred. You've got Twenty20 and you've got 50-over cricket, and we had 40-over cricket, 55-over cricket and 60-over cricket. And then we had three-day Championship games rather than four-day games. And I think we played 25 three-day games and that season we played on virtually every day in June. In terms of keeping up with the schedule it's much more hollowed out now by The Hundred.'

More overseas players fly in and out now as well. 'There are one-day white ball specialists. And there's a big, big difference in the one-day cricket we played and the one-day cricket played now as all the cricket we played was with the red ball. And we didn't play under lights at all, which I rather regret. I'd love to have played under lights wearing pyjamas with a white ball. I think that would have been great.'

So if he was around now, does he think he would have had a longer, more lucrative career, possibly playing overseas T20 leagues? 'I doubt it. It's very difficult to say but I was unbelievably lucky. I got sent in with some fantastic players at the right time. My face fitted and the sort of game I played was consistent with the strengths of the Somerset side. I contributed. I never really intended when I joined Somerset to make cricket a career. I didn't want to play cricket at all costs.'

He taught in the winters. 'That a fantastic combination with playing cricket in the summer. I was just very happy with my lot. People make more money out of cricket now and good for them. It's a great thing the way people can fly around the world and play, and they can be slightly mercenary about it. I think it's a balance of power, but in a way you lose loyalty to causes by that. And I don't think in the county game that's necessarily a good thing. You didn't want to have too many mercenaries playing in Somerset when I played. It was fantastic because it was genuinely a team effort even though you have superstars [playing] in it. But when you come to things like that the T20 and the Big Bash and Hundred it's intended to be a spectacle.'

Popplewell's style might have needed work today. 'You just adapted but I wasn't really a slogger to be honest with you. I could fiddle and fart but I scored most of my runs behind square on the off side, using the pace of the ball. I didn't have a huge heavy bat. But it's like anything, you simply worked it out.'

Nevertheless, in 1983 he managed a 40-minute century: 'I did, but they were short boundaries square. It was quite quick in terms of number of balls faced but it was very quick in terms of time, largely because there were lots of kids there who threw the ball back from the boundary very quickly. And then I got pipped to the post at the end of the season to get the fastest hundred because Steve O'Shaughnessy beat it against Leicestershire. David Gower bowled all sorts of lobby things. I felt slightly aggrieved because I got my runs in proper circumstances. He got his wholly contrived. Whether or not you're allowed to do that or not now because someone thinks you're bringing the game into disrepute I don't know.'

O'Shaughnessy's and Popplewell's centuries are both now *Wisden* footnotes rather than records as they are both described as being scored in 'contrived circumstances' as the bowling side sought a declaration.

Wisden says Popplewell took full advantage of declaration bowling, but Barry Dudleston was the only non-bowler used. Regulars John Shepherd, David Graveney, Gary Sainsbury, Phil Bainbridge and Richard Doughty were the others. The match was a draw anyway, Gloucestershire ended well short, with eight wickets down. Roebuck agreed that as Graveney bowled throughout Popplewell's innings, his team-mate had been unfairly maligned.

Illegitimate centuries from Glen Chapple (21 minutes in 1993) and Tom Moody (26 in 1990) are now top of the fastest footnotes.

In 1980 at Weston-super-Mare, I saw Somerset play against Yorkshire, but Weston isn't as pleasant a memory for Popplewell as it was for many holidaymakers: 'I think the players enjoyed Bath because it had way better wickets in a more interesting setup. But it was a bloody long way to go [for a home game]. We often played Yorkshire at Weston so there'd be a lot of Yorkshire holidaymakers there. And you always seemed to play Gloucestershire at Bath and Gloucester normally came from Bristol, and it took about half an hour to get there and we took ages to travel around the Mendips.

'I don't have happy memories of Weston. The wicket wasn't kept as well as Bath and the Weston pavilion was tiny. When I played my first season, in 1979, I played at Weston and it was during the Fastnet yacht race [13–14 August 1979 when 15 sailors died and 75 boats capsized in force 10 gales]. The sightscreens of Weston were just sheets of canvas; they weren't proper-sized screens and they kept blowing out, these great holes ripped in them. Joel Garner was coming out of the dark background and was a real handful. But I always seemed to celebrate my birthday during Weston week, on 8 August. I used to field short leg to Vic Marks and to Jerry Lloyds and Vic would always give me a pair of shin pads for my birthday. I didn't mind.'

After leaving Somerset, in November 1986, Popplewell spoke out at a Somerset meeting in support of Roebuck's quest to move on from Richards and Garner and look to the future with Martin Crowe as overseas player. Botham heartily disagreed and eventually moved to Worcestershire, while Richards went to Glamorgan. Popplewell had already retired, in his prime. Roebuck wrote about his old housemate's 'crucial speech' supporting the changes and how he missed Popplewell's support at the club.

Roebuck added in *Sometimes I Forgot to Laugh* about the 'engaging' Popplewell's 'fling' in professional cricket. The 'outstanding competitor' delayed his move into a 'more respected profession' after testing himself in a game 'that his conscience never quite managed to persuade him was serious'.

Popplewell was a Radley pupil under headmaster Dennis Silk, a former Cambridge and Somerset batsman who was TCCB chair from 1994–96. He emerged from the Oxbridge first-class scene but that's not around now. Would he have been able to get into first-class cricket now without that?

'I look back and think how fortunate it was that you could go to Cambridge and Oxford and play first-class cricket. Cambridge makes no bones about the fact that they're not interested in all-round people. They are interested in getting people on their academic record, and to get the most out of them academically, which I think is a pity if you're going to say that we stand for excellence. It could be excellence in all sorts of spheres: acting, music, literature, sport, but they're very one-dimensional. I would never have become a professional cricketer if I'd been to Cambridge now, simply because the opportunity to play first-class cricket wouldn't have been there.

'Would I have gone out of my way to try to better my cricket career playing for a major county? I simply don't know because I was brought up in a minor county. And even though I played some second-team cricket for Hampshire, in my year between school and my first year at Cambridge, whether I'd have pursued it, I don't know. I was lucky and I learned my craft at Cambridge against the counties in slightly benign circumstances on uncovered wickets. It was a very good way I found of developing my own style of play. And I got to know my game and what I could and couldn't do well over those three seasons.'

He has few regrets: 'I keep pinching myself, but it was very much a younger me doing it. I look at it now and it all looks bloody hard. But I suppose that was one of the reasons I did it because it was hard work. And I've done a number of things since. I've taught, I've been a lawyer. I am a tax judge. I've been up all night doing deals and that sort of thing, but I've never done anything which is harder than playing cricket, not just because of the physical side or the threat of being hit in the mouth from a bloody hard ball, but because it really mattered to us at Somerset to win. It wasn't like an amateur game, for which you got paid. People really wanted to do well. So you're always under pressure and I seemed to thrive on that and I really enjoyed that. I was fortunate enough to join Somerset at the time and have those fantastic seven years.

'I probably became a better player as I got older. In my last two seasons, I became quite a good batsman. And then I decided to go and do something else, but I knew I wasn't going to ever wait for a benefit or play forever. And I also knew by then, having taught for four years, that I wasn't going to become a teacher, so I had to do something else, and I decided to do it sooner rather than later. But it was just fantastic. I don't regret a moment. I was unbelievably fortunate.'

He was on Somerset's cricket committee but felt he wasn't able to see enough cricket to keep going. Chairman Charles Clark died in June 2019 and Popplewell applied but didn't get the job. 'It was [immediately] pre-Covid, so in a way I was quite pleased I didn't get it because it would have been really, really difficult. And I would not have been able to spend the time I perhaps needed to because I'm doing other things. I'm still working reasonably full-time. I'm on the ECB's Cricket Discipline Commission that reported on the Yorkshire racism charges in 2023.'

The race and cricket argument has since advanced. In the wake of Azeem Rafiq's calling out of racism at Yorkshire and the subsequent ECB judgment, released on 31 March 2023, former England captain Michael Vaughan had a charge of racism brought against him by the ECB 'not proved' as the verdicts from the Cricket Discipline Commission hearing were released. Charges were brought against Vaughan and six other former Yorkshire players, as well as the club itself, following Rafiq's allegations. Tim Bresnan, John Blain, Andrew Gale, Matthew Hoggard and Richard Pyrah all had at least one charge of using racist and/or discriminatory language 'proved'. Yorkshire and Gary Ballance previously admitted their charges ahead of the hearing.

'Have you read the decision?' asks Popplewell. 'It's an overarching decision in you've got within it seven or eight distinct judgments or discrete judgments relating to each of the player charges. And it's very, very good. There is no substitute for reading what the court actually said.' Subsequently, in July 2023, a 317-page report by the

Independent Commission for Equity in Cricket found English cricket suffered from 'widespread and deep-rooted' racism, sexism, elitism and class-based discrimination at all levels of the game and urgently needs reform. The report drew on evidence from more than 4,000 players, coaches, administrators and fans.

Back in his day, a lot of players were banned for playing in South Africa. Popplewell sees the issue with customary intelligence: 'I think people felt two things. One was that the players will have the right, without being told what to do, to go and practice their trade wherever they want subject to their own sense of morality, ethics and political persuasion. The players felt that it was down to the individuals to make a decision and it wasn't for us to criticise them. There'll be lots of players who simply would not have gone there.

'The other thing was that by going out there they did put in jeopardy the livelihood of the domestic cricketers, because it meant that the West Indies weren't going to tour.' He says that could have impacted TV money and gate receipts, revenue that cascaded down to county players.

It's the first day of the 2023 season. 'Until you told me I didn't know,' said Popplewell. 'If I get a chance to go and watch cricket, I will take it, whether it's on television or live. But I like it passively largely during the season. I will always watch Somerset's results but very often what happens is I see they have started the game and then it's two days later that I remember to look at the score. It's great that Somerset have had good seasons over the last 10 to 12 years. They've been regularly successful even though they have not won the Championship, but they've done so with homegrown players. And most of the people I go and watch cricket with would rather see Somerset not do so well with homegrown players than simply find lots of talent to buy success.'

In 1983, Nigel Popplewell (Somerset 1979–85) took 23 first-class wickets at 34.17 and scored 886 runs at 24.61 in 24 matches. In 22 one-dayers he scored 369 runs at 24.60 and took ten wickets at 27.00 with an economy rate of 4.62. In his career (1977–85) he played 143 first-class games, scoring 5,070 runs at 27.11. He took 103 wickets at 43.11 and in 123 List A matches he scored 2,077 runs at 23.33 and took 49 wickets at 32.63. Later, he was a leading tax lawyer.

1983 NatWest Trophy final at Lord's
Kent v Somerset

Peter Roebuck b Dilley 11

Peter Denning lbw Dilley 1

Phil Slocombe c Johnson b Baptiste 20

Viv Richards c Knott b Dilley 51

Ian Botham c Johnson b Cowdrey 9

Nigel Popplewell c Cowdrey b Dilley 35

Jeremy Lloyds lbw Jarvis 10

Vic Marks c Benson b Cowdrey 29

Joel Garner run out 4

Colin Dredge not out 3

Trevor Gard DNB

Extras 20. Total: 193/9 50 overs

Bowling: Dilley 10-2-29-4; Ellison 10-1-35-0; Jarvis 10-0-43-1; Baptiste 10-1-37-1; Cowdrey 10-2-29-2.

Kent

Mark Benson c Lloyds b Garner 0
Graham Johnson b Marks 27
Chris Tavare c Roebuck b Marks 39
Derek Aslett st Gard b Richards 14
Chris Cowdrey c Gard b Marks 0
Eldine Baptiste b Botham 16
Alan Knott c Roebuck b Dredge 17
Richard Ellison b Garner 21
Graham Dilley b Botham 19
Derek Underwood not out 6
Kevin Jarvis c Botham b Dredge 3
Extras 8. Total: 169 all out
Bowling: Garner 9-2-15-2; Botham 10-0-29-2; Dredge 8.1-0-50-2; Popplewell 1-0-9-0; Marks 10-0-30-3; Richards 9-1-28-1.

Somerset

Brian Rose: Left-handed Somerset opener from 1969–87 and captain 1978–83. In 270 first-class matches he scored 13,236 runs at 33.25. He resumed teaching after retiring from the first-class game but maintained his involvement with Somerset. In 2007 he was named part of the committee to review English cricket after the defeat in the 2006/07 Ashes series. A past chairman of cricket, he became the director of cricket at Taunton, until the end of the 2012 season. He was president for three years until 2022.

Rose had a role in a trend of the day. West Country software developer Wyvern Software launched ZX Spectrum (the first popular UK home computer, launched by Clive Sinclair in 1982 which sold a million by the end of 1983 and five million in various forms up to 1987). Its computer game *Howzat!* was released in 1984 and endorsed by Rose.

Rose's benefit year in 1983 seemed an appropriate time to step down as captain, though he played just seven Championship games (138 runs at 19.71) and seven one-dayers, making 124 runs. Roebuck, Botham or Richards were then captains of a disparate group of players, which won the NatWest Trophy and was second in the John Player League. After an innings win at Leicestershire, 'complaining of an injury, Rose did not play again that summer' wrote Roebuck. Rose wanted the conciliatory Marks to be captain to heal rifts between factions, which culminated in Garner, Richards and Botham leaving at the end of 1986 after a fallout with Roebuck, who supported plans to ditch the West Indians, much to their and Botham's ire. But before that, Rose had done his bit.

Jeremy Lloyds (1954–2022): Left-hander and off-spinner for Somerset 1979–84. Gloucestershire 1985–91. Lloyds played 267 first-class matches, scoring 10,679 runs at an average of 31.04 with ten hundreds and 62 fifties. With the ball, in first-class cricket he took 333 wickets at an average of 38.86. In 1983 he scored 803 Championship runs at 25.90 and took 34 wickets at 29.11, plus 206 runs in 16 one-dayers. Umpire from 1996–2020.

Peter Roebuck (1956–2011): Somerset 1974–91. In 335 first-class matches he scored 17,558 runs at an average of 37.27, making 33 centuries with a highest score of 221 not out, and took 72 wickets at 49.16. In 298 one-day matches, he scored 7,244 runs at 29.81 while taking 51 wickets at 25.09. Later a writer and broadcaster. Wrote the 1983 diary *It Never Rains*. Scored 1,235 Championship runs in 1983 at 37.42. Roebuck died after jumping from the sixth floor of the Southern Sun Hotel in Cape Town, when South African police entered to question him about an alleged sexual assault.

Viv Richards: Somerset 1974–86, West Indies 1974–91. 121 Tests, 187 ODIs. World Cup winner in 1975 and 1979. First-class: 507 matches, 36.212 runs at 49.40. Limited overs: 500 matches, 16,995 runs at 41.96. Played for Glamorgan from 1990–93. In 1983 he scored 1,204 runs at 75.25 in 12 Championship matches. Knighted for services to cricket in 1999; later he was a commentator and coach. Topped the first-class averages and was second in the List A averages behind David Gower (1,177 runs at 53.50) in 1983.

Peter Denning (1949–2007): Opener from 1969–84. In 269 first-class matches he scored 11,559 runs at 28.68 and in 269 one-dayers scored 6,792 at 28.06. 'Dasher' scored 659 Championship runs at 21.25 in 1983 and 357 runs in 17 one-dayers. A qualified teacher, he was later a grain merchant.

Ian Botham: Somerset 1974–86, Worcestershire 1987–91. Durham 1992–93. England 1976–92. First-class: 402 matches, 19,399 runs at 33.97 and 1,172 wickets at 27.22. Limited overs: 470 matches, 10,474 runs at 29.50 and 612 wickets at 24.94. In 1983 he scored 570 runs at 43.84 in ten Championship matches and took 12 wickets at 32.33. Also scored 537 one-day runs at 29.83 in 25 matches (40 in seven World Cup matches) with 33 wickets at 23.09

(eight in the World Cup). In four Tests in 1983 he scored 282 runs at 35.25 with 103 at Trent Bridge and took ten wickets at 34.00. Later a broadcaster and member of the House of Lords. Botham's autobiography of 2007 talks of a special meeting at Bath & West Showground to debate a no-confidence vote in the Somerset committee. The result went with the committee. In 2023, I attended an auction, including items from 1983, of Botham cricket artefacts. It raised £300,000. Botham wasn't there

Vic Marks: Somerset 1974–89, England 1980–88. In 342 first-class matches scored 12,419 runs at 30.29 and took 859 wickets at 33.28. In 304 limited-over matches he scored 4,175 runs at 22.56 and took 286 wickets at 27.85. In 15 Championship matches in 1983 Marks scored 498 runs at 23.71 and took 49 wickets at 30.36. He also took 40 wickets at 19.80 in one-dayers including 13 at 18.92 in the World Cup, including an England record 5-39 against Sri Lanka at Taunton. Later a writer and broadcaster.

Phil Slocombe: Somerset 1975–83. In 139 first-class matches he scored 5.634 runs at 27.61 and in 78 one-dayers hit 829 runs at 14.80. Scored 145 runs at 11.15 in ten Championship matches in 1983. Later an antiques and fine-wine dealer.

Trevor Gard: Somerset wicketkeeper from 1976–89. In 112 first-class matches Gard hit 1,389 runs at 13.75 and took 178 catches and made 39 stumpings. In 81 one-dayers he scored 240 runs at 12 and made 57 catches and 13 stumpings. In 1983 Gard scored 440 runs at 16.29 and made 42 catches and eight stumpings, plus another 60 runs,

25 catches and four stumpings in 22 one-dayers. Lived and worked in his native Somerset after retirement.

Joel Garner: Somerset 1977–86, West Indies 1977–87 (58 Tests, 98 ODIs). In 214 first-class matches he took 881 wickets at 18.53 and in 256 limited-over matches took 397 wickets at 16.61. In 1983 he took 34 wickets at 19.38 in nine Championship matches and took 29 one-day wickets with an economy rate of 2.97, including five in the World Cup. Later had various roles in West Indian cricket.

Hallam Moseley: Somerset 1969–82. Took 557 wickets in 213 first-class matches and 313 in 212 one-dayers. Did not play in county cricket after 1982. West Indies Test player Shayne Moseley is his nephew.

Colin Dredge: Somerset 1976–88. He played 194 first-class and 209 one-day matches taking 443 wickets at 30.10 and 253 at 25.42 respectively. The 'Demon of Frome' took 48 Championship wickets at 27.56 in 1983, plus 28 one-day wickets. A toolmaker, he later worked for Network Rail.

Chapter 20

Surrey: Graham Monkhouse

'WE PLAYED at Chelmsford on a very nice day,' remembers Graham Monkhouse, an all-rounder for Surrey in the 1980s. Setting the scene, 'Farmer' recalls the most famous 87 balls of the era: 'We lost the toss. We batted first. They got about 300 which was par for the course at Chelmsford, which was a small ground, tree-lined. There was a good crowd as there always was for Surrey.'

All seemed calm. But why, for years, would there be a framed, signed scorecard from this match on the hall wall of my childhood Keswick home, just 20 miles from Monkhouse's farm in Cumbria's Eden Valley?

'Back then after 100 overs there were no bonus points so they used to declare the first innings and might be three quarters of an hour left,' he explains, retaining his rich Cumbrian accent. I was thinking how lucky I was to talk to an inspirational figure from my childhood, and find out how he had served the game since his heyday in the 1980s, when he played in some of the best-remembered matches of the era.

'So, there was always this nasty period before the end of play. We trooped off. I bowled about 15 overs. The bowlers have got their boots off and are looking to relax. It did come over a little bit cloudy because it had been a very nice day. And suddenly the ball just swung all over the place.'

Monkhouse is recalling a remarkable innings, that he could scarcely have contemplated being part of when he made his debut for Cumberland in 1973. He joined Surrey in 1980 and developed into a line and length bowler, with often standing up to the stumps. Monkhouse could bat too, top-scoring with 100 not out against Kent at The Oval in 1984. He retired back to Cumbria in 1986. His highlights included a NatWest Trophy winners' medal in 1982 (0-36 off eight overs). Surrey won by eight wickets as the late-season curse of losing the toss and being put into bat at 10am took its toll on Warwickshire.

But back at Chelmsford in summer 1983: 'Literally within two or three overs we were four wickets down for six runs. I was probably batting eight. I did stay there for a little while. The good story I missed at the time because I was in the middle was that Sylvester Clarke, the West Indian fast bowler, who'd bowled 18-20 overs earlier in the day, had stripped off and was lying in the bath relaxing and one of the lads went in and said, "Sylvester we've lost four or five wickets. I think you'd better get out and get your kit on."

'Well, of course, Sylvester just thought it was a wind-up and took absolutely not notice whatsoever. And then we lost another wicket and another wicket. And [manager] Micky Stewart went in and said, "Silvers you've got to get out." They frantically got Silvers dried and he came out to bat with no socks on and first ball he slogged through midwicket for four which made him our highest scorer. And then he was out next ball and walked back in again.

'I edged the ball through about fourth slip and I stayed there for a while but I got an lbw which I thought I was outside the line. But the ball was swinging so much that you were having to play balls that were quite wide, and it swung back in at me. But you never think you're out.

'And we were all out for 14 and we walked off and the dressing room was, as you can imagine, very, very, very quiet. And Micky Stewart didn't say anything. Micky could give us a bit of a roasting at times, but I think he realised that this wasn't the time and that this was just a one-off. Neil Foster and Norbert Phillip bowled magnificently. The ball had swung like a boomerang for some reason. Some balls do and Chelmsford is a swinging ground because it's tree-lined. We had to go and play a John Player game at Trent Bridge on the Sunday, which was rained off. Then Essex made us follow on the Monday and we got 280 for two. Roger Knight and Graham Clinton got hundreds. It was just a complete and utter cricket one-off that no one can explain.'

In the late 1970s, Monkhouse was the best player in Cumbria. But at 24, was it too late to step up? 'My entrance into first-class cricket was very strange to say the least. I'd been a decent sportsman and I played professionally for Workington in the Football League and I hurt my knee quite badly when I was 20 or 22. And we had quite a big family business as animal feed manufacturers at Langwathby. I'd been to agricultural college [in Nottingham]. My father wouldn't let me go and play football when I was younger, I had to finish my education. I came back into the business, played semi-pro football and minor county cricket and I was thoroughly enjoying life. I was single and I was reasonably well off because I had three incomes coming in, and I came to Penrith as professional in 1979 and had a fairly decent year.'

Monkhouse got his chance when he took his National Cricket Association coaching awards. He'd done his intermediate award and really enjoyed coaching the kids at Penrith. The next step up was the advanced award, which required a week at Lilleshall, where England's footballers used to train.

'We didn't play cricket. We netted and we did all the necessary coaching and everything. I became quite friendly with Micky because he'd never done any coaching awards and there's a certain amount of technical stuff in it and I'd been doing that, I knew how to write it down and how to organise.

'Micky asked if I'd thought about playing first-class cricket? I was quite happy and at 24 thought I was a little bit past my peak. Then he asked me to come to London in December 1979 to coach some juniors. I thought I'd have three days in London and they're paying my expenses.

'So I went down and of course it had nothing to do with coaching. It was basically he wanted me to have a trial. They offered me a contract because Robin Jackman was retiring to take up a job in South Africa. Micky said, "I really think you're the ideal replacement for Robin Jackman. We really want you to come." I came home and

I told my father who said: "Well look, son, you're 24 and if you don't go you will regret it for the rest of your life." I rang Micky and told him I'd give it a go.'

He started in April 1980. In a flat in London, unmarried, he could do what he wanted because he had no commitments. 'And I had a very, very happy six years. I didn't play any first-class cricket at all in the first year, but the second team virtually had a fixture every week. It was a much stronger level because the staffs were much bigger.'

Monkey, praised in a Surrey yearbook for 'his immaculate turnout and attention to detail [which] are typical of his approach to professional cricket'. had a good season (31 wickets at 16, one behind Intikhab Alam). He turned from being a sort of an all-rounder for Cumberland into more of a bowler who batted. South Africa that winter he played good club cricket and learned a lot about his bowling because he had to really be on top of his job on good wickets against good players. But when he came back, Robin Jackman had decided not to retire, because he'd taken 121 wickets in 1980, been named as one of the *Wisden* cricketers of the year and been picked for England. In 1981 Monkhouse played virtually in all of the one-dayers, but just four first-class matches, taking seven wickets.

He lived in Dulwich, had a flat in Wimbledon and lived in Thornton Heath for two years. He then shared an upstairs flat in Clapham. The downstairs garden flat came up for sale. An elderly couple offered it to him for £33,000 cash. 'It needed a bit of work doing. I'd get someone to share with me to help pay the mortgage. My dad was a pretty hard-nosed businessman and I'll never forget the look he gave me when I told him the price: "£33,000! You could buy a farm here for that!" That was the end of the conversation. Those flats now will be worth a million quid.

'I was really lucky actually because Surrey paid my rent and gave me a car because I was going to earn £2,000–£3,000 less when I went there, which was a lot of money on those days. Micky didn't want to upset the wage structure.'

Monkhouse was allocated to Wimbledon to play club cricket because the second team didn't play at the weekend. 'It was the best move I ever made in my life because Wimbledon is a super club. I made some great friends down there because I was a club cricketer at heart. I enjoyed the social side and it was a ready-made group of friends for me.'

Chris Brown, the son of former England captain Freddie, was captain of Wimbledon and asked Monkhouse to play for the MCC. He became a member in 1986 and played 150 games for them. 'I enjoyed the cricket and went on tours and in 2013 I was approached to stand for the main committee.' He did three years, then was voted on to the cricket committee, where he remained until 2023. 'It was very enjoyable and I learnt a lot. The MCC have 18,000 members and turns over £52 million a year. They play 450 matches a year so it's a big organisation and I met a lot of very, very interesting people, a lot of high-fliers and a lot of ordinary people.'

He is well-placed to comment on differences between 1983 and 2023: 'Cricket is completely different. As with most sports, cricket has changed enormously in terms of preparation and fitness. The money has improved. I wouldn't say we played for the love of it but we were never going to be wealthy playing cricket. That's why benefits were so important in our day because you could make £40,000 or £50,000 tax-free and in the 1980s that was a lot of money. You could buy a house in London or a pub after you'd finished playing.'

He tells a good story about a Surrey IPL player who after tax was left with £80,000 for 42 days work. 'He got more money from the IPL than he got for the whole season playing for Surrey. So you can understand why young players are looking at one-day cricket, in terms of not only it being maybe slightly easier physically than Test or four-day cricket, but also the financial rewards available playing all over the world.'

Brought up on the intensity of short-form cricket, because all the midweek cricket in Cumbria was 20 overs, he would have loved to have played T20. 'It's been great for cricket, because it has regenerated a lot of interest from the public. I go down to Lord's for Middlesex versus Surrey T20 and it's a sellout, 27,000. When I played red ball cricket for Surrey we would walk out and they would announce the crowd changes. It's introduced a whole array of new shots. I mean, I've never done a reverse sweep or a scoop in my life. It's only been good for cricket.'

In 1983 Surrey planned to spend £865,000 on executive boxes, as detailed in the 1984 yearbook, funded mostly by a loan from brewers Watney Mann. Subs paid were £134,000 and the cricket spend was £327,000. The pitch was quick, and the team had won the NatWest Trophy in 1982. But in 1983 Warwickshire bowled them out for just

138 in the second round and they only beat the universities in the B&H. They won just four Sunday League games. Their mid-table Championship campaign will always be overshadowed by the 14 all out against Essex.

But perhaps beyond the results, there was more of a soul to the game back then. Monkhouse misses the sociability of cricket during his era: 'I think, possibly in all sports, the camaraderie in my day was better. There was a more social aspect. People must be terrified now. They can hardly go out and have a quiet drink or a meal without people taking pictures of them. We were lucky in that respect, and you built friendships with other players, not only from your own club. Micky Stewart was always adamant that we went down to The Oval Tavern and mix with the opposition and with the umpires.

'Micky used to say to me "always go and have a chat with the umpires" and because the umpires were all ex-players they would give you little tips and advice. Jack Birkenshaw said to me one night, "Farmer, you've got to get a little bit closer to the stumps because it'll be easier for me to give lbws when you're bowling wicket-to-wicket." You didn't want to fall out with them and you got to know the opposition.'

He was friendly with Tim Tremlett and Nick Cook from Northamptonshire. He would go round to Cook's house during away games for something to eat. 'Now you hear stories that they all go back and play on their PlayStation in hotels because they're terrified to go out. There wasn't much money, but it was a lovely time of my life I can assure you.

'I also had four seasons in South Africa and that was a real learning curve. I went to Pretoria, which was predominantly Afrikaans and a lot of them didn't even speak English. I had to make my way and prove to people that I was a good cricketer and that I was there on merit and I deserved to be there.'

He has roles at Edenhall and Langwathby in Cumbria and has just been appointed president of Penrith Cricket Club, the patron of the county club: 'So I am still heavily involved in recreational cricket and will be as long as I can because it gave me a fantastic life. I've played cricket in 23 countries, including some very strange places like Swaziland, Ghana, Gambia, Sierra Leone, Namibia and Botswana. That's all due to the MCC because I've been on eight tours with them.'

But it is the big names and big games that stick in the mind.

'I got Richards out for nought. Wow. In a John Player game at Bath, there was about 8,000 in for Richards's benefit game. Bath was a club ground and surrounded by hospitality tents. And down at fine leg there was a big beer tent and of course they were all giving big licks in there.' Surrey batted first and made a decent score, 175, Monkhouse 20 not out. 'That was a good score in 40 overs in our day.'

Monkhouse opened the bowling on Sundays because they were very strict on wides and Clarke used to swing the ball in a lot and go down the leg side. 'It was quite a raucous atmosphere because the boys were getting more and more cider into them and anyhow I bowled Peter Roebuck and I got Peter Denning caught behind after about two or three overs and then Viv walked in. He had a distinctive walk, almost a strut and he used to walk with his chest out, swing his hips and tap the top of his bat. The crowd went absolutely crackers, because he was their big hero. I bowled a ball just outside off stump and he lent into it and knocked it into extra cover for none and the ball came back to me and I bowled him virtually the same ball, but it was maybe just a little bit shorter and he went to push it into through extra cover but it came back on him and knocked over his off stump. There was silence.

'It must have taken him about two minutes to walk off because he was so disappointed. The only person like that I didn't get out in my career was Geoffrey Boycott. I got Graham Gooch out for none, but that was caught. It was a poor shot whereas I felt as if I bowled Vivian out. He hadn't got himself out. I had a decent career. I finished with 170-odd first-class wickets. I got 100 one-day wickets. I averaged about 27 with the ball and 22 with the bat, and I got a first-class hundred as nightwatchman.

'I was probably the first Cumbrian to be capped in first-class cricket [in 1984]. In those days the county caps were much prized as it meant that you were much more secure. You got a pay rise as a capped player and that was the start of the countdown to your benefit.'

Monkhouse's Twitter handle is @legcutter54. The name came about after press called for a traditional English seamer to play against New Zealand in 1983.

At Headingley, Lance Cairns took 7-74 to propel New Zealand to their first Test win in England. Monkhouse says: 'He was medium paced at best. I played it a lot against him because he was pro for Durham when I played Minor Counties. They called me a medium pace but I was a yard and a half quicker than Lance. He bowled big inswingers off the wrong foot.'

Monkhouse and his team-mates were driving to Swansea for a Sunday League match listening to *Test Match Special*'s Trevor Bailey's views (Monkhouse adopts a posh accent): "Yes, Lance Cairns bowled very well. He berls a genuine leg catter. When I played every canty side had someone who berls a genuine leg catter. I can only think of one person now in canty cricket, who berls a genuine leg catter and that's Menkhice of Surrey. And he doesn't berl it veh well." And the whole car erupted in laughter.'

Monkhouse became a popular player on the county circuit before retiring in 1986. In the fixture against Lancashire in early August captain Pat Pocock asked him to open the batting.

'Now I used to do nightwatchman and I quite liked that because it gave me the opportunity to have a bat. And I always thought I was a better batter than they'd give me credit for.' Opener Alan Butcher was injured and Pocock wanted to keep the balance of the side. 'I thought okay, then I realised Patrick Patterson was the overseas pro at Lancashire. He was fast for sure, but he wasn't express pace. But then we had a little rainstorm, which freshened up the pitch. He bowled a ball which bounced a little bit and it hit me on the hand right where the knuckle was, and it had broken my finger.'

Monkhouse asked Micky Stewart if he could have two or three days back home. Stewart agreed but said to keep fit ahead of the upcoming NatWest final. But Surrey lost to Lancashire by four runs in the semis.

Recuperating in Cumbria, his mother was unwell and his father wanted him back home. 'I was on £11,500 a year at Surrey in 1986 and there weren't all the jobs that there are now in coaching and media, so I decided to retire because I didn't want to lose my position in the family business.'

Surrey offered another two-year contract and on reflection Monkhouse wishes he'd played longer. He played professionally in the northeast for a couple of years then for Penrith, Edenhall and Wigton until he was 50 and for the MCC for a few years after that. He also got married and had two children.

'I'm basically retired now. I got divorced, and I had no one else involved in the business and it needed a little bit of a shake-up and a bit of capital investment because the EEC altered some rules and we couldn't do this and we couldn't do that. We also had six farm shops and the High Street shops and the supermarkets were starting to impinge upon our trade so in 2006 I rationalised the business. I sold one of the farms and I used some of that capital to buy some more property. And now I've got a property portfolio for my retirement, and I turned the big farm into industrial units that I rent out. I'm nearly 70, I got married again and I've got a 16-year-old daughter so that keeps me on my toes.

'I play a lot of golf. I've had some health problems this last two or three years but I'm hopefully over those and everything's going quite nicely. I do a bit of biking. My knees are terrible. I put up with them and watch a bit of cricket and enjoy life.'

Looking back, the early 1980s was the time of his life: 'I can't over emphasise how much that chance meeting with Micky Stewart changed my life when he signed me for Surrey. He had never seen me play, it was like Liverpool signing a player after watching him in a five-a-side game.'

Stewart invited Monkhouse to his 90th birthday party at The Oval in 2022, a great honour. Among the guests were former Prime Minister John Major, ex-England captain Graham Gooch and former England tour manager Peter Lush. Monkhouse was on the Stewart family table, which included another former England captain, Micky's son Alec. 'Farmer' was one of a handful of former players among the 70 guests in The Oval's Long Room.

The entertainer and former Surrey president Richard Stilgoe sang a song about Micky. 'It was a lovely evening. I was so honoured to have been invited when you think about how many players he's been involved with in his career.

'When Micky finished playing he went to work as marketing manager for Slazenger. When he came back to The Oval he brought a little bit of business organisation and was the first coach that really organised pre-season training. The lads couldn't believe it, whereas now it's just standard for everybody.

'They ran round Richmond Park. Some players would hide. Sylvester Clarke was the least fit man in the world but he could bowl quicker than me in his plimsolls, so you just didn't find fault with him.

'I was a lad from Langwathby, population of 450–500 at most, and suddenly I'm thrust into the middle of London. And we weren't as worldly-wise in 1980 as kids are now. There was no internet and no mobile phones. I suddenly had to make my own way.

'They were great days and I probably wish I'd done it for longer, but I enjoyed what I did and it kept me in touch with people all over the country. And I've been all over the world with the MCC on tours as a player and a manager. I'd never have done that if I hadn't played cricket for Surrey.'

In 1983, Graham Monkhouse scored 291 first-class runs at 22.38 in 18 matches and took 47 wickets at 22.12 with a best of 7-51 against Nottinghamshire at The Oval on 27 July. Surrey won by nine wickets. Peter Such, who took 1-51 and 1-13, was one of Monkhouse's victims, bowled for a duck. In 15 List A games he scored 70 runs at 11.66 and took 17 wickets at 23.70 with a 3.91 economy rate. In his career, he took 173 wickets in 103 first-class matches at 27.06 and 103 in 94 List As at 29.64. He scored 1,158 first-class runs at 21.84 and 395 in one-dayers at 13.62.

Essex v Surrey at Chelmsford, 28–31 May, 1983
Surrey First Innings

Alan Butcher c D East b Phillip 2
Grahame Clinton c D East b Phillip 6
Andy Needham b Foster 0
Roger Knight lbw Phillip 0
Monte Lynch lbw Phillip 0
Jack Richards c Turner b Phillip 0

David Thomas lbw Foster 0
Ian Payne b Phillip 0
Graham Monkhouse lbw Phillip 2
Sylvester Clarke b Foster 4
Pat Pocock not out 0
14.3 overs. Total: 14
Fall of wickets 1-2, 2-5, 3-6, 4-8, 5-8, 6-8, 7-8, 8-8, 9-14, 10-14
Bowling: Norbert Phillip 7.3-4-4-6; Neil Foster 7-3-10-4.

Surrey

Roger Knight: Surrey captain from 1978–83 who retired in 1984. Played 387 first-class matches and scored 19,558 runs, took 369 wickets and also played 310 List A games. He was Surrey president in 2008, MCC secretary then CEO from 1994–2006. MCC president 2015/16. In 1983 he scored 1,235 Championship runs at 38.59 and took 15 wickets at 45.13, plus 12 one-day wickets and 272 runs in 16 matches.

Alan Butcher: Surrey 1972–98 and Glamorgan 1987–92. Left-handed opener who played 402 first-class and 359 List A matches including one Test and one ODI. Scored 22,667 first-class runs at 36.32. 1983: 24 matches, 1,341 Championship runs at 33.52 and 524 in 18 one-dayers. Later a coach for Essex, Surrey and Zimbabwe.

Grahame Clinton: Surrey 1979–90 after five years at Kent. In 270 first-class games the left-handed opener scored 13,118 runs and also played 185 List A matches. In 1983 he scored 371 runs at 20.61 in 12 Championship matches. Later a Surrey, Kent and schools coach.

David Smith: Surrey 1973–83. Moved to Worcestershire for 1984–86, returned to Surrey until 1989 then Sussex until 1994. Played 319 first-class games with 15,265 runs at 36.17. Two Tests in 1985/86. In 1983 he scored 748 Championship runs at 46.75 in 13 Championship games plus 286 in 11 one-dayers. Later a Sussex coach.

Monte Lynch: Topped Surrey 1983 averages with 1,558 runs at 53.72 in 24 matches. Left in 1994 for Gloucestershire. Three ODIs for England in 1988. In 1983 he also scored 390 runs in 18 one-dayers. Played 359 first-class matches (18,325 at 35.17) and 378 one-dayers. Was in the West Indies rebel squad for their 1983/84 South Africa tour. Later a coach with his own academy.

Andy Needham: Left Surrey, where he debuted in 1977 after the 1986 season for Middlesex where he stayed until 1988. Off-spinning all-rounder, in 1983 he scored 88 runs and took ten wickets in eight Championship matches. Later a schools coach.

Jack Richards: Surrey 1976–88. Cornish wicketkeeper who played eight Tests between 1986 and 88 and 22 ODIs between 1981 and 88. Played 286 first-class and 264 List A matches. In 1983 he made 718 runs at 27.61 in 24 Championship matches and made 58 dismissals. Later moved to Belgium with his Dutch wife; he runs a Dutch shipping company and is a director of a crewing agency.

Sylvester Clarke (1955–99): Surrey 1979–89, West Indies 1978–82 (11 Tests, ten ODIs). Toured with the West Indies rebel team to South Africa. In 1983 the fast bowler took 79 Championship wickets at 22.44 in 24 matches and 19 in one-dayers with 942 at 19.52 in his 238 first-class games. Later a carpenter in Barbados. There is a Sylvester's Bar at The Oval.

Robin Jackman (1945–2020): Four Tests and 15 ODIs 1981–83. Surrey 1966–82 with 1,402 first-class wickets at 22.80 in 399 first-class matches. The opening bowler also played 288 List A Matches, taking 439 wickets at 21.10. Retired after an ODI defeat in Christchurch, in February 1983, when he took 2-32 (New Zealand won the series 3-0). Later a broadcaster.

Kevin Macintosh: RFM seamer who left Surrey after 1983. Nottinghamshire 1978–80. Played 33 first-class matches (59 wickets at 35.45 and 33 one-dayers with 30 wickets at 26.56). Later worked in IT in the USA. One Championship match in 1983 and no wickets.

Dave Thomas (1959–2012): Left-arm bowler for Surrey between 1977 and 87. In 150 first-class matches he took 336 wickets at 33.97 and scored 3,044 runs at 20.02. Played 153 one-day matches (142 wickets at 33.71 and 1,556 runs at 18.74). In 1983 he took 57 Championship wickets at 31.24 in 23 matches and also hit 937 runs at 36.03. He took 21 wickets in one-dayers and scored 244 runs in 18 matches. Died in 2012 of complications from MS aged 53.

Pat Pocock: Off-spinner for Surrey from 1964–86. Recalled to Test cricket in 1984 after eight years. Took 1,607 first-class wickets in 554 matches. In 1983 he took 68 Championship wickets at 26.08 plus 14 in one-dayers. Later founded a sports/hospitality events company.

Chapter 21

Sussex: John Barclay

SUSSEX CAPTAIN John Barclay declared the innings closed at a packed seaside Scarborough festival during the summer holidays in 1982, setting Yorkshire 251 to win. There was a plague of ladybirds that weekend. Thousands of tourists switched from watching the toy battleship World War Two re-enactment at Peasholm Park to North Marine Road to watch the match.

'I remember that match really well,' says Barclay. 'I'm so glad you reminded me. I'm assuming there were rain interruptions earlier in the match. It was a lovely day. I may have tossed up shyly as he [Yorkshire captain Ray Illingworth] was such a heavyweight character, though he would have been getting on a bit then.'

Barclay set Yorkshire 195 minutes to score the runs. *Wisden* said it was a 'generous' target. Sussex were only one bonus point behind Middlesex in the Championship by mid-season, having come second in 1981.

'It might look like my declaration was a bit foolhardy, but our team respected that sort of declaration. It was the best chance to win. Boycott played the best innings I'd seen him play. He took control and hit the ball very, very hard. I remember bowling and he hit me hard through midwicket. It was not a bad ball, though it may have been quite easy for him. I put men out there but he still breached the field. Setting Yorkshire 250 in the last afternoon, I wouldn't have thought we bowled more than 50-odd overs. Chris Waller, who was a very good bowler, and I bowled quite a lot.

'I liked to back our bowlers. In the dressing room they may have thought "he's gone a bit mad and declared too soon" sometimes, but the great thing I said to them is if they knock them off we'll get off earlier, and get home earlier.

'It was a really good game, and I don't regret it at all. Hanging on two or three more overs when batting was what I always did regret, declaring maybe too late. It was a fine game and the crowd loved it, especially as Yorkshire won, and it was good for cricket.'

Boycott hit 122 not out including a rare six, but both teams finished mid-table. That was riches compared to 1983, when Yorkshire came bottom and Sussex suffered all sorts of calamities. Star all-rounder and future Pakistan prime minister Imran Khan was among those injured.

'Imran had a problem that year with shin soreness, a little stress fracture. He went to a specialist who came up with the idea that it would be good if he exercised, but not too much, and suggested five or six overs bowling at the most in an innings. We had a bit of a laugh at that. You had to be really strategic and bowl him at the best moment, because I didn't want to waste those overs. Imran bowled better with the older ball as he found the new one slipped around, which was unusual.'

Imran battled through the World Cup, unable to bowl in the semi-final, which Viv Richards won for the West Indies with 80 not out. But two months later, in late August against Warwickshire at Edgbaston, the world-leading all-rounder, who thought he may have to give up bowling, had his first, and only, golden spell of the year.

'Somewhere after 40 overs, he came on. He only bowled off six paces at most. I don't know why he was so successful that day. He should have won us the game. [Wicketkeeper] Ian Gould was helpful tactically about when we bowled Imran. What fun it was but we got it right; it's a lovely story.' Imran took six wickets in 23 balls including a hat-trick and followed his 94 with 64 but Sussex still lost by 21 runs, chasing 219. Barclay second top-scored, with 27. 'Paul Smith was a little bit wild as a bowler and I probably fancied him so probably had a flash at a wide one.'

The season had started brightly: 'In 1983, right at the beginning of March and living in Brighton I walked up the road and, though I'm not a betting man, I pottered into Ladbrokes just for fun. And the odds were there on the cricket and Sussex were at that stage favourites to win everything. But we were like the Grand National favourites falling at every fence. Everything went wrong.'

Barclay's *Life in the Airing Cupboard* describes a pre-season visit to La Manga, Spain, in 1983, with Surrey as opposition. Trouters dislocated a thumb trying to catch Alan Butcher off his own bowling and felt despair. He couldn't even play golf. Sylvester Clarke bowled to him off four steps as he attempted a comeback net. It hurt. The trip was Pat Pocock's well-intentioned idea. Neither Sussex nor Surrey had a particularly distinguished season after recent successes. 'Perhaps the English climate and home territory have their merits after all.'

As well as Imran's injury, the World Cup took him and Ian Gould out. Fast bowler Garth Le Roux injured his groin in early July and barely played afterwards. In May, all-rounder Ian Greig fell off a balcony at his flat. He'd broken his key in the lock and was trying to break in. He badly injured his ankle and was out for eight weeks. 'We lost a lot of armoury. I broke a finger on my right hand but kept playing as we didn't have any more players. I was a wounded soldier, without the zip. Paul Parker was a wonderful player but couldn't get any runs. His form ran out for some unknown reason. Form is fickle and was always an unknown. In one or two matches it was quite hard to get a side. There were no loans in those days, so we were struggling a bit.'

Forty years on, Barclay is an elder statesman of the game, his career and personal battles with depression well documented in a series of insightful autobiographies.

'There's been so much evolution. Four-day cricket and two divisions and covered pitches from 1981. The covering then became much more sophisticated so much more cricket is played than there used to be in wetter conditions.

'In the 70s and 80s there really were tip-top class overseas players at each county and every county would have a couple of good, or more than useful, spin bowlers because conditions warranted it. Now you are quite hard-pressed to find the conditions and pitches because of the nature of the County Championship. Starting in early April doesn't really help.

'And much more recently, since 2000, short-form cricket T20 and The Hundred altered the context and perception of the game sometimes for good and some not quite so good. Most of these changes have been led by finance, the wish to make ends meet or more than meet and create a healthy financial setup for what are some beleaguered counties. Some things are much the same. England fast bowers like Ollie Robinson since the year dot are all exactly the same; very, very good seam up, swing, tall and fast. Jimmy Anderson's use of swing and seam and his stamina; Stuart Broad was the same, tall and with great fitness.

'The influence of sports science in general and the way people train and look after themselves is completely different. That shows most clearly in the difference in fielding, which is outstanding now by comparison. You don't see many ponderous cricketers, as there might have had back in the day.

'We played three-day cricket with a sandwich weekend. A Saturday start, then a Sunday League match not always in the same place, then Monday and Tuesday back at the Championship match, so travel days were Tuesday and Friday night in cars, three per car usually. There were no coaches or not many. Travel was a big thing. I don't know how we did it. After a long day it was a very long way back to Hove from Scarborough, probably to play a match the next day. The lifestyle was sometimes quite fun but if you played for Sussex or were in the north there was a lot of travel. Warwickshire and Leicestershire were well-placed. But make no mistake, I enjoyed it all. They were great days to play for Sussex.'

He waxes lyrical about the halcyon days: 'Top players played for every county, the more the merrier. Graham Gooch was unbelievable, performing for England then incredible for Essex. He just loved batting. John Emburey was the same. He loved playing cricket. He just liked to turn up and play. John Lever was a freak almost. But some found it much harder to lift their game having played a tough Test.'

All three of the above were banned for playing for England for three years after taking part in the 1981/82 rebel tour to South Africa, much improving the county game, though diminishing England's options.

'South Africa? I don't remember it being talked about. Within professional circles where people were earning their living. People respected choice.'

Barclay's books *The Appeal of the Championship*, *Life Beyond the Airing Cupboard* and *Lost in the Long Grass* were published by Stephen Chalke's Fairfield Books. Another, *Team Mates*, saw 27 writers, mainly cricketers, profile their favourite fellow players.

'I loved doing the books with Stephen Chalke. They were so wonderfully edited. *Team Mates* raised £35,000–£40,000 for Arundel Castle Cricket Foundation. We chose people who wrote well. Being for charity helped.' Barclay chose John Spencer, who was seen as a journeyman.

Barclay is an old Etonian. In a bid to look less elitist, the MCC is seeking to end the Eton v Harrow match being held at Lord's, which has been held there since 1805, the longest-running annual cricket fixture in the world.

'It's a very interesting question. On the whole the MCC has been very good in two ways to progress as best as possible. There's a balance with history and heritage the MCC is responsible for and to spread opportunity to as many as possible to enjoy the game. From that point of view, it becomes less exclusive and at the same time it's important to promote the history and heritage and the MCC has done that very well.

'They perhaps may have consulted a bit more on history and heritage with historical matches but in the end they came up with a solution, albeit temporary to see how things go. There's a balance between progress and history and it's very hard to satisfy everybody. The Media Centre is a remarkable building you might not expect at Lord's or from the MCC.'

In 1983, Oxford played Cambridge at Lord's in a high-profile first-class fixture. Oxford played nine first-class matches and Cambridge ten. Neither won a match and few players graduated to become professionals, though Tim Curtis did go on to play for England.

'Oxford and Cambridge attracted gifted sportsmen. Because of the admissions policy, plenty of fine sportsmen were admitted. They might not be totally blessed academically but that has changed for years and years now with the current admissions policy. The result is not many current players will come through to play first-class cricket.'

Half of the 2022/23 England cricket team had private educations (Joe Root, Jonny Bairstow, Stuart Broad, Zak Crawley, Ollie Pope, Ben Duckett, Harry Brook, Ollie Robinson) though Ben Stokes, Jofra Archer, James Anderson, Chris Woakes, Jack Leach, Ben Foakes, Moeen Ali and Mark Wood went to state school. A higher proportion of England's women internationals were state-educated.

'With independent schools there are no doubt more opportunities for scholarships for talented young people to have an education. It looks as though many of the best players had private education. When I was playing it was much less.

'Some very good players do come up through the state schools and Ben Stokes is a very good example of that. There's a whole lot of different routes at Sussex. To take a generalised route and identify a strict pathway to Sussex only half works.'

I told Barclay I'd talked to Graham Monkhouse yesterday. 'A lovely man, lots of fun, we called him the Farmer. I remember him with great affection as a stalwart county player and a good fast bowler. Kevin Emery? I remember facing in 1982, a very good bowler, never really seen him since.' He recommends Geoff Miller and Vic Marks as good interviewees.

Trout, an utter gentleman and charming conversationalist, told me that when he travelled north close to where Farmer lived, he visited John Norris's fly fishing shop in Penrith. He is a man with class. Among others I interviewed for this book, Ole Mortensen, as a Dane, did not suffer, or benefit, from being part of the England class system. Monkhouse, a Cumbrian farmer, broke barriers and played for the MCC.

Barclay is the sort of man who keeps in touch with his old cricket pals and seeks to broaden the game's appeal to new ones. He is president at Sussex CCC: 'I don't have to do much except be nice.' Post-Covid-19, he enjoyed meeting the crowds at Hove again. 'It was difficult for everyone in all walks of life but the management at Hove handled it adeptly to create minimum upset. Obviously other areas of life were much more important than cricket; we were alright and probably stronger for it. It put it all into perspective.'

Sussex

John Barclay: In 1983 he played 21 first-class matches and scored 743 runs at 21.85 and took 17 wickets at 45.52. In 21 one-dayers he scored 142 runs at 14.20 and took 16 wickets at 28.87 at an economy rate of 3.54. In his career (1970–86), he played 274 first-class games with 9,677 runs at 24.81 and 324 wickets at 30.66 and 236 List A games with 2,792 runs at 21.81 and 167 wickets at 25.49. He was later a cricket manager and writer.

Gehan Mendis: Opener for Sussex 1975–85, Lancashire 1986–93. In 226 first-class matches scored 21,436 runs at 36.83 and in 313 one-dayers scored 8,327 runs at 29.42. Scored 1,608 Championship runs at 41.23 in 1983 plus 463 in 21 one-dayers. Later a teacher.

Allan Green: Sussex 1980–89. Played 164 first-class games with 7,932 runs at 28.94 and in one-dayers scored

2,333 runs at 26.21. Scored 519 runs at 19.22 in the 1983 Championship campaign. Later worked in HR.

Paul Parker: Sussex 1976–91, Durham 1992–93. England 1981 (one Test). Played 371 first-class matches with 19,419 runs at 35.05 and 341 one-dayers with 8,606 runs at 30.51. In 1983 he scored 507 runs at 21.12 and 513 in 20 one-dayers. Later a teacher.

Imran Khan: Sussex 1983–88, Worcestershire 1971–76, Pakistan 1971–92 (88 Tests, 175 ODIs). Played 382 first-class matches with 17,771 runs at 36.79 and 1,287 wickets at 22.32. In 425 one-dayers he scored 10,100 runs at 33.22 and took 507 wickets at 22.31. In 1983 took 12 wickets at 7.16 in the Championship and scored 1,260 runs at 57.27. In the 1983 World Cup he scored 383 runs at 70.75 and captained the side to the semi-final, scoring 17 as Pakistan lost by eight wickets to the West Indies. In all, he scored 695 runs in 20 one-dayers in 1983. Later he was Pakistan prime minister.

Colin Wells: Sussex 1979–93, Derbyshire 1994–96 England 1985 (2 ODIs). Played 318 first-class games with 14,289 runs at 33.07 and 428 wickets at 34.45 and scored 6,192 runs in 322 one-dayers at 25.80 with 233 wickets at 30.93. In 1983 he took 32 Championship wickets at 35.46 and scored 857 runs at 25.20 as well as 505 runs and 15 wickets in 21 one-dayers. Later he was a cricket teacher in UAE.

Ian Greig: Sussex 1979–85, Surrey 1987–92, England 1982 (two Tests). Played 253 first-class matches with 8,301 runs at 28.72 and took 419 wickets at 31.08. In 235 one-dayers he scored 3,136 runs at 20.10 and took 212 wickets at 28.08. Brother of former England captain Tony Greig. In 1983 he scored 177 runs at 19.66 and took 17 wickets at 40.05 in eight Championship matches, plus 15 one-day wickets. Later a coach in Australia.

Ian Gould: Middlesex 1975–80, Sussex 1981–90, England 1983 (18 ODIs). Scored 66 runs at 22 in the World Cup; 'Gunner' took 11 catches and made one stumping. Scored 473 runs at 29.56 in 17 Championship games in 1983 and played 26 one-dayers in all with 373 runs, 22 catches and one stumping. Played 298 first-class matches with 536 catches and 67 stumpings and scored 8,756 runs at 26.05 and played 315 one-dayers with 242 catches and 37 stumpings and 4,377 runs at 19.11. He coached Middlesex before becoming an umpire from 2002.

Paul Phillipson: Sussex 1970–86 with 153 first-class wickets at 34.07 in 168 games and 104 one-day wickets at 28.43 in 228 matches. Played one Championship match in 1983 scoring 23 and 28 and played 17 one-dayers with 152 runs. Later a teacher and coach in South Africa.

Garth Le Roux: Sussex 1978–87. Played 239 first-class matches taking 838 wickets at 21.24 and 250 one-dayers with 378 wickets at 19.97. In 1983 he took 37 Championship wickets at 25.51, playing just 12 games because of injury, plus 22 in one-dayers. Later a property agent.

Tony Pigott: Sussex 1978–93, Surrey 1994–96, England 1984 (one Test). Played 260 first-class matches with 672 wickets at 30.99 and 270 one-dayers with 377 wickets at 24.39. In 1983 he took 72 Championship wickets at 26.09

and 24 one-day wickets. Later 'Lester' was Sussex's chief executive and is now an ECB pitch liaison officer and sales and marketing director of the Turf Club.

Chris Waller: Surrey 1967–73, Sussex 1974–85. Played 267 first-class matches with 630 wickets at 29.06 and took 125 one-day wickets in 149 matches at 29.46. In 1983 took 53 Championship wickets at 35.24. Later a coach.

Chapter 22

Warwickshire: Norman Gifford

I WAS getting anxious again having not talked to any players since Mike Selvey and Peter Such at Easter. May Day had gone. I'd been back to Lord's Library to research and take stock and put off finishing the book, and I had no hot leads.

Leafing through my increasingly worn Panini album, near the back, I still hadn't talked to an old player from Warwickshire and Worcestershire. I find out Norman Gifford (who took 100 first-class wickets and had been playing since 1960 but wasn't in the album) and Tim Curtis, who was entering his breakthrough year, were both Worcestershire presidents. My Worcestershire Supporters' Association contact Mike Hitchings sent me their email addresses.

First, a wild goose chase. As a garden writer, I remembered former Warwickshire batsman Asif Din used to work for A. Mir Garden Furniture in Oldbury. I watched a video of him with Dermot Reeve talking to fans at Edgbaston. Reeve did most of the talking. Asif just said he had a fear of failure in the first half of his career but got rid of the shackles in the second half with subsequently better results. So I called the garden furniture company. They said he didn't work there anymore.

Giff began before many people's time too. One of the greatest servants of the game and in my mind a bit of an unsung hero too, he appeared in the last Gentlemen v Players match at Lord's, in 1962, four months before the distinction between amateurs and professionals was abolished. *Wisden*'s reporter was unaware, more concerned with who would captain England in Australia that winter. 'Lord' Ted Dexter was elevated to the role during the match, ahead of future Bishop of Liverpool David Sheppard. Fred Trueman, from a Yorkshire mining village, captained the Players, who were denied victory by rain.

The Gentlemen had only won the fixture three times since the war – the First World War. However, those leaving the amateur ranks for 1963 included sometime England captains Tony Lewis and M.J.K. Smith as well as Dexter and Sheppard. Micky Stewart opened for the Players and became Surrey's first professional captain, in 1963. Also in 1963, Australian Ken Grieves replaced specialist captain Joe Blackledge (who had replaced Gents' opener Bob Barber for 1962 at Lancashire). He averaged 15 with the bat and Lancashire came second bottom of the Championship. Lancashire had wanted to sign Gifford in 1958, but he decided Worcestershire was a better fit.

Meanwhile, Worcestershire's pro captain Tom Dollery won the Championship in 1964 and 1965 after coming second in 1962 and his team were runners-up in the first Gillette Cup in 1963. A final Gents v Players match, the

274th, was played at Scarborough in September 1962. Tony Lock replaced Giff and took 7-213 in the match and the Players won by seven wickets.

The 60s marked a watershed for county cricket. Writers such as E.W. Swanton blamed the end of carefree amateurism for safety-first slow scoring which meant lots of draws and falling crowds, who had plenty of other things to do, such as watch TV, a pastime that had become the UK's number one since the coronation in 1953 which was the first time Giff had watched one. I spoke to Giff the day before the next coronation, 70 years later. One-day cricket was the answer to bring back interest, trialled in 1962 with a Midland knockout and begun in earnest in 1963 when Sussex won the first Gillette Cup.

If he'd been in it, Gifford would have been the oldest in the Panini album apart from Ray Illingworth. Giff is six months older than Boycott. He's 24 years older than the youngest in the album, Peter Such. Illingworth, the last player born in the 1930s to play county cricket, was 33 years older than Such. Eddie Hemmings retired aged 46 in 1995. Graham Gooch and John Emburey were both 44 when they made their final appearances in 1997. Giff was 48 when he retired in 1988, with more than 2,000 wickets to his name.

He played his first Test in 1964 in an Ashes team where all the players are now gone, apart from Peter Parfitt. He took 2-14 and 1-17 in 29 overs. Almost 20 years on, he moved from Worcestershire to Warwickshire and took 104 first-class wickets in 1983. He'd taken just 23 the season before. At Worcestershire he won the Championship three times, including as captain in 1974, when his Test career was already over. Giff was one of *Wisden*'s five cricketers of 1974: 'He cannot be written off or underestimated, as he has proved on countless occasions.'

He played two one-day internationals a decade later, in Sharjah, aged 44.. A highlight was removing Imran Khan's first ball.

Teenager Richard Illingworth was Gifford's replacement at Worcestershire for 1983. At Warwickshire, Giff and fellow newcomer Chris Old bowled more than half their overs in the Championship. Gifford was an inspiration and wouldn't let games drift, said *Wisden*. He stood in for England captain Bob Willis (who still played 12 Championship matches), with the side winning ten games to move up from last to fifth in the table. This was their most wins since 1964, when Giff was winning the Championship with Worcestershire.

Eight wickets against Lancashire, the county he had nearly joined 23 years before, helped bring a win at Old Trafford. This included 5-31 in 35 second innings' overs. He can't even remember the 6-22 that helped beat Middlesex, who scored 78 then 74 on an overly dry pitch at Edgbaston in July. It was a sixth successive Warwickshire win and Gifford did as well as England's two top spinners Phil Edmonds and Emburey, both a decade younger.

Taking a break from watching an under-11 match, I retreated to the pavilion, and rang Giff, as arranged. 'I hope you've got some information, mate. Ask me what you want to know, and I'll try my best to answer it,' Giffy rasps in his deep north Lancashire accent.

He was on the scrap heap at the end of 1982: 'They released me at Worcestershire. A few months after that [Warwickshire manager] David Brown rang me and asked me to meet with him and Bob Willis for a chat to see if I could help some youngsters at Warwickshire. It was a big, big surprise when David Brown spoke to me.

'I was disappointed when Worcestershire said I could go. I didn't kick up any fuss, but after everything I'd done for the county ... I was captain for about eight years.' He'd been stock bowler supporting opening bowlers Len Flavell, Jack Coldwell and medium pacer Jim Standen, who in 1964 won the County Championship with Worcestershire and the FA Cup Final with West Ham. Gifford wants him properly commemorated at New Road.

Gifford seemed from another time: 'When I started, there were uncovered wickets. For spin bowlers, if it was uncovered from Saturday evening to Monday morning and you'd get to Monday, the sun's shining, you fill your boots. It made a big difference.'

The almost-retired spinner had been England assistant manager on the 1982/83 Australia tour and could have pursued management as a career. He'd been linked with Lancashire in early 1982, but had stayed loyal, and suddenly it all seemed over after decades of service.

Yet he appeared in 43 games in 1983, bowling more than 1,000 overs. He didn't really know how much he would play when he joined and did not expect to deputise as captain in his first season. Willis, who was also England captain from 1982–84, was skipper when he joined, holding the role from 1980–84. 'I didn't expect to captain Warwickshire in 1983. I thought over and I'd just be setting my own fields.

'But it's not difficult to captain once you get to know the characters you play with. As a captain you've got to get to know your bowlers and understand them. That's where the majority of decisions are made on the field. You're lucky when there's Allan Donald. And we had Anton Ferreira, a South African lad who was a good guy who would do anything you asked him. He was very good at mixing everyone together. The dressing room contained a good set of people. Chris Old was a fine bowler when he was fit and on the pitch. He put it in good areas and made the ball talk at times.'

But how did Giff make such a comeback and take five times more wickets in 1983 than 1982? 'You have to bowl the overs to get rhythm. There's no substitute for the work you put in and the overs you bowl. You might bowl 20 or 30 on a flat wicket but that experience will pay off when you start to play on something that does a bit more. I didn't feel reborn. I just enjoyed playing the game. I played with motivation from within myself.'

He took four or more wickets in the season 16 times in 1983, more than anyone else. John Lever was second with 14. Derek Underwood and Emburey had 11 each. His 6,262 balls for 104 wickets were more than anyone and he bowled 100 overs more than Emburey (5,610 balls for 106 wickets) and Underwood (5,619 balls for the same number). Giff also bowled 930 balls in 21 one-day matches for 22 more wickets. Underwood took 37 one-day wickets in 25 matches for 143 in all. Only

Bob Willis (45 in 24 matches), Vic Marks (40 in 28 games), and Malcolm Marshall (38 in 26) took more than Underwood in one-dayers, though Steve Malone also took 37.

Gifford remembers that in 1983 it rained all spring. 'If you had a wet start to the season the outfield would be damp, but the wickets were now well covered so there would be no moisture on the pitch, not like you used to get. One of the biggest problems bowling spin is to be confident with the grip on the wet.'

He also helped the young spinners at Warwickshire such as Asif Din and Adrian Pierson, passing on his experience and adding even more to the value Warwickshire got from one of their best signings: 'I'd chat to them about various things, what they were looking to control, the length and line, that side of things.'

It had all begun a quarter of a century before. 'My father's friend played cricket for Ulverston and his son Kenneth played as well. I said to my father I'd go with Kenneth to keep him company and take the trial as well.'

Aged 18, they asked Giff, but not Kenneth, to stay on another two days and then offered him a contract. He needed permission from the county of his birth, Lancashire, to sign. 'I had to go to Old Trafford for a trial. I did alright and they wanted to sign me as well. I asked my dad what to do. I'd been to Worcestershire and it was a very friendly place. Old Trafford had just come out of the amateur/professional era and coming from a little town it was a big shock so I decided Worcestershire was where I wanted to go and it was one of my better decisions.'

Members of the Indian cricket team for the Prudential World Cup series arriving at Heathrow. Back row, from left: Dilip Vengsarkar, Krishnamachari Srikkanth, Yashpal Sharma, Balwinder Sandhu, Ravi Shastri, and manager Man Singh. Front row, from left: Roger Binny, Sunil Gavaskar and wicketkeeper Syed Kirmani.

Enid Bakewell, pictured at Lord's Cricket Ground to mark the 50th anniversary of the first ever Women's World Cup.

John Holder, pioneering umpire, with the author at Cheltenham

Essex CCC 1983 (back row): Alan Lilley, Graham Gooch, Derek Pringle, Neil Foster, Keith Pont, Brian Hardie, David East. (Front row) Ken McEwan, David Acfield, John Lever, Keith Fletcher, Ray East, Stuart Turner

Jack Russell at Chris Beetles Gallery for his 60th birthday paintings exhibition in 2023

Gloucestershire's David Graveney with the author

Hampshire's Kevin Emery with the author

Hampshire's Tim Tremlett with the author

Lancashire opening batsman Graeme Fowler, batting at Old Trafford.

Leicestershire and England's Nick Cook with the author

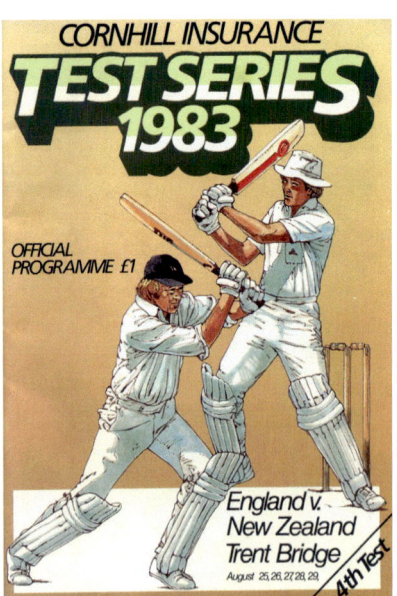

1983 Official Programme cover. England v New Zealand. Trent Bridge, Nottingham. 25–29 August Fourth Test. Nick Cook took nine wickets in England's 165 run win. Graeme Fowler had been dropped.

B&H 1983 scorecard Essex v Middlesex

Members of the Middlesex County Cricket Club team for 1983. Left to right (back row): Colin Metson, Neil Williams, Bill Merry, Norman Cowans, Kevan James, Rajesh Maru and CWV Robins. (Centre row): Coach – Harry Sharp, Don Bennett, Simon Hughes, Keith Tomlins, Colin Cook, Paul Downton, Andy Smith, Keith Brown and physiotherapist – John Miller. (Front row): Wilf Slack, Wayne Daniel, Philippe Edmonds, captain – Mike Gatting, John Emburey, Clive Radley, Graham Barlow and Roland Butcher.

Mike Brearley with the author 2023

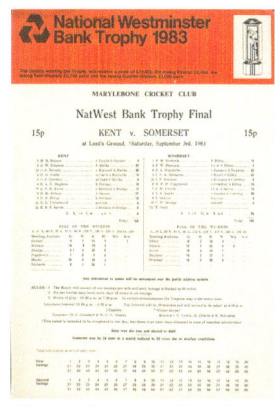

Kent v Somerset NatWest final scorecard 1983

New Zealand's batsman Lance Cairns with his middle stump removed when he was bowled for 34 by Surrey's Graham Monkhouse during the one-day friendly at The Oval.

The Oval 2023 for a Hundred match

Cheltenham Festival 2023

Lord's Championship match 2023

Drawings of the cricket heroes of 1983

Geoff Boycott

Geoff Boycott in a typical pose batting for Yorkshire

Indian supporters run on to the field at Lord's in 1983 after India's captain Kapil Dev had caught West Indian batsman Viv Richards, during the Prudential World Cup Cricket Final. India defeated West Indies by 43 runs. India caused a major upset in world cricket by lifting the trophy at Lord's against a West Indies side that had won the two previous editions and featured Viv Richards, Clive Lloyd and Desmond Haynes.

Anyway, Lancashire had three Test spinners in Tommy Greenhough, Roy Tattersall and Malcolm Hilton.

'I left school at 15 and my father found me a job as an apprentice decorator. In those days there were no strength and conditioning people. There was a physio and that was it. But at Worcestershire the strength and conditioning man worked out why I was a good spinner. At 15 I painted ceilings with a big seven-inch brush left-handed, which was ideal for them because I could start at one side with the other right-handed painter starting at the other. That built a lot of strength in my wrist and fingers and I'm sure it helped when I started county cricket. There were no rollers. Everything was brushes and I'd not realised until then why I could spin it more than others.'

He'd never seen a first-class game until he joined Worcestershire. He's always been drawn players from the far northwest, Langwathby's Graham Monkhouse and Paul Nixon, Ulverston's Willie Hogg and young Barrovian Liam Livingstone.

Gifford was a big success at Worcestershire, so much so he was picked for the Ashes Test at Lord's in 1964. Until you walk out onto the pitch there's no cap. It rained Thursday and Friday. Eventually captain Ted Dexter handed over the cap on the Saturday.

But he played just 15 Tests in his ten-year England career: 'Derek Underwood was never going to retire before me. The only chance I'd get was if he was injured. One big positive was Ray Illingworth preferred me to Derek. He was the best captain. We both played at Karachi against Pakistan. I get on well with Derek. He's a nice guy. On a wet wicket he was unplayable. He bowled quicker than I did. He was more a cutter than a spinner.'

Gifford was recalled in 1971 under Illingworth, who he admired most as England captain. 'Top class. He knew what I could do and what he could ask of me. His tactics and field placing were good as well. He went to Australia and captained John Snow, who he knew how to handle.'

The 'biggest mistake' of his life was taking up smoking, on a Rest of the World tour of Australia in 1971, captained by Garry Sobers. With pipe smokers Bob Taylor, Tony Greig and Richard Hutton, they were invited to a shop in Sydney by Dunhill and Giff was asked to pick a pipe. He might have a cigar with a beer at night but didn't really smoke. He jokes that in the Worcestershire dressing room he'd sit in the corner with an open window and send smoke signals to people on the field.

Gifford now lives in Pershore, in Worcestershire's cider country, which is apt as he is known for his apple-cheeked complexion. Reflecting on today's game, he says: 'One of my great disappointments was the end of the John Player League. You used to get good crowds on Sunday afternoons. I thought that was a good format. I know it was the start to the build-up to T20. And The Hundred is what it is. I go to Worcestershire reasonably often to watch some cricket, but I prefer four-day cricket to 20 overs. I've never seen The Hundred.'

Giff was the last bowler to reach 2,000 first-class wickets: 'I don't think anyone else will get to what I got to.' But what was the secret to his longevity? 'I never suffered any injuries to my knees or shoulders. I had the odd broken finger playing and I'm suffering with my hips now after all the overs I bowled.'

He captained England in Sharjah in 1984/85 in a round robin against Australia, Pakistan and South Africa. Some enjoyed the social side and the team could have done better.

After retiring aged 48 he coached: 'You've got to believe in the people you're coaching and get them to believe in themselves. As time went on I knew I could bowl. I knew the things I needed to work on, changes in pace and flight, and those sorts of things I'd try and instil in the people I was coaching.'

When coaching Durham, pace bowlers dominated, including Melvyn Betts and Steve Harmison. He enjoyed working with captain David Boon. Giff asked why at his age Boon would bat in the nets against Harmison and he replied that it was a 'bloody good way to get him going for the day'.

At Sussex he coached leg-spinner Ian Salisbury and thought he was a really great talent. Giff would hear commentators say 'another bad ball' but all leg-spinners bowl bad balls. He was a big spinner and had one of the best googlies of anyone: 'I was so disappointed when he got such criticism from commentators who should have known better.'

On revolutions, Giff says he'd be up there as a left-arm spinner. Moeen Ali, who started at Warwickshire before moving to Worcestershire, 'spins the ball a lot' and has been not a bad successor for England since Graeme Swann retired.

Gifford's not so sure about four-day rather than three-day county matches, revealing his relatively ambitious captaincy technique: 'For three days a lot of thought had to go into it. If you batted first, you had to think about how to go at them overnight, not just bat until lunchtime on the second day. We never had that luxury in three-day cricket. There were always thoughts about moving the game on. I was keen on looking for a result. If you felt there were enough runs in the first innings you were brave enough to have half an hour bowling at them.'

At 82, he's retired: 'I'm happy to pop down to Worcester when I get half a day to watch the cricket and see some young kids play.' There are kids who he coached before Covid at Malvern College who he is still expecting to play first-class cricket.

He ends our chat by recalling a cricket tour to Barbados he hosted when a young lad asked if he knew how many overs he bowled in first-class cricket. 'He must have looked it up overnight because at breakfast he told me 128,000 balls, and 17,000 in one-day cricket. He did me proud but it made me feel even more knackered than I was. But if you're going to take 2,000 wickets, you're going to bowl a lot of overs.'

In 1983, Norman Gifford took 104 wickets at 23.00 in 22 first-class matches and 22 at 35.13 in 21 one-dayers with an economy rate of 4.98. In his career from 1960–88 (Worcestershire 1960–82, Warwickshire 1983–88) he took 2,068 wickets in 710 first-class games at 23.56 and 443 wickets in 397 one-dayers at 26.01.

He played for England from 1964–73 (15 Tests) and in two ODIs in 1985. He was later a coach for Durham and Sussex.

Warwickshire

Bob Willis (1949–2019): Surrey 1969–71, Warwickshire 1972–84, England 1971–84 (90 Tests, 64 ODIs). Played 308 first-class matches and took 899 wickets at 24.99 and 293 one-dayers with 421 wickets at 20.18. Took 11 wickets at 18.72 in the World Cup in 1983 with an economy rate of 2.79 and 20 wickets at 13.65 in four Tests v New Zealand as captain. In 1983 he took 21 Championship wickets at 36.76 plus 45 one-day wickets in all. Later a commentator.

Dennis Amiss: Warwickshire opener from 1960–87, England 1966–77 (50 Tests, 18 ODIs). Played 658 first-class matches with 43,423 runs at 42.86 and 404 one-dayers with 12,519 runs at 35.06. In 1983 he scored 1,571 Championship runs at 43.63 plus 590 in 23 one-dayers. Later Warwickshire chief executive.

David Smith: Warwickshire opener from 1973–85 playing 197 first-class matches with 8,734 runs at 27.55 and 108 one-dayers with 2,772 runs at 28.87. In 1983 he scored 1.133 Championship runs at 29.81 and 325 in 15 one-dayers. Brother Paul played for Warwickshire between 1982 and 96 and scored 335 runs and took 16 wickets in 11 Championship matches in 1983. David Smith was later chief executive at Leicestershire and Northamptonshire. He also ran a sandwich shop and worked in marketing.

Alvin Kallicharran: Warwickshire 1971–90, West Indies 1972–81 (66 Tests, 31 ODIs). Left-hander who played 505 first-class matches with 32,650 runs at 43.64 and in 383 one-dayers scored 11,336 runs at 34.66. In 1983 he scored

1,637 Championship runs at 54.56 and 626 in 22 one-dayers. Later a coach.

Andy Lloyd: Left-handed opener for Warwickshire from 1977–1992. England 1984 (one Test, three ODIs); 17,211 runs at 34.28 in 312 first-class matches and in 287 one-dayers scored 7.562 runs at 30.86. In 1983 he scored 1,659 Championship runs at 47.40 plus 512 in 19 one-dayers. Later a stud-farm manager.

Asif Din: Warwickshire 1981–94. Played 211 first-class games with 9,074 runs at 30.55 and in 256 one-dayers scored 5,943 runs at 31.11. In 1983 he scored 361 Championship runs at 22.56. Later worked for an outdoor leisure firm.

Geoff Humpage: Warwickshire wicketkeeper from 1974–90, England 1981 (three ODIs). Played 351 first-class games with 18,108 runs at 36.36 and took 672 catches/72 stumpings and in 324 one-dayers he scored 6,594 runs at 25.55 and took 249 catches and 32 stumpings. In 1983 he scored 1,003 Championship runs at 31.43 and took 23 catches and made five stumpings in first-class matches, plus 362 runs and 17/5 in one-dayers. Later a policeman.

Anton Ferreira: Warwickshire all-rounder from 1979–86. Played 245 first-class matches and scored 9,064 runs at 28.68 and took 583 wickets at 30.37. Played 230 one-dayers with 3,199 runs at 22.52 and 297 wickets at 25.24. In 1983 he took 39 wickets at 31.71 and scored 399 runs at 22.16 in 16 Championship games plus 195/21 in 19 one-dayers. Later a coach in South Africa.

Gladstone Small: Warwickshire 1979–99, England 1986–92 (17 Tests, 53 ODIs). Played 315 first-class matches with

852 wickets at 28.62 and 390 one-dayers with 462 wickets at 26.47. In 1983 took ten Championship wickets at 29.90. Later worked in corporate hospitality and as a speaker.

Willie Hogg: Lancashire 1976–80, Warwickshire 1981–83. Took 222 first-class wickets in 96 appearances at 28.99 and 91 wickets in 88 List A one-day games at 30.87. In 1983 he took 31 Championship wickets at 34.61 plus ten in one-dayers. Son Kyle played for Lancashire and father-in-law Sonny Ramadhin for West Indies.

Chris Old: Yorkshire 1966–82, Warwickshire 1983–85, England 1972–81 (46 Tests, 32 ODIs). Played 379 first-class games taking 1,070 wickets at 22.20 and 314 one-dayers taking 418 wickets at 20.86. In 1983 'Chilly' took 61 Championship wickets at 29.27 plus 15 in one-dayers. Later ran a restaurant in Cornwall and worked for Sainsbury's.

Chris Lethbridge: Warwickshire 1981–85. Played 50 first-class games with 77 wickets at 38.90 and 59 one-dayers with 59 wickets at 32.89. In 1983 he took six Championship and eight one-day wickets. Was a miner before becoming a professional cricketer; he later worked as a service engineer in a quarry.

Chapter 23

Worcestershire: Tim Curtis

A PROMISING start: 'I'd be very happy to talk with you. I might need to revisit my *Wisden*s to find a significant match about which to talk! Tim.'

In *Cricketers' Who's Who 1983* Curtis's view is that he is not convinced four-day county matches are a good idea because of the reduction in batting opportunities and the tendency to slow the game down even more. He thinks the reduction in overseas players was necessary and hopes the consequent reduction in crowd-pulling potential will be made up by a greater sense of county identity and loyalty and support.

I ring TC. He's as friendly as the email suggested. The mention of *Wisden* sounded hopeful. Curtis was an English teacher and director of sport at Royal Grammar School Worcester, where he was educated and was head boy and cricket (and rugby) captain. He retired from teaching in 2016.

When he was a pupil RGS was a state grammar school but between his leaving for university and returning as a teacher the school went independent. Education reorganisation in

Worcestershire took place in 1978 and the grammar school was going to lose its sixth form, so they went private. The head who came in used sports and particularly cricket to help attract pupils. This meant players such as Curtis, Phil Neale and Phil Newport, who is current master in charge of cricket there, ended up teaching the game.

Curtis had won a Cambridge Blue in 1983 after moving there to study following a degree at Durham. He'd been playing for Worcestershire since 1979, and didn't do that much in 1983, though he showed promise with a 74.14 average for the second team, which featured future international players Phil Newport, Richard Illingworth, Greg Matthews and Joey Benjamin.

His first really good year was 1984 when he hit his first hundred and he ended the summer with 1,405 runs at 42.57 – the first of 11 seasons he was to pass 1,000.

But 1983 saw Worcestershire's young players progress and hint at promise for the future, although they won just two Championship games out of 24. Illingworth, Newport and Curtis were emerging, as was future England coach Peter Moores and New Zealand all-rounder Dipak Patel. Graeme Hick was in the Zimbabwe World Cup squad and arrived at New Road still aged 17 in 1984, as did David Smith, who had no future at Surrey after a falling-out with them in 1983. Neal Radford and Steve Rhodes were both signed for 1985 and Ian Botham for 1987. Most were fringe internationals, so were county regulars, the perfect formula for domestic success.

Worcestershire won the Championship in 1988 and 1989 (Curtis played for England in both years) and the Sunday Refuge Assurance League in 1987 and 1988. There was also the B&H and Sunday League in 1991 and 1994 NatWest Trophy, after Curtis became captain in 1992. He made five Lord's final appearances, winning twice.

Curtis has the *Wisden* 1983 in his hand. He's looked up the Cambridge against Worcestershire game, when he scored just eight and five. But was something brewing at Worcester in the early 1980s? 'Sports teams talk in terms of half-lives, a bit like radioactive substances and decay and Worcestershire were decaying around the end of the 1970s and beginning of the 1980s, with players coming to the end of their careers.'

In Curtis's *Wisden* he finds a game where he played against Lancashire in 1983. Alan Ormrod saw them home with 72 not out in the second innings and TC scored 32 and 27. It was effectively Ormrod's place Curtis took in 1984. Ormrod retired, Patel emigrated, Ted Hemsley and Basil D'Oliveira had come to the end of their time. There was a good crop of young players coming through. There's a parallel with the seconds. Before Worcestershire won the County Championship in 1964 and 1965 they won the second XI Championship in 1962 and 1963. Curtis remembers the same happened in the mid-to-late 1980s. In fact, though he averaged 74, they were eighth in the second XI Championship in 1983 (having won in 1982) and third in 1984 with Hick and Newport leading the batting and bowling respectively. In 1985 and 1986 they were tenth and eighth as the second-team stars graduated and the first XI improved to finish fifth in both years.

Curtis says: 'We recruited Richard Illingworth, Newport, Steve Rhodes and the crucial fact of all was that Hicky appeared in 1984 and he was the one that really galvanised the whole successful period that we then went on to have. None had massive Test match careers but the fact that they played suggest they were at the top end of the county game and then we added a bit of gilding when Both and Graham Dilley arrived as well.'

In 1983 Younis Ahmed was sacked early on after being accused of breaking betting rules. The Pakistan batsman explained in his autobiography that it was a 'joke that backfired' and a 'sad misunderstanding'. Curtis says: 'It was at a time when we never thought of betting in cricket but obviously subsequent events have shown that it was probably there all along and was about to make quite a significant appearance across world sport in general.'

The run machine at the county for a decade or more had been New Zealander Glenn Turner: 'He was amazing to watch. I remember one year when I came back from Durham University, and I think I played four matches towards the end of the season which was characteristic of what would happen. If things weren't going particularly well, then Worcestershire would bring in some younger players. In two of those matches Glenn got a hundred in both innings and I barely got to the crease batting at six. But watching him play was an influence on me, seeing how he would completely dominate county cricket. He'd become the most remarkable player at that stage in his career and he was really quite dismissive of bowlers. His departure in 1982 [after debuting in 1967] was a signal of a team that was very much changing.'

Australia fast bowler Terry Alderman, a hero of the 1981 Ashes series with 42 wickets, was due to play for Worcestershire in 1983, but he dislocated his shoulder tackling teenage English expat pitch invader Gary Donnison in the Ashes match at the WACA in November 1982.

West Indian Collis King only played a few games as he had a Lancashire League contract, so the Pears managed without overseas help between Turner and Hartley Alleyne, who'd also left after 1982, and Graeme Hick in 1984. Hick then spent seven years qualifying by residence to play for England, averaging between 50 and 90 in each season from 1985–90, helping win all those late 1980s titles. On King's stint at the county, Curtis says: 'I imagine that purse strings were probably tight and we grabbed him when we could.'

Tellingly, without overseas professional spearheads, Yorkshire and Worcestershire were bottom and second bottom of the Championship: 'They were much more significant, absolutely. The international calendar has changed so much. The thought back then that other countries would put on international fixtures during England's cricket season just seemed totally alien.

'It's been a concern of mine with promotion and relegation. You might have a couple of good overseas players for a season and the next season you might not have them so there isn't that sense of a team getting promoted because they are a good team, but because they are benefitting from the performances of individuals. You knew then that if you were playing Hampshire, you're playing Malcolm Marshall and Gordon Greenidge, and Somerset it was Joel Garner and Viv Richards. It was very much more of a pattern.'

At the start of his career varsity cricket felt competitive. Oxbridge sides could make a decent effort with the bat, though he was conscious it was a struggle to bowl county sides out.

'The plan had always been that my parents weren't happy for me to go into professional sport with nothing behind me, so I was always going to go to university.' He did his degree at Durham and teaching qualification at Cambridge and is now president of The Quidnuncs, the former Cambridge cricket Blues society (fellow Magdalene College student and university team captain Steve Henderson, who played for Worcestershire 1977–81 and Glamorgan from 1983–85, is on the committee and is immediate past president).

Talking to current men and women players, they recognise they are not first-class cricketers and Cambridge is not worthy of first-class status. Curtis says: 'It's an inevitable consequence of how universities have changed and what students are required to do and the pre-eminence of academia, I suppose. It's a shame. You still get some people who can combine the two successfully. From my point of view it's absolutely right that university cricket is no longer first-class. But that doesn't mean it can't be a pathway for players to come through.'

But he warns: 'My understanding is the pressures for players to develop as professionals mean a number of players are choosing not to go to university and to go straight into professional cricket, even with the MCCU setups that offered a channel which some people certainly took. Joe Leach is very successful at Worcestershire now and he was at Leeds MCCU. Fewer people are taking that route. Do I think that's a shame? Yes, I'd always say it's great if you've got university behind you because it's such an education in life and means you have something else to fall back on if the cricket doesn't work out.'

Ed Pollock was at RGS Worcester for five years and although he wasn't outstanding at school is now a pro at Worcestershire. His father is Angus Pollock, a team-mate of Curtis's from Cambridge in 1983 and brother Ali was an RGS pupil and Cambridge Blue (and Quidnuncs treasurer) too. Tim's son Andrew was in the same team as Ed and was a star batsman but didn't kick on as Ed did. Neil Pinner was on Worcestershire's staff too but didn't make the runs to stay around for more than three years. 'Only a small percentage go on to make it professionally, either because of desire or because of ability,' says Curtis.

He was Professional Cricketers' Association chairman from 1989–96, following Geoff Cook (1984–89) and Chris Balderstone (1980–84). As PCA chairman, he had to get time off from school for winter meetings in the grand setting of the Liberal Club off Pall Mall with Lawrie Doffman and Harold Goldblatt, a lawyer and an accountant, who were 'incredibly far-seeing, because one of their ideas was to set up funding for cricketers who had fallen on hard times and needed help for medical treatment after they had finished playing'.

There was a sense of being 'at loggerheads' with the TCCB, trying to make a case for the PCA to have a decision-making place at cricket's top table: 'We were very much cast as the trade union that was on the outside that should be kept in its place. I look at it now as a commercial organisation and the clout that it carries is absolutely massive and they do really good things looking after players during the off-season, helping their career development when they've finished, and also through the Players Benevolent Fund. We fought some of those early battles to try and get ourselves established.'

One of Curtis's successors, Richard Bevan, who was at the PCA from 1996–2007, changed it from a body with no employees to one with 20 and helped the ECB develop central contracts before becoming the (football) League Managers Association CEO. 'He opened our eyes in terms of what was possible,' Curtis explained.'

'In 1988 we played 28 days on the trot, seven three-day matches with seven Sunday League matches in between through August. It was full-on, and three-day cricket tended to be a bit unsatisfactory. It went through a formula. The side batting first got 300-350 in 100 overs, declared half an hour before the end of the first day's play, then the other team got something similar, then you worked out a declaration on the third and fourth innings. Unless you got a pitch where there was a really good balance between bat and ball, a lot of three-day cricket was a bit contrived. I was an advocate of four-day cricket but in some ways it's gone the other way because if you play four-day cricket in April on pitches that were a bit juicy, then matches were over in two days. Not only have you got fewer fixtures going on but you've also got far less cricket for people to watch and I think that's a bit sad. Getting the pitches right is so important.

'In the 1960s the flooding at New Road was responsible for the pitches being bouncy with the natural deposits creating a good top surface. It was definitely slow and low through the early 1980s. We then got a decent side together and used to talk about quadrilateral movement at Worcester because it moved not just side to side but up and down because the surface was quite cracked and the grass was tufty. It wasn't a great surface but when you've got Dill and Radders and Beefy and Phil Newport and Hicky, who could bat on any surface and score all the runs, you always had a chance.'

Curtis had a sticky career for England. In contrast, to bat for them in the Bazball era you need to blast it. 'I'd have loved to have played as an amateur. Wouldn't that have been great not to have to pay our mortgage on the basis of your contract? Those sort of thoughts, consciously or subconsciously, tend to dominate. I'm a safety-first person in life. You see me on a golf course or any sport. Would I have adapted? I adapted to Sunday League cricket and one-day cricket. I remember we played Surrey in 1994 and got almost 360 [357] and Tom Moody got 180 and I got 137 [adding a record 309 for the third wicket] and I played a fine lap off Adam Hollioake to the short boundary down to the pavilion at The Oval and that shot hadn't really been played a great deal at that point.

'So I hold that close to my heart as an example that maybe I could have adapted. But could I have become the power hitter and had the mentality to keep striking it ball after ball? The mantra for us in those days was if you get a boundary, make sure you get one off the next ball, rotate the strike, don't get out after you hit a boundary as it gave the initiative back to the opposition. The mentality nowadays is totally different.'

The dressing room back then was split into two at Worcester, upstairs and downstairs, junior and senior. 'My wife used to be appalled when I'd come back and my clothes would stink of cigarette smoke. It was a fuggy, sweaty place. If I got out cheaply, I could sit and swear quietly to myself for a while until the world returned to normal a bit and people would know to leave me alone.

'It was a place that felt clubby because it was just you and these guys who you shared a shower with, shared a changing room with and shared ups and downs with. It had an intimacy about it, but I think ours was reasonably harmonious.'

Bookmaking was closer to the mark than reading books in the dressing room, says the former English teacher. One book would last a summer as he was emotionally caught up in the cricket and could not concentrate on reading. He remembers reading Gabriel Garcia Marquez's *Love in the Time of Cholera*: 'I sometimes think I just chose books because they had funky-sounding titles. I think I would have been one of the less-well-read English students.'

The camaraderie remains: 'I remember Giffy with his pipe. I saw him the other day and he asked me who my first first-class wicket was. I worked out it was Neil Mallender in 1982 at Stourbridge against Northamptonshire. I dropped a catch that game off Giffy at short fine leg off Ned Larkins and then Larkins hit Giffy out of the ground for two big sixes and then got out and I went up to Giffy and said, "I'm glad my dropped catch didn't cost too much," and he wasn't terribly impressed. Giffy was very much part of my initial impressions that a dressing room was full of older, wiser cricketers.'

In his first Test, in July 1988 against West Indies, as one of seven new faces under new captain Chris Cowdrey, Curtis lasted an hour and a half in each innings against Marshall, Ambrose, Walsh and Winston Benjamin. He dug in even longer in the last Test of the series, but England lost again, to go down 4-0. But in the next summer's series, against Australia, he began doggedly but kept getting out to Terry Alderman and was dropped for good, aged 29.

'I'm chuffed to have played for England but I found it very difficult to be recorded and analysed. I wasn't terribly successful. I got 40-odd in one game and at the other end of the scale at Trent Bridge we didn't take a wicket all day and Geoff Marsh and Mark Taylor got big hundreds, despite the fact that the first ball Devon Malcolm bowled to Geoff Marsh was plumb lbw and wasn't given out. I got 0 and 1 in that Test.

'It was lovely to get a few in that one game and I took a couple of decent catches and when I hit Marshall for consecutive fours at The Oval you can imagine the crowd went berserk. I was in great form but I was picked when I'd scored runs in one-day cricket and it was like that then. People popped in and out according to whether they were scoring a few runs at the time. We had 26 players play in 1989 against Australia, the whole England setup was a mess. Central contracts came a bit after that and made a massive difference. If central contracts had been around before, I really believe they would have changed Graeme Hick's world, because he was a sensitive soul and he needed to be loved and a central contract would have given him the continuity rather than being chopped and changed. I was delighted to have played and would have loved to have done better. I wanted to sing the national anthem before we went out, but it wasn't like that then. You had to control your emotions and try and do your best.'

Taking early retirement from WRGS when his youngest left six or seven years ago means nowadays it's the 'life of Riley' watching cricket and playing golf. His garden looks immaculate.

Until Covid, he was travelling to all the places he might have travelled to when he played cricket but never enjoyed 'because all we saw was the inside of a hotel room or a cricket ground'.

Our chat comes to an end. 'I notice gardening is your sideline. I've just planted my first asparagus bed, which I should have done years ago.'

Worcestershire

Phil Neale: Worcestershire 1975–92. First-class matches 354 with 17,445 runs at 36.49 and 338 one-dayers with 7,253 runs at 30.22. Worcestershire captain from 1982, he was also a professional footballer. Scored 1,500 Championship runs in 23 matches in 1983 plus 451 in 18 one-dayers. Later a coach, then England operations manager from 2000–2020.

Martin Weston: Worcestershire 1979–93. Played 161 first-class games with 5.597 runs at 23.91 and 213 one-dayers with 3.476 runs at 22.28. In 1983 he scored 314 runs in 16 one-dayers and 823 runs in 19 Championship matches. He managed a car dealership and then health facilities and played football for England over-60s.

Alan Ormrod: Opened for Worcestershire from 1962–83, then Lancashire until 1985. Appeared in 500 first-class matches scoring 23,206 runs at 30.90 and 286 limited-overs games with 6,398 runs at 25.18. In 1983 he scored 883 runs in 23 Championship matches. He ran a flooring company then coached Lancashire and became director of cricket at Nottinghamshire.

Mark Scott: Worcestershire 1981–83. Played 32 first-class matches with 1,383 runs at 24.26 and 24 one-dayers with 392 runs at 16.33. In 1983 he scored 155 runs in five Championship matches. Later played for Sussex and Worcestershire seconds and became a coach.

Younis Ahmed: Worcestershire 1979–83. Appeared in two Championship matches in 1983, he played 460 first-class matches scoring 26,073 runs at 40.48 and 326 limited-overs matches with 8,297 runs at 29.52. Also played for Surrey and Glamorgan in England and in four Tests and two ODIs for Pakistan.

Tim Curtis: Worcestershire 1979–93 and England 1988–89 (five Tests). The opener played 339 first-class matches, scoring 20,832 runs at 40.68, and 304 one-dayers for 10,280 runs at 39.69. In 1983 he scored 880 first-class runs at 27.50 in 19 first-class games for Cambridge University and Worcestershire and 86 in eight one-dayers at 14.33. He hit 75 in the drawn 1983 varsity match. Later, he was a teacher.

Damian D'Oliveira (1960–2014): Worcestershire 1982–95. Son of England and Worcestershire cricketer Basil and father of Worcestershire's Brett, he played 234 first-class matches with 9,504 runs at 27.62 and 265 one-dayers with 4,822 runs at 22.96. Scored 775 Championship runs in 19 matches and 283 in 17 one-dayers. Later a coach.

Dipak Patel: Worcestershire 1976–86, New Zealand 1987–97. He played 358 first-class matches with 15,188 runs at 29.95 and 347 one-dayers with 5,567 runs at 19.32 and took 654 first-class wickets at 33.23 and 250 one-day wickets at 32.99. In 1983 he took 45 Championship wickets and scored 1,537 runs in 23 matches plus 314 runs and 23 wickets in 18 one-dayers. Later a coach in New Zealand.

David Humphries (1953–2020): Leicestershire 1974–76, Worcestershire 1977–84. Played 175 first-class matches with 5,116 runs at 24.83 and 294 catches and 60 stumpings and 167 one-dayers with 1,639 runs at 14.25 and 138/35. In 1983 he scored 496 Championship runs at 21,56 and took 27 catches and made nine stumpings in first-class matches. Scored 192 runs and took nine catches/nine stumpings in one-dayers. He was later a member of Worcestershire Golf & Country Club. He died in 2020 aged 67 after a long illness.

Paul Pridgeon: Worcestershire 1972–89. Played 240 first-class matches and took 530 wickets at 32.76 and in 229 one-day matches he took 219 wickets at 32.65. In 1983 he took 59 Championship wickets at 28.59 and 72 first-class wickets in all, plus 16 in one-dayers. He was later a coach.

John Inchmore: Worcestershire 1973–86. Played 218 first-class matches with 510 wickets at 28.97 and 227 one-dayers with 278 wickets at 24.92. In 1983 he took 32 Championship wickets at 34.59 plus six in one-dayers. He later worked in financial management.

Alan Warner: Worcestershire 1982–84, Derbyshire 1985–96. Played 200 first-class games with 426 wickets at 31.45 and 227 one-dayers with 275 wickets at 27.81. In 1983 he took 21 Championship wickets at 23.85 in seven matches plus 17 in one-dayers. He played league cricket in the Midlands after leaving Derbyshire.

Chapter 24

Yorkshire: Simon Dennis and Geoff Boycott

I FOUND Simon Dennis on Twitter, the weekend after talking to Ole 'Stan' Mortensen. I followed him and he followed me back. I direct-messaged a now familiar story about the album.

He's 62 now. After working in IT for nearly 30 years he just retired in 2022. Aged 31, it was hard to not take a full-time job when it was offered. He was always interested in computers and after a career outside the game has the perspective to offer insight into what has always been the most dramatic of county clubs, Yorkshire.

His uncles were Sir Leonard Hutton and Frank Dennis and his cousin is Richard Hutton. His father Geoff was instrumental in Scarborough becoming one of the best club teams in the country.

In 1969, a national club knockout competition was established, sponsored by *The Cricketer* magazine. In 1972, under Geoff Dennis's captaincy, Scarborough progressed all the way to Lord's to meet Brentham CC in the final. The trophy was brought back to North Yorkshire in style after a six-wicket win. In 1976, John Haig whisky became sponsors and in the seven years of the Haig Trophy, Scarborough were winners four times and semi-finalists once.

'Scarborough was the strongest club side in the country and Dad started that in 1960. He retired and I started playing the season after. My uncle Len was not that much of an influence because I didn't see that much of him. My cousin Richard Hutton I hero-worshipped a bit. He was in the Yorkshire side when I was young and I saw a lot of him, more than Uncle Len who I'd heard everything about. So Richard Hutton definitely had an influence, particularly as he was a bowler. I just wish a bit of Len's batting genius had rubbed off.

'People forget Frank Dennis. I never met him, but we spoke on the phone a bit when he moved to Christchurch. [Frank emigrated in 1948 to become a New Zealand fruit farmer and later a Canterbury cricket selector after playing 89 matches for Yorkshire from 1928 to 1933.] I was genetically linked to Frank but not to Len and he was a bowler more than a batter.'

The highest county membership in the land paid £185,000 in subs in 1983, making Yorkshire the richest club too.

At county level, under 51-year-old Ray Illingworth, Yorkshire were captained astutely. At the start of the season he felt Yorkshire were 'genuine challengers' for the Championship if Alan Ramage and Graham Stevenson could stay fit. Illingworth could read the game after a lifetime of cricket. But vice captain Neil Hartley had a back injury and was so out of form he requested to play in the seconds and the John Player League was so important that Illingworth rested Dennis from July's Championship game against Kent so he could be fresh for Sundays. But the Championship was another story.

Overseas players overwhelmed Yorkshire, taking 40 per cent of five-wicket analyses against them, and scoring 25 per cent of the half-centuries. The April 1982 club referendum had voted 4,493 to 537 in favour of only playing Yorkshire-born players. This did not change until 1992, when Sachin Tendulkar was contracted, after 25 seasons when overseas pros were employed without residential qualification at the other counties.

The White Roses won just one Championship match all year, at Southampton in June, thanks to Dennis and Stevenson reducing the home side to 29/4 before Arnie Sidebottom removed the last five batsmen for six runs. Even then Yorkshire took 163 overs to dismiss Hampshire, without World Cuppers Malcolm Marshall and Gordon Greenidge, second time around. Dennis this time shifted the tail, before the Tykes made 71 to win with three balls to spare, Boycott getting a red inker for 22. A bruised Illingworth, his tactical triumph in the Sunday League not respected by many members or committeemen, had already said he would retire at the end of the season.

Illy had been hit on the head by Essex's Norbert Phillip in a final Championship defeat. Bill Athey and Nick Taylor went too, disillusioned, as Chris Old had at the end of 1982. The final straw for Illy was Boycott's 347-ball first day 140 not out against Gloucestershire in mid-August.

His captain was at his wits' end trying to persuade Boycott to accelerate so Yorkshire could get a fourth bonus point. Yorkshire managed just 11 wickets, Dennis five of them, and lost, again. Boycs had scored a quicker 97 in the second innings. For the majority of Yorkshire fans, it wasn't his fault. He scored 163 and 141 in the next match, including 100 runs before lunch, under Hartley who had replaced Illy, a victim of fluid on the knee, as captain.

A brighter day was Yorkshire v Derbyshire at Bradford on 28 August 1983. I was there with my brother and Dad (2,394 paid £4,289 to get in plus members), in Marks & Spencer flared jeans, a Mr Tickle T-shirt, a parka and a Yorkshire bucket hat. My mum was at her widowed mother's bungalow in Baildon. We ate her parkin and salmon paste sandwiches out of old ice cream tubs and hunted autographs at the ramshackle Horton Park Avenue ground. Yorkshire were in a state of disrepair too, split by the traditional rows, for or against Boycott – but against the odds were vying for the Sunday League title.

'That match against Derbyshire when I hit Ole for six? I remember it very clearly,' says Dennis. 'That was probably the most important cricket shot in my batting career. Bill Athey had been involved in a car crash the night before with Martyn Moxon, and Martyn was not fit but we were a bit short so Bill said he'd play. But after the first shot he played he collapsed in a heap and we found he'd broken two ribs so he retired hurt.'

Derbyshire scored 168/7 off their 40 overs, Dennis 0-33 off eight. Yorkshire lost wickets in pursuit and Athey had to go back in with Neil Hartley as a runner, 'which is always chaos'. With 19 still needed, number ten Dennis came in after Michael Holding ripped out the middle order. He and Athey were the last hopes. Illy was number 11 and had barely scored a run all season.

They whittled them down until they needed four off the last over, bowled by Mortensen: 'I'd worked out they had mid-on and mid-off up for me but back for Bill so I thought that if the ball's up, I'll take a chance and go for it and it could run away for four or three and I got it a lot better than I expected and it went all the way. It surprised everyone in the ground, including me.

'It was really important because we were terrible in the Championship and at the bottom but in the Sunday League Ray organised us pretty well. I opened the bowling with Geoff Boycott in several games and some of the big players didn't like playing shots at Geoff because they were scared of him getting them out, so he'd bowl four overs for nothing in every game. It was the second-to-last game with Somerset breathing down our neck, it was a full house with an intense crowd and I remember they came on at the end and me and Neil Hartley had run off jumping and leaping and forgot about Bill with his two broken ribs. We had to go back and find him and get him off with all these people slapping him on the back and the head.'

Yorkshire beat Somerset to the title (and £13,000) after the final round of matches were washed out thanks to having five away wins against Somerset's three as the two sides were tied on 46 points. Their eight home games attracted 46,700 people as Yorkshire won its first trophy since 1969 after coming 16th in 1982.

Illingworth remembered how Somerset's Ian Botham wrote in *The Sun* that Yorkshire was a Mickey Mouse outfit. Botham was sent a telegram when Yorkshire won the title: 'Weather fine in Disneyland, wish u were here love Mickey Mouse.'

I tell Dennis a story about getting Boycs' autograph at Bradford when he asked me to carry his bags in return for the prized signature. 'I can empathise with that because I grew up in a cricketing family and I was dressing-room attendant at Scarborough from when I was 11 to when I was 15 or 16 and that was such a learning curve for me. I remember getting their coffee and putting the odd bet on, which you wouldn't be allowed to do now, so I know that feeling.

'When I got into Yorkshire seconds I had to give up my dressing-room job because it didn't seem the right thing to be making coffees for my team-mates!

'Bradford was an interesting dressing room because it was at the back and you had to walk through the other one to get to the balcony. It felt pretty unsafe and you were worried the balcony would collapse. It's all gone now.'

Back in 1980 at Weston-super-Mare, the then teenage Dennis made his debut: 'People always had the misconception back then that my first wicket was Sunil Gavaskar, but that was my second. It was a guy called Martin Olive [caught by Phil Carrick for seven] and I remember the cheer. My dad and his friend had travelled down from Scarborough overnight and they led the cheering. My second wicket was Gavaskar [for 14]. It was a long hop and Neil Hartley caught him at midwicket.

'There were big characters at Yorkshire and you had to be a big character too. The Yorkshire dressing room, in those days, just before the 'winter of discontent' as they called it, was a tough school and always a hard place but Boycott v Illingworth did not find its way into the dressing room. We had a really good team spirit. Even though we were bottom of the Championship we weren't as bad a side as that suggests. A few results could have gone our way. It was one season where nothing went our way in close games and if we'd won two or three games, we'd have been in the top half.

'Everyone had two overseas players and if we'd had Clive Rice and Richard Hadlee or Joel Garner and Viv Richards, we'd have been really up there. We were strapped by everyone having two world-class stars. But we were pretty close in the dressing room, and I have fond memories. Cricket in the 1980s were good days. The England Test players played a lot more for their counties. You'd expect to play against six or seven with international experience from England and overseas.'

Dennis played in South Africa in 1982/83: 'Orange Free State did me a lot of good. I went out with Neil Hartley. Neil was a bit older and was captain of the club and he handled me well, not over-bowling me. Mentor was probably the word.

'I remember when I played for Orange Free State against Eddie Barlow, and he nicked me a couple of times and didn't walk and I gloved him to short leg and didn't walk. We were in the bar on the second day and he said he wanted to talk to me outside, and he was quite a fiery character. He took me to the middle, took the covers off and said, "I've been watching you bowl. You've got a great future," and spent half an hour out there telling me about the game when I thought he took me outside for a telling-off.

'I came back in 1983 and Chris Old had gone to Warwickshire so there was a bit of an opening at Yorkshire and I managed to take it and keep my place. It was a breakthrough season.' He took 52 wickets in 20 Championship games and bowled 525 Championship overs, compared to 86 the year before.

Wisden said, 'Dennis displays real persistence. He has emerged as the best of the younger quicker bowlers. But relying on native-born players meant Yorkshire will continue to struggle.'

He was capped on 6 August that year, exactly three years on from his debut on 6 August 1980 at Weston. They were 'happy years'.

What about the ructions now as Yorkshire is blown apart by the Azeem Rafiq racism scandal? Dennis is reluctant to get involved: 'I don't think I should. It's a massive shame for cricket. It could have been handled in a better way. A lot of people involved have had their careers ruined. It shouldn't have happened. It should have been sorted in a different way. I won't say any more.'

He believes T20 is good for the game 'but we need to be careful' as 'a lot of finishes can be much the same with one side needing 30 off two and a half overs or something like that. Cricket is at the crossroads. Are we going to end up just playing T20?' He says losing 50-over cricket would be a shame as bowlers have more of a chance in a world of big bats and smaller boundaries. He wants to protect Tests by protecting four-day cricket and is not sure about The Hundred. 'It takes up prime cricket time in August, and there's no Test in August 2023, which is absolutely shocking.'

He added: 'British people like supporting counties, not the franchises. People like to see players coming through the system, not just who is available in the IPL bidding war.'

As well as formats, fitness has changed too since the 1980s: 'From a training point of view we didn't know anything about what to eat and drink. Bowlers did some running in the off-season and a few press-ups and sit-ups, then they just bowled. Seeing the number of fast bowlers injured now, I'm not sure our method was that bad. Some are overdoing it with gym work maybe.'

Then again, the travelling in the 1980s wasn't good for fitness: 'One weekend I played for the seconds at Dover on the Friday then drove to Leeds to play on the Saturday then off to Taunton for the Sunday. It was madness really, fitness-wise. It was a good lifestyle but by August you were pretty tired. You would always see tailenders get a few runs by then because the bowlers were tired. We'd play 24-25 days on the trot but no one moaned too much. You just got on with it. There was no social media and you weren't under that pressure like you are now.

'Fans, including me and my dad, used to go to the same Headingley pub after the match to see the players – The Original Oak. 'We were very limited in our knowledge, we always had a few beers after the game,' says Dennis. 'It was definitely not very good for us as we really needed to rehydrate for the next day. When you look back that must have been why we were so tired every morning, playing cricket all day then having three or four pints every night. But you always learnt a lot in the bar from other players. I suspect that doesn't go on now, though I'm not involved in cricket.'

Boycott would have a drink occasionally. 'He was very much his own person after the game. Probably the first to look after himself, he'd have ginseng tea and honey and things like that. When I started in our dressing room he was a very established international figure and he did his own thing. In his opinion if you scored runs, you were good for the side.'

His final story is also from 1983, again against Derbyshire at Abbeydale Park, Sheffield. The Championship game was on 22–24 June on 'not a very good wicket' which was reported as substandard because of its uneven bounce. Dennis came in at number 11, with Boycott: 'We still needed 60 and I managed to hang around until he got his hundred. It was one of the most disappointing things. We got to less than 20 needed and I started to think we might win it. That was a bad thought and Ole Mortensen had me caught at gully.' Derbyshire won by 22 runs, their first Championship victory since 1957 against Yorkshire.

But two months later, in the John Player Sunday League, Dennis's batting saw Yorkshire home to the title with the stricken Bill Athey earning his place in Yorkshire folklore.

In 1983, Simon Dennis took 52 first-class wickets at 30.76 with a best of 4-32 and scored 71 runs at 4.93 with a best of 17 in 20 first-class games. In List A matches, he scored 32 runs in 16 matches, with a best of 16 not out and took 12 wickets at 42.83 with an economy rate of 4.11.

Yorkshire v Derbyshire at Bradford 28 August 1983

Kim Barnett c Athey b Illingworth 29
Iain Anderson c Sidebottom b Carrick 40
Alan Hill b Carrick 5
Geoff Miller st Bairstow b Carrick 8
John Morris st Bairstow b Carrick 3
Roger Finney not out 41
Bill Fowler c Bairstow b Boycott 8
Paul Newman c Athey b Stevenson 6
Bernie Maher not out 13
Paul Newman, Michael Holding, Ole Mortensen DNB
Extras 15. Total: 168/7 (40 overs)
Bowling: Dennis 8-1-33-0; Boycott 6-0-32-1; Stevenson 6-0-28-1; Sidebottom 4-0-20-0; Illingworth 8-0-27-1; Carrick 8-1-13-4.

Yorkshire

Geoff Boycott c Maher b Mortensen 8
Bill Athey not out 21
Kevin Sharp run out 56
Neil Hartley c Miller b Mortensen 0
Jim Love c Maher b Miller 19
Graham Stevenson c Anderson b Miller 0
David Bairstow c Barnett b Holding 18
Phil Carrick b Holding 5
Arnie Sidebottom b Holding 5

Simon Dennis not out 16
Extras 23. Total: 171/9 (39.2 overs)
Bowling: Holding 8-0-25-3; Mortensen 7.2-0-39-2; Newman 8-3-16-0; Miller 8-0-34-2; Fowler 6-0-24-0; Finney 2-0-10-0.

Geoff Boycott

Mortifyingly, I had missed messages on my phone. One was from *Downton Abbey*'s Jim Carter. One was from my childhood hero Geoff Boycott: 'Hi, Geoff Boycott here. Ring me when you get this. I'll do what I can for you.'

A household name as much as Botham, Boycott's imprint had been on most things that happened in English cricket for almost 20 years by 1983, and indeed for 40 years after. From being England's most prolific batsman to endless controversies as a player and then for his archetypal blunt Yorkshire views as a commentator, Boycott was and is cricket to many people. I'd contacted him on Twitter, not really expecting to hear back. But at 82, he's still keen to express his views.

'Alright then, what do you want to know?'

Were Yorkshire judged unfairly for coming bottom of the Championship in 1983 for the first time, when they won the John Player League, a first trophy since 1969? 'Because of Yorkshire's history and tradition, we're always going to be judged on how we do in the Championship. We've won more Championships than anyone else and produced more players than anyone else. That's a fact. Some of the greatest players in the history of the game came from Yorkshire. And we did it playing proper cricket so we're going to be judged by that. We always are. It's never going to change, even now. We're in the second division and people are not happy – members, spectators because of the heritage, the tradition and the history.

'What I saw was spectators that were all thrilled to bits with us winning a trophy. A trophy is a trophy. Ask anybody. Ask Manchester United. Winning the League Cup is not the Championship, but it's a trophy. I know they were pleased about it.'

Founded in 1863, by 2023 Yorkshire has won a record 33 County Championships, were joint champions twice, plus five one-day trophies. Yorkshire has also produced more England players in history than any other county. There are 125,000 recreational players at 850 clubs and schools.

In 1983, bowlers Graham Stevenson, Arnie Sidebottom, Paul Jarvis and Alan Ramage were often injured. This left youngster Simon Dennis to step up. Were injuries the problem?

'No, we just weren't good enough,' says Boycott. 'We weren't a very good side to be brutally frank, but because of our history and tradition many older ex-players feel we have the right to be top of the Championship. They played and watched when Yorkshire were the best. But it's not always possible to find 11, 12, 13 players who come together at the right time.

'Nobody has a right, and these things come in cycles. Purely and simply, in one period you have enough good players around, or excellent players and one or two good players, and that's when you have a good side. From 1863, for 150 years were we always going to have the best players in the country? That's bloody nonsense. I try and talk sensibly. That's not going to happen in life. Manchester United is a great club and they had Matt Busby and Alex Ferguson but in between they had some shit times. Look at Chelsea. Look at Arsenal. Fortunes change and that's good for everybody. No one should be on top all the time.'And now it's going to be almost impossible because every time you produce top players they play for England and never play county cricket. Joe Root has 4,000 runs for Yorkshire and he's 30-odd. That's nothing. There's more internationals now, and one-dayers and tours in winter and they have to have rest. That didn't happen until 20 years ago. There were just five Tests and back to the County Championship. Now they play for England most of the time. Harry Brook, Jonny Bairstow and Root, you never see them. Yorkshire spend all that money and time having kids from 15 years of age through the academy, the second team and the first team and then they become ready for England, and you never see them again.

'They might turn up for a couple of games pre-season to get into nick for the internationals. So, it's going to be harder and harder for clubs like Yorkshire who keep producing good youngsters. I'll eat my hat if Finlay Bean doesn't play for England and he's only 21.

'You almost have to get a team with no internationals but that's not Yorkshire's way. We produce lots of youngsters because of our league cricket and we teach them the right way. Look at Surrey. They have those openers [Dominic Sibley and Rory Burns] who have played for England but are not quite good enough and one or two others who have had a game or two for England but aren't regulars. That's the best way if you want to win it but it's not the way of Yorkshire. But Yorkshire is still always going to be judged on Championship cricket.'

None of Yorkshire's Panini players had won anything before the 1983 JPL title, apart from Boycott and Illingworth, back in the 1960s. 'We didn't think we'd win the John Player League until after a few games. We kept winning. We lost one ten-over slog and another was rained off but we won the rest.

'My bowling was better than my batting. I just bowled a bit in the nets but Raymond Illingworth came in as captain and wanted options. He was right. In one-day cricket it doesn't matter how good you are because somewhere along the line someone is going to collar you. So you need a sixth and seventh bowler. By using me I somehow found a way to bowl around the wicket with my cap on, bowling inswing and to my field, drying up runs. That was the key. Not that I was any good. I wasn't. Getting people out was very difficult but that's what 40-over cricket is, stopping people scoring too many. I gave another option.'

Boycott conceded 4.44 runs per over in the JPL, less than, for instance, Derek Underwood (4.75). Boycott's bowling gave the team a rare reliable serenity amid the relentless friction of the overall season.

When we spoke, I've just come back from the Cheltenham festival, scene of some classic Yorkshire and Boycott dramas. In 1979 Mike Procter took a hat-trick of lbws in a match I was at. Boycs, spectating at the non-striker's end, went on to be lbw John Childs for 95. 'Procter was bowling big fast inswingers. Len Hutton said the good player was at the other end. We were 20/5 that night and they [the lbw victims] were all out!'

At Cheltenham, four years later, Boycott was reprimanded for slow scoring. Yorkshire drew and chaos ensued. Boycott was sacked at the end of the season, then reinstated after a winter of war in the committee room. Boycott wrote in his 1987 *The Autobiography*: 'The 1983 season may be remembered for two features as far as Yorkshire are concerned: we finished bottom of the Championship for the first (and hopefully only) time in our history; and Geoff Boycott was reported for scoring too slowly in a match against Gloucestershire at Cheltenham.'

He remembers all his innings. 'I made 140 *and* 97 in the second innings,' he reminds me. He also made 39 and bowled eight overs for 38 in the intervening Sunday League four-wicket win. The 97 was scored much faster than the 140 (375 mins, 347 balls with 262 balls to reach his century), which took all day as Yorkshire failed to get their fourth batting point, by one run.

Illingworth wrote: 'A lot has been written and spoken about Saturday 13 August, the day that broke the camel's back. That particular camel being me. Boycott in one of those moods.' Leo McKinstry's Boycott biography likened Yorkshire CCC's love of strife to that of Prime Minister Margaret Thatcher.

Boycott said because Yorkshire lost at Cheltenham by five wickets the bonus point didn't matter. He rejected suggestions that he refused Illy's instruction to hurry up. 'I went, as far as I recall, as quickly as I could.' He is critical of how Illy managed the reprimand and felt he was obsessed about getting rid of him.

From 1979, Illy was part of the rise of the manager along with Micky Stewart (Surrey), Ken Taylor at Nottinghamshire from 1977, David Brown at Warwickshire and Jack Bond at Lancashire. But only Illy went back to playing.

Don Mosey's book on Boycott says of Cheltenham 1983 that it was all about treading warily ahead of his testimonial in 1984, which had been granted in July 1983. After the 140 not out, 'all hell broke loose'. Illy offered to resign. That didn't happen. The (anti-Boycott) reformers showed righteous indignation.

'I didn't get scolded by anyone,' Boycott tells me. 'It was only after the match. No one has said anything. We were all flabbergasted. David Bairstow was driving me home and we heard it on the radio for the first time. Raymond Illingworth had told the committee and they were going to have a meeting. That was the other side of Raymond. He was a fine captain tactically, but we knew nothing, lad, nothing.'

After scoring 136 runs in nine innings (including just 53 in the Championship by the end of soggy May 1983) the summer bloomed for Boycs. Another run-scoring triumph was 163 and 140 not out at Bradford against Nottinghamshire on 20–23 August, in another draw. The 163 came the day after the Cheltenham affair. Boycott was heading to 1,941 Championship runs for the season, almost double the next best by a Yorkshire batsman and second most in the 1983 first-class season, behind only

Ken McEwan of champions Essex. His seven centuries were second most behind McEwan too. In 1984 Boycott was again Yorkshire leading scorer, though he took almost 1,200 overs to score 1,567 runs.

'Look, I was getting old, way past my best, but I could make runs. As Jack Hobbs said, he made a hundred hundreds after turning 40. I was a better player before I was 40, because of instinct, quickness, eyesight, everything is better when you're younger than when you're 40.

'I was a better player before, but I could still make runs and more than the others. It was a period when we didn't have enough good players. We had some wonderful lads and team-mates, but not enough talented players to be a great side.'

The real excitement of 1983 came a month after Cheltenham. On a wet and windy day at Chelmsford, hardly anyone changed into whites, and Yorkshire won the John Player League.

Perhaps the excitement of the first trophy in 14 years, perhaps the champagne, but Illingworth said he would continue as Yorkshire skipper, if they wanted him to. They didn't want.

'In the Championship we won only one match but lost only five,' Illy wrote defensively. 'The five losses were the same as Essex, who won the title and they included two declaration games … another half hour we might well have won them and shot up the table.'

Boycott says: 'Sunday League was a different format, not like the Championship when you had to take wickets. It was about denying others ways of scoring.

'We were very good at that with Phil Carrick and Raymond Illingworth. He wasn't in the Championship much because his finger was arthritic, so he tried not to bowl Saturday before a Sunday match once we were up there. He was still a very good player but after eight overs he wasn't fit to bowl the next day. He was 50-odd, for Christ's sake! We had young kids and were a good fielding side and we bowled to our field. It was different to the Championship where you had to bowl people out.'

Boycott was banned by England after the 1981/82 rebel tour to South Africa, but he thinks his 108-Test England career would have been over by 1983 even if he had been available. England picked Graeme Fowler, Chris Tavare and Chris Smith instead: 'In 1983 I was 43 so they were not going to pick me. If I hadn't been banned, I don't think it would have mattered. I think they'd decided to move on and try and find others.

'Could I have made runs? That's a different matter! I think I would have made some, but I couldn't have scored as quickly as I would have done years before. You can't run as fast when you're 43 as when you're 26 or 28. Usain Bolt can't run as fast now as when he won Olympic gold medals. It's a fact of life. It's a shame but it happens to everyone.'

He says the game is different today. 'The IPL more than anything is the biggest influence on the game now. It's made India the powerhouse of cricket. They get £1bn a year TV revenue and that's without Test cricket. No one else is anywhere near what they get. They have the biggest number of people to watch compared to other nations. They have 1.4 billion people who are nuts on cricket.

'Look what's happened to football with Sky and other money rolling in; it's gone crazy, the Premier League. It's way above any other league in the world. It's like rolling stones downhill, the TV money is a rolling stone and the game has gone on from there.'

In 1983 there was warfare in the committee rooms of Yorkshire as they fought over whether to sack Boycott and move onto younger players. There was a £76,000 surplus in 1983, reduced to £48,000 by the costs of the special general meeting, which ultimately led to Boycott's reinstatement and another three years at the county. And there was fighting in 2023 too, this time over the Azeem Rafiq racism scandal.

In 2023 the Independent Commission for Equity in Cricket report commissioned by the ECB found that the game is institutionally racist, sexist and classist. There has never been a women's Test at Lord's. Women players should be paid the same as men. The elitist Eton v Harrow at Lord's must end. Non-whites are hugely unrepresented in professional cricket.

'It was not just in 1983,' says Boycott. 'There's always been strife, trouble at mill. In 1896/97 there was the Bobby Peel scandal at Bramall Lane, the great player who bowled Australia out for England at The Oval. Go on a few years and there's some amazing things. Ellis Robinson was due a benefit and was sacked and went to Somerset.

'The sacking of Johnny Wardle. He'd been picked to tour Australia for England but Yorkshire wouldn't give him a contract. After that, Raymond Illingworth. We never had contracts but in 1968 Raymond Illingworth asked for a contract and the committee didn't want to do it. They had always had lots of players so said you can fuck off if you want.

'They sacked Brian Close, who was a successful captain, but they had the crackpot idea he was not doing as well as Lancashire at one-dayers. They were always sacking me.

'You seem to know your cricket. You'll know there were so many issues. There was always bloody trouble at mill. It's not just me. It's always been the same. Now they're in trouble over racism, and whichever way you look at it, they handled it badly, but that seems to be Yorkshire County Cricket Club. We just make a mess of it. I don't know how the hell we ever win owt, but we do. But it's been good fun. Now, is that enough? I've got to write my *Telegraph* report about the Ashes going down the drain.'

The final day of the fourth Ashes test was washed out when England had been in a dominant position to bring the series back to 2-2. The next week, at The Oval, Root, Brook and Bairstow batted England into a winning position in The Oval (fifth) Ashes Test.

On 28 July, midway through that match, Yorkshire were docked 48 points from the 2023 County Championship and four from the Vitality Blast and fined £400,000 (with £300,000 suspended for two years), for their handling of the Azeem Rafiq racism scandal.

Yorkshire

Ray Illingworth (1932–2021): England all-rounder (1958–73 61 Tests, three ODIs). Yorkshire 1951–68 and 1982–83 and Leicestershire 1969–78. In 1983, took 32 Championship wickets at 29.71 and 25 List A wickets at 14.92 to top the averages for those who took over 20 wickets. In his career, he took 2,072 first-class wickets at 20.27 and scored 24,134 runs at 28.06 in 787 matches and 186 one-day wickets at 25.19 in 218 matches with 2,380 runs at 26.74. Worked in the media from 1984 and then became England coach and chairman of selectors. Awarded a CBE in 1973.

Geoffrey Boycott: England opening batsman who since his career (1962–86) ended has been an outspoken media commentator and is a former Yorkshire president. In 1983, he scored 1,941 Championship runs at 55.45 in 23 matches (with seven centuries) and also carried his bat in two Sunday League wins as well as taking 3-15 in a victory against Middlesex, who had 11 Test players in the team. In 18 List A matches in 1983 he scored 421 runs at 28.06 and took five wickets at 34.60 at 3.26 an over, bowling 318 balls in all. In 1984, his contract renewed, he scored 1,567 runs at 62.68, though critics pointed out that took 1,187 overs. In his career he played 108 Tests between 1964 and 82 and 36 ODIs. Played 609 first-class matches with 48,426 runs at 56.83 and 10,095 in 313 one-dayers at 39.12. His 1984 testimonial year raised £147,954, with his 1974 benefit having raised £20,639. Knighted in 2019.

Richard Lumb: Opening batsman for Yorkshire from 1969–84. Played 245 first-class matches with 11,723 runs at 31.17 and 137 one-dayers with 2,784 runs at 25.30. In 1983 he scored 328 Championship runs at 23.42. Father of England batsman Michael. Has run his own coaching business in South Africa. His 1983 benefit raised £52,000.

Bill Athey: Yorkshire 1976–83, moved to Gloucestershire in 1984 and Sussex in 1993, staying until 1997. England 1980–88 (23 Tests, 31 ODIs). In 1983 he scored 758 Championship runs at 24.45 plus 596 in 19 one-dayers. Played 467 first-class matches with 25,453 runs at 35.69 and 459 one-dayers with 13,240 runs at 33.86. Later a coach at Dulwich College.

Jim Love: Yorkshire 1975–89, England 1981 (three ODIs). In 1983 he scored 1,020 Championship runs at 32.90 plus 298 in 15 one-dayers. In 250 first-class matches he scored 10,355 runs at 31.09 and in 238 one-dayers hit 4,962 runs at 26.67. Became Scotland's director of cricket before running a pub and was later regional manager for the Cricket Foundation.

Neil Hartley: Yorkshire 1978–89. A middle order batsman who scored 4,667 first-class runs at 24.95 in 142 matches and 2,859 one-day runs at 22.87 in 173 games. In 1883, he scored 261 runs at 14.50 plus 341 in 19 one-dayers. Went into insurance. Has also been chairman of the Yorkshire CCC Players' Association.

Martyn Moxon: Yorkshire 1980–97, England 1986–89 (ten Tests, eight ODIs). Opening batsman who played 317 first-class matches, scoring 21,161 runs at 42.83, and in 256 one-dayers he scored 7,813 runs at 34.41. In 1983 he scored 780 runs at 33.91 in 12 Championship matches. Became director of coaching at Yorkshire before coaching Durham, then he returned to Headingley as director of cricket.

Kevin Sharp: Yorkshire 1976-90. Played 218 first-class matches scoring 9,962 runs at 30.84 and 217 one-dayers with 5,049 runs at 27.44. In 1983 he scored 597 runs in 12 Championship matches at 29.85 plus 398 in 18 one-dayers. Was Yorkshire's batting coach and has also coached Shropshire and Worcestershire.

David Bairstow (1951–98): Yorkshire wicketkeeper-batsman from 1970–90. England (1979–84, four Tests, 21 ODIs). Played 459 first-class matches with 13,961 runs at 26.44 and 961 catches/138 stumpings and 429 one-dayers with 5,439 runs at 20.68 and 411/36. In 1983 'Bluey' scored 1,102 Championship runs at 38.00 and took 47 catches and made eight stumpings in first-class matches plus 145 and 11 catches/eight stumpings in 19 one-dayers. Father of England player Jonny Bairstow and former Derbyshire player Andrew.

Graham Stevenson (1955–2014): Yorkshire 1973–86, Northamptonshire 1987. England 1980–81 (two Tests, four ODIs). In 1983 he took 56 wickets at 25.00 in the Championship plus 18 in one-dayers. Took 488 wickets in 188 first-class matches at 28.84 and scored 3,965 runs at 20.33 and 307 in 225 one-dayers at 23.07 with 1,794 runs at 13.00. Worked as a scaffolder, milkman and bailiff.

Arnie Sidebottom: Yorkshire 1973–91, England 1985 (one Test). Played 228 first-class matches with 596 wickets at 24.42 and scored 4,508 runs at 22.42. In 240 one-dayers he took 264 wickets at 26.65 and scored 1,304 runs at 14.98. In 1983 he took 39 Championship wickets at 27.69 plus 17 in one-dayers and scored 490 runs at 35.00. Father of England bowler Ryan, Arnie played football for Manchester United and Huddersfield. Later a coach in Yorkshire.

Phil Carrick (1952–2000): SLA. Yorkshire 1979–93. In 1983 'Fergie' took 62 Championship wickets at 28.2 plus 13 in one-dayers and scored 697 runs at 29.04. In 444 first-class matches he scored 10,300 runs at 22.00 and took 1,081 wickets at 29.82. In 311 one-dayers he scored 2,188 runs at 14.88 and took 249 wickets at 30.67. Led Yorkshire to a Benson & Hedges Cup win in 1987, by losing fewer wickets in the final against Northamptonshire. Paul Jarvis (4-43) removed Geoff Cook, Carrick took 0-30 from ten overs and scored ten in six balls as Jim Love's 75 not out saw the Tykes home in the season after Boycott left. Became an umpire before dying of leukaemia in January 2000.

Chapter 25

Faces for the Future: New Song

Colin Cook played 11 first-class matches in his career with none for Middlesex in the Championship in 1983. He is Bill Athey's brother-in-law and was later a coach in Australia.

Nigel Felton played for Somerset from 1982–88 and Northamptonshire from 1989–94, scoring 10.242 runs at 30.12 in 211 first-class games and also playing 160 List A games. He was Northamptonshire's commercial director from 1999–2002. In 1983 the opener scored 376 runs at 34.18 in seven Championship games including 173 not out against Kent at Taunton in an end-of-season draw.

Neil Foster played 29 Tests and 48 ODIs for England from 1983–93. He won the Championship five times with Essex (1983, 84, 86, 91, 92). He took 52 first-class wickets at 23.38 in 1983 plus 13 in one-dayers. The opening bowler debuted for England in the 1983 Lord's Test against New Zealand (taking 0-40 and 1-35). In all he took 908 first-class wickets at 24.44 including 51 at 22.37 in the 1983 Championship success. He also played 215 one-dayers, taking 292 wickets at 24.41. He toured South Africa in

1989 but returned to England after a ban in 1993, retiring that year to become a physio.

Richard Illingworth took Norman Gifford's place at Worcestershire as a slow left-armer and went on to play nine Tests and 25 ODIs between 1991 and 96 and took 831 first-class wickets at 31.54 and 412 at 27.08 in 381 one-dayers during his career. He became an umpire, and had stood in 188 internationals by 2023. In 1983 he took 41 first-class wickets at 40.97 plus 18 in one-dayers.

Paul Jarvis opened the bowling for Yorkshire until 1993 then joined Sussex (1994–98) and Somerset (1999–2003). He played nine Tests and 16 ODIs (1988–93) before touring South Africa in 1989. In 1983 he took three first-class wickets in two games. Overall, he took 654 first-class wickets at 28.92 and 399 at 24.22 in 276 one-dayers. He then worked in the player agent market, coaching and in property development.

Hugh Morris opened for Glamorgan from 1981–97, scoring 19,785 first-class runs in all plus 8,606 in 274 one-dayers at 35.85. He played three Tests in 1991 and was Glamorgan captain from 1986–89. In 1983 he scored 228 runs at 20.72 in seven Championship games. He was later the ECB's chief executive officer and CEO and cricket director at Glamorgan.

Chris Penn played 128 first-class games for Kent from 1982–94. The seamer took 296 first-class wickets at 33.24. He played 99 one-dayers taking 104 wickets at 31.88. He was later a PE teacher and bowling coach for the ECB and Kent. In 1983 he took two first-class wickets in two matches.

Tony Wright opened for Gloucestershire from 1980–98, scoring 13,440 runs at 28.84 in 287 first-class games. He also played 284 List A games with 7,216 runs at 28.85. He scored 354 Championship runs in nine matches in 1983. He became Gloucestershire Academy director in 2002.

Roger Finney was a Derbyshire all-rounder between 1982 and 88 and in 1983 played 20 first-class matches with 30 wickets and 578 runs, plus 241 runs and ten wickets in 15 one-dayers.

Paul Johnson was a Nottinghamshire batsman from 1982–2002 and later Nottinghamshire, ECB, Canada and Leicestershire coach, In 1983 he played 15 Championship matches with 524 runs and nine one-dayers with 125 runs.

Robert Leiper played two first-class games for Essex in 1981–82; all-rounder (and Geordie rebel)'

Paul Smith was with Warwickshire from 1982–96, played 221 first-class games and 270 List A matches with 11 Championship games in 1983, scoring 335 runs at 30.45 and taking 16 wickets at 39.2. He played in six Lord's one-day finals and two Championship-winning teams.

Roger Watson played two first-class matches for Lancashire from 1982–85.

Jack Russell we know about.

Chapter 26

Conclusion: Everything Counts

CRICKET HAS been transformed since 1983, which was a pivotal season for the game. The players interviewed have shed light on the differences between then and now. The game continually seeks to reinvent itself.

In 1983, *Wisden* proposed a two-division Championship (with an 18th county) and complained about pressure on umpires (which might be fixed by TV technology, suggested Sir Donald Bradman), bouncers, too much appealing, a lack of spinners, lack of state-school cricket (though there were 45 pages on the boys' public school game) and contrived finishes. Boycotting South Africa was an issue, as was sponsorship and overseas players. By 2023, some of this has been addressed through better technology, a greater media emphasis on women's cricket, race and class in the game, and changes in format.

The thread running through these interviews is that the players mostly had happy memories and would not have missed it for the world. They are reaching retirement age and have time to reflect on their halcyon days. Some have sadder memories, of injuries, premature ends to careers, being overlooked. Most have remained connected to the game, as coaches, writers, broadcasters, administrators, umpires and in figurehead roles. Hardly any play anymore.

Many say developments such as short-form cricket have been good for the game. Others rue the decline in popularity of longer formats. But women's cricket, diversity and more exciting white ball games are boons for many.

In 1983, England beat New Zealand 3-1 in four Tests (a first win for NZ in England) but on tour in 1983/84 lost three-match series 1-0 to both New Zealand and Pakistan 1-0. England lost 39 out of 105 Tests in the 1980s.

County champions were Essex (won £14,000); NatWest Trophy: Somerset; Benson & Hedges Cup: Middlesex; Sunday League: Yorkshire.

The Championship increased from 22 to 24 matches. It's now back to 14. There were 16 points for a Championship victory, while the first innings bonus points available were four each. The required over rate was 19 per hour or 100 a day (in 2023 it was 16 an hour) with Tests at 96. Now it's 15 an hour in Tests, and in The Hundred, 100 balls in 65 minutes or for T20, 20 overs in 85 minutes.

India, 66/1 outsiders, won the World Cup, beating West Indies.

Cricket is getting shorter: T20 and The Hundred have replaced the John Player Sunday League and Benson & Hedges Cup.

The best overseas players, and some of the home ones, will not be available to play in England because of international T20 contracts.

CONCLUSION: EVERYTHING COUNTS

The Championship has reduced from 24 three-day games to 14 four-dayers. This means less travelling, one of the biggest bugbears of the players in 1983, but also means less use of out-grounds and opportunities for members to watch the stars. The Strauss report unearthed strong opposition to further reduction in the county game. But The Hundred has frayed the edges of the traditional 17–18 team formats.

Minor counties, universities and second XIs have less prominence and fewer opportunities to play against the best.

Central contracts mean England players rarely play for their counties, but they earn a lot more and are injured less.

Mark Wood, injury-prone and aged 33, did not play for his county, Durham, in 2023. He played three Ashes Tests in July, taking 15 wickets in 526 balls (87.4 overs) and bowling at 96mph. He did appear in the IPL for Super Giants four times in April though, taking 11 wickets in 96 balls. England's fastest bowler in 1983, the 33-year-old injury-prone Bob Willis, played 24 one-day and 20 first-class matches in the English season. He bowled 1,249 List A balls, taking 45 wickets at 16.24 and 2,261 first-class balls (585 overs in all), taking 41 wickets at 25.80. Wood made his first-class debut in 2011 and in 12 years had played fewer than Willis's 44 county first-class matches from 1980–83 outside Tests (72 first-class matches including 31 Tests) by September 2023.

Pay has risen hugely for top players thanks to globalisation and competition from satellite TV. A player might have earned £9,000 a year as an average county salary in 1983 (Graham Monkhouse negotiated £11,500 a year at Surrey in 1986) and around £8,500 to tour with England. Benefits after ten years' capped service for a county could be £40,000 tax-free. The average national salary in 1983 was £8,500 (in 2023 it was £29,500). In 2023, England contracts are worth up to £900,000. White ball contracts are worth £250,000–£350,000. Players also get a county salary, £14,500 per Test (£1,500 in 1983, up from £210 in 1977).

In 1977 a five-year £1m Cornhill Insurance sponsorship deal helped to stop players leaving for Australian media magnate Kerry Packer's lucrative breakaway World Series cricket competition, which ran from 1977–79. In 2023 players also got £4,500 per white ball international appearance and any IPL money they can earn. There were 18 full contract holders, including Wood, plus six incremental and six pace bowling development contracts, including Olly Stone, who played two Championship games and bowled one ball in a T20 in 2023. Wood was bought for the IPL for around £735,000. Ben Stokes was bought for £1.6m. County salaries could be a basic £30,000 plus £500–£1,200 match fee and performance bonuses. The county salary cap is £2m, rising to £2.5m in 2024.

In 1983, the BBC showed cricket. Sky's 2020–24 ECB broadcast contract is worth £1bn, the BBC's £100m. Sky has live England (men's and women's) Tests, white ball, county (selected), T20 Blast, plus ICC World Cups, IPL, Big Bash and other international leagues. The ICC contract lasts until 2031.

CONCLUSION: EVERYTHING COUNTS

The BBC boasted of 27.3 million listening requests for *Test Match Special* on BBC Sounds or the BBC Sport website during the 2023 Ashes with nearly 60 million people viewing video clips, almost 500 million page views on the BBC Sport website and 194 million views on social media. The BBC also showed some matches in The Hundred, though Sky has rights to them all.

Runner Steve Cram won BBC Sports Personality of the Year in 1983. David Steele won in 1975, Ian Botham in 1981, Andrew Flintoff in 2005 and Ben Stokes in 2019. Geoff Boycott was second in 1977 (behind Wimbledon winner Virginia Wade). These were all for Ashes performances. Steve 'Interesting' Davis, who won the World Snooker Championship in 1983, won SPOTY in 1988. Among ball sports, only snooker got more TV hours than cricket in the 1980s.

In 1983, the India World Cup team received 200 rupees/day and 1,500 rupees match fee each. The BBC showed live coverage of the World Cup in 1983 (as it had in 1975 and 1979). For the first time, on 6 January 1983, the Channel 9 broadcast of the fifth cricket Test from Sydney was shown on the BBC (two hours for £10,000, watched by two million). This was the first time cricket from abroad was shown live in England. On World Cup final day, Peter West introduced BBC2 coverage of 'the final stages and finish' of the third World Cup Final from Lord's (commentary Richie Benaud, Jim Laker and Tom Graveney), alongside the 'vital moments' of Wimbledon and *The Daily Mirror* Greyhound Derby presented by Harry Carpenter. The BBC had shown Sunday League cricket every Sunday afternoon from 1.55pm during the season on BBC2 since 1969. The BBC also broadcast the New Zealand Tests of 1983. Managers, coaches, analysts and trainers have transformed how players prepare. However, in 1983 all the counties had a coach, from Phil Russell at Derbyshire to Doug Padgett at Yorkshire. But from the 17 counties only Kent (Brian Luckhurst), Lancashire (Jack Bond), Leicestershire (Mike Turner), Surrey (Micky Stewart), Warwickshire (David Brown) and Yorkshire (Ray Illingworth) had managers.

There were 68 players who left county playing staffs in 1983, while 35 joined. Of those, only seven came from other counties, including Mike Selvey and Norman Gifford. In 2023, there were 122 joining counties and 97 leaving, including 63 swapping to other counties, with 22 loans.

Third and fourth TV (and neutral for internationals) umpires and referees are innovations. Technology has improved decision-making, not just for player analysis, since the implementation of the Decision Review System (DRS) in 2008.

Playing staff: Yorkshire list 46 for 2023, including a women's squad. In 1983 it was 18. Lancashire and Warwickshire had the most at 25.

The fulcrum of cricket has moved from Lord's to India, a process that began with India's 1983 World Cup win and accelerated with the IPL, founded in 2008, which has led to the international franchise tournament circuit that increasingly dominates cricket now.

The greatest players of 1983, using the statistics and ratings available, were Viv Richards, Gordon Greenidge,

CONCLUSION: EVERYTHING COUNTS

Clive Lloyd, Malcolm Marshall, Michael Holding, Andy Roberts and Joel Garner, all West Indian, though you could include the all-rounders Richard Hadlee, Imran Khan, Ian Botham and Kapil Dev, plus Zaheer Abbas and Ken McEwan. Every county had two overseas stars on the books apart from Kent, Middlesex, Worcestershire and Yorkshire. Cricket was ahead of the game compared to patriotic football (England used a bulldog as a mascot for the 1982 World Cup in Spain) which struggled to accept non-British Isles players in that era. Argentinians Ossie Ardiles and Ricky Villa were huge novelties, and the Falklands war exacerbated the xenophobia that hindered the internationalism of the game.

In 2023, the greatest cricketers are mostly Indian and Australian, with short formats and the IPL more important in making a judgement than the Test and county cricket (and World Cup) of 1983. Virat Kohli, Steve Smith, Rohit Sharma, Ravichandran Ashwin, Pat Cummins, Ravindra Jadeja, Jasprit Bumrah, Kagiso Rabada, Shaheen Afridi, Mitchell Starc, Kane Williamson. The best Englishmen: Joe Root, Harry Brook, Ben Stokes, Stuart Broad, James Anderson, Mark Wood and Moeen Ali; for them read Geoff Boycott, Graham Gooch, David Gower, Ian Botham, Bob Willis, John Lever and John Emburey.

Sports sponsorship hit £100m in 1983, double that of 1980, according to the Central Council of Physical Recreation (now the Sport and Recreation Alliance). In cricket (and darts and snooker) this was led by cigarette companies such as Benson & Hedges, John Player and Embassy, banned from advertising on TV since 1965.

Sponsoring sport by tobacco companies was phased out from 2003.

Social media has largely replaced newspapers as the way of reporting the game, and the way players communicate with fans and each other. The tabloid culture of the 1980s, obsessed with celebrity and royal scandal, and sports (often combining the two with, in cricket, Botham most often at the centre) has, arguably, waned. Privacy laws are stronger.

Women's cricket was virtually invisible in 1983, but is on mainstream terrestrial TV in 2023, with professionalism growing. The Hundred has been instrumental in driving this.

Race remains an issue the game is still trying to tackle.

At Yorkshire, there's still 'trouble at mill'.

Panini had another go in 1995 with a 168-sticker cricket album. Much had changed. This might be my next book.

Postscript

Mike Brearley

AS THE 2023 World Cup in India reached its climax, I finally caught up with Mike Brearley, the writer of the foreword of the 1983 Panini sticker album.

Brearley is one of the few cricketers who went on to do something in another field after retiring from cricket. In fact, he did something else beforehand, only becoming a full-time player aged 30 after spending the 1960s studying at Cambridge University and then teaching philosophy at Newcastle University.

In contrast, his successors as England captain all work or worked in the cricket media, administration and/or in coaching: Mike Atherton, Michael Vaughan, Andrew Strauss, Nasser Hussain, Graham Gooch and David Gower.

Indeed, after retiring from playing, most of the 195 featured Panini players of 1983 continued to work in cricket, as coaches, commentators or umpires. Brearley hasn't; he's been a psychoanalyst for 40 years.

His 'memoir of the mind' *Turning Over the Pebbles* speaks of eschewing lecturing to use the brain for reasoning on the cricket field. He writes: 'Like chess, it calls for planning, calculation of probabilities and intuition.'

Speaking at a book festival, he talks of the balance between mind and body and snobberies that can come from each direction, from 'mere hearties who throw buns in restaurants and so-called intellectuals, who can be scornful. I was torn between the two. Should I spend a lot of my life playing with a bit of leather and a bit of willow?'

Sledging, 'an Australian word', is an example of Brearley's brain/cricket conflict. He is aware that to win you must do what a batsman least wants. It is a legitimate part of the game to make a batsman 'feel he can't do something or provoke him to try and do something he doesn't want to do'. He stayed at opponent Derek Randall's house before a county match and tempted 'Arkle' into being out hooking for nought in both innings by asking the Nottinghamshire batsman whether Middlesex's Simon Hughes was going to bowl a bouncer first, second or third ball. 'It wasn't saying "we'll break your fucking arm".' To Brearley, as ever, there's a 'borderline' between gamesmanship and shrewdness.

Brearley played for Cambridge University between 1961 and 1968. He got a job as a philosophy lecturer at Newcastle University. In the summers he played for Middlesex.

After giving up lecturing to captain Middlesex in 1971, he was 'a decent county player and getting better', when he made his England debut in 1976, aged 34.

Tony Greig joined Kerry Packer's World Series Cricket 'circus' in 1977, so Brearley took over the captaincy, and won 18 out of 31 Tests, losing only four before retiring in 1981.

When Brearley was unavailable, Geoff Boycott and Botham captained, both unsuccessfully, winning one out of 16 Tests between them and losing nine.

Brearley's first move as captain was to persuade Boycott to return to the England team after three years' self-imposed exile.

Boycott told his skipper: 'If I had your posh accent and had been to a fancy school in southern England I'd have been captain ten years by now.' Nevertheless, Brearley won Boycott round, unless the Yorkshireman was in a bad mood, or hadn't scored any runs, in which case he was a flea in Brears' ear. Boycs said: 'You leave batting to me and I'll leave man-management to you.'

Walking off not out at tea at 50/0, Brearley's opening partner went ahead 'as if I wasn't there, I had to run to catch up. I asked: "Are we going to the same place?"'

Boycott replied: 'I don't want any of your egghead intellectual stuff.' He may well have been right, concedes Brearley.

Brearley motivated alpha male Ian Botham by calling him the 'sidestep queen' when he altered his direct approach to the wicket while bowling. The riling of his talisman made him bowl quicker. Bob Willis was more sensitive, so if you used that approach, 'He might feel that's what he is. He needed to be much more encouraged.'

This showed how Brearley's study of psychology helped his captaincy (though he says if anything it was the other way round). He sums this up as getting the best out of people, man-management, emotional intelligence and finding what makes different people tick and, for the opposition, discovering what they least want, psychologically and tactically.

While his cerebral approach worked as a skipper (he won 18 out of 31 Tests in charge from 1977–81) it did not as a Test batsman – he averaged 22 in 39 Tests, blaming being unable to free his mind for not doing better. By 2023, Test skipper Ben Stokes's Test win rate was 68 per cent, though he had already lost more Tests than Brearley did, in about half as many matches.

Brearley says Stokes's Bazball co-creator, England coach Brendon McCullum, was motivated by trying to recover playing with the same motives and feelings of when he was a boy, thinking what he can do rather than what might go wrong. This echoes Brearley's Panini introduction, about getting his great-aunt to bowl to him in the garden, joining in games on the beach at Bognor, and when you begin to understand it, you're too old to play.

Acknowledgements

DAVID JACKMAN (Everything Essex Cricket), Steve Dolman (Peak Fan Blog), David Griffin (Derbyshire CCC), MCC Library (Alun Cruz Rees, Matthew Hau, Neil Atkinson, Charlotte Goodhew), Chris Beetles, Peter Sibson, Nick Hoult, Mike Hitchings (Worcestershire), Glen Birkwood, Paul Douglass (Middlesex), PCA, Pitch Publishing (Paul and Jane Camillin, Graham Hales, Duncan Olner), Peter Sibson, Jeremy Squire, Duncan Dine, James Bielby, James Lowman, Martin Chandler, Simon Wray, Andrea Dunn, Greg Lansdowne, Bethan Norris, all the players interviewed.

Bibliography

Wisden, WCM, The Cricketer, Playfair, Cricketers' Who's Who, County yearbooks, *Indian Cricket*, Cricinfo.

Biographies and autobiographies about/by: Mike Brearley, John Holder, Bob Taylor, Peter Kirsten, Keith Fletcher, Graham Gooch, Derek Pringle, John Lever, Ray East, Javed Miandad, Malcolm Nash, Alan Jones, Chris Broad, Zaheer Abbas, Franklyn Stephenson, John Shepherd, Alistair Hignell, Gordon Greenidge, Mark Nicholas, Malcolm Marshall, Bob Woolmer, Chris Cowdrey, Alan Knott, Graham Dilley and Derek Underwood, Clive Lloyd, Graeme Fowler, David Lloyd. Jack Simmons, Chris Balderstone, David Gower, Mike Gatting, Graham Barlow, Roland Butcher, Phil Edmonds, John Emburey, Simon Hughes, Wayne Larkins, Allan Lamb, David Steele, Kapil Dev, Basharat Hassan, Derek Randall, Eddie Hemmings, Brian Rose, Viv Richards, Ian Botham, Vic Marks and Peter Roebuck, who wrote a diary of 1983's season, *It Never Rains: A Cricketer's Lot*, Roger Knight, Alan Butcher, David Smith, Robin Jackman, Pat Pocock, John Barclay, Ian Gould, Imran Khan, Bob Willis, Dennis Amiss, Alvin Kallicharran, Phil Neale, Younis Ahmed, David Bairstow, Ray Illingworth and Geoff Boycott. *A Corner of a Foreign Field*: Ramachandra Guha.